LETTER DESIGN
in the graphic arts

MORTIMER LEACH

ECHO POINT BOOKS & MEDIA, LLC

In addition to the author's text, this book contains information provided by many specialists in the graphic arts field. When interspersed among the writings of the contributors, the author's writing is identified by this monogram

To my wife, Betty

Published in 2017 by Echo Point Books & Media
Brattleboro, Vermont
www.EchoPointBooks.com

Letter Design in the Graphic Arts
ISBN: 978-1-63561-804-4 (paperback)

Interior design by Harvey Thompson
Cover design by Justine McFarland
Photo composition by Graphic Services, Inc.

CONTENTS

ACKNOWLEDGEMENTS

The development of this book depended upon the cooperation of many people. In every case, these were busy people, active in their various capacities in the fields of advertising and graphic arts. I am grateful for the willing help of those whose examples and comments appear and are credited in the book.

Many advertising executives, executive art directors, and artists also gave valuable assistance in providing the reproduction material and in securing permission to reproduce the examples. I wish to acknowledge, with gratitude, the helpful cooperation of Frederick W. Boulton, Charles T. Coiner, Al Camille, Wallace W. Elton, C. K. Eaton, Glen J. Frost, Claire F. Friedman, Phil Filhaber, Robert J. Flatley, Richard D. Gaul, David C. Gibson, Claire Harmon, Joseph C. Hochreiter, James Hastings, John H. Kies, N. Lee King, Folke B. Lidbeck, Elizabeth Low, H. C. McNulty, Hortense Mendel, Arthur G. Petry, Richard Reins, Allen C. Smith, Jr., Mary Sheridan, Francis E. Smith, Blount Slade, William J. Stevens, Jr., William Tara, Austin Thomas, John H. Tinker, Jr., Harvey Thompson, James Yates, Doyald Young, as well as all those whose names may have been inadvertently omitted.

As this book concentrates on the applications of letter forms, art credits have been given to the lettering artists and art directors only. I ask the indulgence of the illustrators and photographers whose work is shown without credits. Their fine work has added much to the presentation of the letter examples, and I wish to thank them all.

FOREWORD

This book deals with the use of letter styles within the field of graphic arts in this country. During the past generation, great strides have been made in the design field, and the pace is still accelerating. New materials and new technologies in reproduction methods are steadily increasing the opportunities for design applications. The lettering and typographic arts continue to be an important factor in this fast-developing field.

My recent book, "Lettering for Advertising," contains a study and analysis of letter styles that have exerted an influence upon the design of many subsequent styles. Because it was written as a textbook, with a "how to do it" section for beginners, I felt it necessary to hold to conservative forms on the premise that understanding these styles would serve as a base for the beginner. He could then go on to attempt the design of more stylized and sophisticated interpretations, without violating the rules of good taste.

Included among the letter styles in this book are individual expressions of the forms shown in "Lettering for Advertising." I have endeavored to present a rounded picture of the uses of letters—of how and why individual letter styles are employed.

The lettering examples shown may serve as inspirational material for students and young lettering artists, but they will be of greater value if they also make the beginner aware of the possibilities for new and personal interpretations of letter forms.

I sincerely hope that the information provided by type experts, art directors, lettering artists, and producers of photo-lettering will stimulate the thinking of art students and beginning designers by making them aware of how much thought is given to the designing of letter forms and to their artistic and practical application.

In all good design arrangements, planned for space advertising, posters, packages or products, some elements may be of secondary importance in terms of display, but no element should be considered secondary in terms of the complete design. Well-selected type or lettering, whether playing a dominant or secondary part in a design pattern, can often make the difference between a mediocre and a fine presentation.

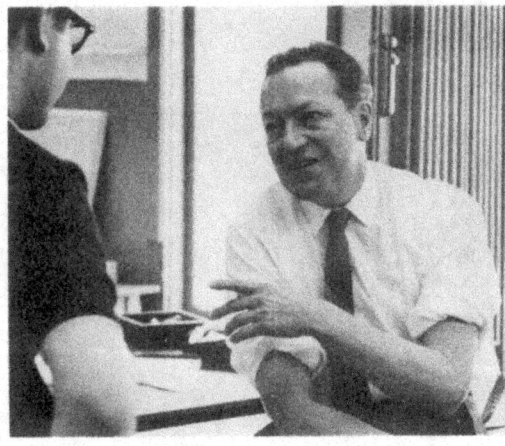

Mortimer Leach

1

LETTER DESIGN

In this country, the graphic artist is offered three major sources from which to choose letter styles to serve his purposes. Type foundries, here and in Europe, provide numerous alphabets cast into metal. Lettering artists are available to produce their interpretations of type forms, tailored to fit individual advertisements, as well as to produce other lettering styles not available in metal types. In comparatively recent years, photo-lettering has become another source of supply.

Although the technologies of these crafts differ, they are related to each other by one common need, all their letter designs must be provided by lettering artists.

Each one of these crafts has affected the others. Type letter styles, although originally derived from the early calligraphic writings, have long been the basis for many lettered interpretations, which, in turn, have stimulated the redesign of type forms. The success of new or redesigned type styles challenges the lettering specialist to produce more objective stylings in order to compete with the successful new type forms. Photo-lettering organizations, with their large supply of alphabet styles, compete with both, often on the basis of lower cost and higher speed of production. Although one sees many fine examples of work done by the suppliers of letter forms, the need for improvement still remains. Each can, and surely will, continue to improve his letter designs and methods of production.

In order to give a clearer picture of the current thinking concerning trends and problems in letter design, the following pages present statements and information provided by men from the separate crafts who are highly qualified to speak for their respective fields of work.

Several questions were sent to Professor G. W. Ovink, art consultant to Typefoundry Amsterdam, The Netherlands, a company represented in the United States by Amsterdam

Continental Types and Graphic Equipment, Inc.; to Mr. Jan van der Ploeg, director of type design for American Type Founders Co., Inc., Elizabeth, New Jersey; and to Mr. James Blake of Stephenson Blake and Company, Limited, Sheffield, England.

Through a reprinted article, Mr. Freeman Craw, designer of Craw Clarendon and Craw Modern, contributes the thoughts of an American type designer. Mr. Ward Ritchie, of Anderson, Ritchie and Simon, Los Angeles, widely known as the designer and publisher of books for the Huntington Library, the Limited Editions Club, and several California colleges, including the University of California Press, also offers his thoughts on the art of printing.

From information gathered through correspondence and personal talks with more than twenty of this country's highly rated lettering artists, I have endeavored to present their thinking concerning the current status of their specialty and the problems imposed by new forms of competition, and also their thinking about the future and what they believe it holds for artists who do lettering specifically designed for individual advertisements or advertising campaigns.

Mr. Robert M. Greve, president of Lettering Inc., Chicago, and Mr. Edward Rondthaler, director, Photo-Lettering, Inc., New York City, have written about the part that photo-process lettering now plays in the graphic arts field and how they think it may affect the use of metal type and hand lettering in the future.

That there are divergences of opinion and areas of disagreement between these fields, is obvious. Though the competition may become keener, I believe that the use of metal type, hand lettering, and photo-lettering will continue far beyond our time and that the competition may be a healthy one for all.

Following are the questions I asked and the answers received from Mr. Ovink, Mr. van der Ploeg, and Mr. Blake. It should be noted that in the course of continuing correspondence the questions changed both in phraseology and in number, so that all questions have not been answered by all three of these gentlemen.

Q. Is there any direction in the design of book and display types today? Can a trend be anticipated?

G. W. OVINK . . . The present approach to type design is predominantly functional: a type foundry, composing machine manufacturer, or any other type producer is not concerned with making the ideal type for all uses but with creating a suitable type for a given purpose or demand (either actual or anticipated).

This purpose can be the obtaining of a type with a certain boldness, or width, or X-height; with a certain openness (for a uniformly gray page) or closedness (for a pronounced ribbon-effect of the lines); rigidity or liveliness; a certain contrast between thick and thin (for even color or sparkling brilliance); cool precision and sharpness or mellow "impressionism" and roundness; formalism or spontaneity; sensitivity or hard-hitting realism; etc.

The purpose can be to maintain a clear and clean print in rotary newspaper printing with thin ink at high speed on rough paper; or in gravure, where the screen breaks up the clear outlines of the type; or in offset, the process which tends to present the type thinner and grayer than ordinary letterpress will make it.

Finally, the purpose can be to obtain a psychological effect with the type, to give it a certain emotional value (atmosphere-value, feeling-tone). This can consist in the suggestion of a period of style, as for instance the Louis XV style by the Cochin family, early nineteenth century classicism by Bodoni or Didot types, or pioneer days by Davy Crockett types and similar old-timers, or by the suggestion of delicate fragrance for perfume ads, of sturdiness for steel and concrete ads, of old-fashioned reliability for banking and investment publicity, etc.

This functional approach means that a type producer must be able to supply a wide range of types for the customer to choose from.

If he has no classical design, he will produce one: he will produce a true Garamont if he has nothing of that kind in stock, or a modernized version if he wants to kill two or more birds with one stone.

There seems to be a tendency to avoid extremes: to produce classical designs that are more regular than the original Garamont and Granjon types; to use Walbaum, as the mellowest of classic types, instead of Bodoni or Didot; to return from the strictly geometrical Bauhaus-Sans to (modernized) nineteenth century sans forms etc. That is, for *most* work; for special effects some designers are always prepared to take the liveliest or most monotonous types available.

JAN VAN DER PLOEG . . . To some extent, possibly by carefully watching design activity in other fields: architecture, furniture design, industrial design, etc. Still, one can easily be wrong, as most type founders have been, at one time or another, much to the dismay of their treasurers.

In display types, the nineteenth century letter forms such as Bodoni, Craw Moderns, sans serifs on the order of News, Franklin, Alternate Gothics and Spartans, the Craw Clarendons, Century Schoolbook and Century Expanded will be in use for a long time. These are basic styles, not fads or temporary "revivals."

For text styles, there are few discernible major trends. Clean-cut, legible faces will always be used and the standard classics will remain in use. There is little need for additional text faces.

JAMES BLAKE . . . It is difficult to predict or anticipate present-day trends in display-type design with any degree of accuracy. It does seem, however, that there is a strong swing towards revivals of the best of the nineteenth century.

With reference to the design of book and newspaper type, there does not appear to be any very strong swing in one direction or another, but the main thing in influencing successful designers seems to be that the type must be extremely legible and not too wide, as the amount of paper to be used still seems to be of considerable importance.

Q. How many separate drawings are employed by your organization in the cutting of a complete range of point sizes for roman types and sans-serif types?

G. W. OVINK . . . This depends on the type design in question and the working methods of the engraving department; the latter varies from one type producer to another and usually also from design to design. The more handwork, the fewer drawings. A composing-machine manufacturer will often use a separate drawing for each size, a type foundry may use only one for all sizes but produce the necessary variations by hand. A certain amount of variation can be done on the machine, viz. of the width and boldness of a type. I do not think that on the European continent "italicizing" on the machine is still practiced.

JAN VAN DER PLOEG . . . One set of drawings, although separate drawings of certain characters are often needed, especially for the smaller sizes, in order to preserve the character and "optical consistency" of the face in the entire size range. However, for most of the sizes, usually 18 point and up, our Benton matrix engraving machines are adjusted to carry out a carefully precalculated plan of "grading" the size range, i.e. expansion, condensation, and weight corrections, all to compensate for optical problems.

The artist chooses a size most comfortable for him to work in, usually not smaller than 2 inches.

JAMES BLAKE . . . Probably three sets of drawings in a full range of bodies, but the number depends to a certain extent on whether the face is narrow or wide, since owing to the automatic cutting on a pantograph as the sizes come down in proportion, the counter is lost.

The question of how many drawings are required in the cutting of a range of type is not affected by whether they are roman types or sans-serif types. The number of drawings has to be decided by eye and this is influenced by the width of the type and the size of the counter; for example, if a type is drawn for say 36 or 48 point, as the sizes get smaller and the size of the counter is reduced in proportion, the design appears to be different. In the old days when a punch-cutter cut each size separately, he always enlarged the pro-portion of the counter as the sizes came down, and by this means all the sizes looked even, although, in fact, they were not. In enlarging this counter, some allowance may have to be made in the width of the face and in the thickness of the various strokes. In the old days considerable allowance was made by the punch-cutter in the gauge or X-height, but in modern practice considerable effort is made not to interfere with this.

Q. How many letter combinations are used to ensure fit?

G. W. OVINK . . . For fitting new types, we start first with a test word, containing the most important lower-case characters, plus a round and a straight capital; in our case mostly "OHamburgefions." These characters serve to test typical combinations such as oo, nn, ee, ss, rr, gg, etc.; combinations of each vowel with one of the others; words consisting of straight characters, such as "minimum" and others predominantly consisting of round characters. Next we make sentences with all the 26 characters, such as "a quick brown fox" and include these on our test prints.

JAMES BLAKE . . . This justifying proof shows the combinations of letters we use.

COMMOONWEALTH? WARWICKSHIRE; BALACLAVAH!
BIRMINGHAM OSSORY'S MUZZLEM ENJOYMÆNTS
SUPPROSSŒNS LIVEERPOOL SOCIETIES QURQUHARTS
SHEFFIELD UNITED: VECCHI-HITTING

HHAAHBBHCCHDDHEEHFFHGGHIIHJJHKKHLLHMMH
HNNHOOHPPHQQHRRHSSHTTHUUHVVHWWHXXH
HYYHZZHÆÆHŒŒH&c.,&c.   HHOOH.   nnoon.

hammond; welchpool: carboniferous! weed-haarlem hoddledop
moggorton's divines excellent quinquennial ixias maccabees
commoonwealth? tarquin possessions patriarchs inflame
muzzlem (sanctified) deschœpeles sumœtra nwaveyn

nnaanbbnccnddneenffnggnhhniinjjnkknllnmmnoon
nppnqqnrrnssnttnuunvvnwwnxxnyynzznœœnœœn
nfiflnffinflfinfffnffifflinffflfflln&c.,&c.   November 26th, 1958

nn,,n..n::n;;n--n   HH!!H??H"H"H

£0011022033044055066077088099£
$03192834754159261483759171$

Q. What problems may be encountered in the design of a new type style, such as necessary redrawing and reproportioning of some letters to assure compatibility with other letters and their proper "fit" in words?

JAN VAN DER PLOEG . . . This is a very large and complicated subject. The design of a type face and its transfer to metal consists of a series of carefully weighed compromises. There are numerous technical and optical reasons for this. Correct fitting of the characters in relation to each other is of vital importance if words and lines set in the type are to look well. In precision-cast foundry type, it is possible to reduce fitting problems to an absolute minimum by kerning of letters, or casting them with an overhang to permit a narrower body or "set" than would otherwise be the case. Complicated body structures such as "wing bodies" and "angle bodies" permit the correct fitting of scripts with an extreme degree of slope, such as Bank and Type scripts.

Q. To what extent is the pantograph employed in the cutting of types from your foundry?

G. W. OVINK . . . Again, this depends on the kind of type, and sometimes on the specific character or sign too—there is less handwork on a point or dash than on a lower-case "g"—but at Typefoundry Amsterdam, as a rule, every character or sign is machine cut and hand finished. We do not work in steel any more, but cut either "upwards" (i.e. patrices, or dies, in soft metal) or—in the case of simple designs with not too sharp corners and for short runs—"inwards" (i.e. matrices in some brass alloy). The metal alloy used in our casters demands a high temperature, and therefore brass matrices will burn too soon. The standard practice, therefore, is to make nickel matrices from hand-finished, machine-cut patrices in lead alloy.

JAN VAN DER PLOEG . . . Although we sometimes prepare "nickel matrices," using the electroplating process, we believe that superior results are obtained with our Benton matrix engraving machines. These machines are not mere pantographs, in that they are adjustable to correct the optical problems encountered in a straight reduction or enlargement below or above the size for which the drawings were prepared (in our case, usually 36 point). We use the Benton machines for most of our matrix engraving.

JAMES BLAKE . . . The pantograph is used entirely in our Works for the cutting of both matrices and also types for the electrolytic bath—the types having to be finished by hand.

Q. Do you feel that the pantograph produces letters as pleasing to the eye as those produced by punch-cutters? What are its shortcomings and advantages?

G. W. OVINK . . . The shortcomings of the pantograph consist in its being unable to cut sharp corners, ideally smooth surfaces, and side-walls of the desired slope, in all cases. The drawbacks of relying entirely on the machine are the difficulties one has in visualizing the effect of a design in small sizes, when starting from a large drawing, and of then translating the adaptations of the design called for by these small sizes into alterations of the drawings. The usual method is to make trial cuttings in small sizes, recut them by hand, enlarge the prints to drawing size, and make new drawings for the small sizes.

The advantage of the pantograph is its speed and the uniform result. It can (and, for good results, should) be operated by a skilled mechanic rather than by a hand punch-cutter. The latter has a different skill and training and is scarcer than a mechanic. The product of the punch-cutting machine can be controlled by anybody through comparison with the patterns or drawings; the product of a hand cutter is unique; it cannot be reproduced any number of times and has to be controlled by a highly qualified artist or type expert.

For a single font of a very sensitive subject, such as a small-size book type, hand cutting of steel punches may yield a better result in less time, but machine cutting is indispensable for the mass production of punches or patrices for entire type families, and once the various drawings have been okayed, it is quicker, cheaper, and more reliable, too. A certain amount of hand finishing remains necessary.

JAN VAN DER PLOEG ... I feel that the Benton matrix engraving machine definitely produces letters of the same quality or, in some respects, better than those done by punch-cutters. In fact, this system produces far more even and consistent results, so vitally important in modern type design (faces with sharply contrasting thick and thin strokes, such as the Bodoni types, the Craw Moderns, sans serifs on the order of News, Franklin, Alternate Gothics and Spartans, the Craw Clarendons, Century Schoolbook, Century Expanded and other letter forms that characterize the machine age, the nineteenth century).

JAMES BLAKE ... The shortcomings of the pantograph are simply that it is mechanical. The best simile is the difference between a photograph and a painting. When people say that a painting is photographic, they are usually being rude. If a pantograph is being used to cut type instead of matrices, the type can be touched by hand and to some extent eliminate the faults. No doubt if a skilled punch-cutter could be found, his work would be preferable to that of a pantograph.

Q. *What effect has photo-lettering had upon type design from a competitive standpoint?*

What is your feeling about Mr. Edward Rondthaler's article in the 1959 *Penrose Annual,* Volume 53, in which he states "... we cannot fail to recognize that perhaps within no more than a generation, the era of metal type may be passing, replaced by some form or forms of photographic or 'cold' composition?"

G. W. OVINK ... I agree that photo-composition will take over a large share from lead composition, but I definitely do not agree that metal type may entirely disappear in one generation. There is too much capital invested in metal composition and it has many advantages over photo-composition.

JAN VAN DER PLOEG ... The ease with which photographic "masters" are made in photo-process display lettering constitutes a danger. It has caused catalogs of such services to be badly overloaded with inferior design and much duplication or near duplication.

Type foundries, because of their far greater investment in developing a new face in metal, must of necessity think carefully before a new face is accepted for production. This, in many respects, is a good thing (as most printers will agree!). It helps maintain higher standards of design and keeps much inferior lettering from being cut in metal. In the larger cities, photo-process lettering competes with use of foundry type. For reasons outlined above, it is not considered that the photo-process lettering services have much influence on the type design efforts of a creative type foundry.

 During my correspondence with the gentlemen quoted above, the sales potential of recently offered type styles was discussed. Type styles mentioned as being used by designers include Consort, Melior, Palatino, Torino, Craw Clarendon, Studio, Rondo, and Libra among others.

There was also some discussion about the different thinking in Europe and the United States in relation to type design and usage. Dr. Ovink wrote:

". . . It strikes me that there is more going into detail on the use of type in the U.S.A. than in Europe. This is apparent from the reactions of type directors in the big advertising agencies. On the other hand, however heart-warming this interest and detailed knowledge of the functioning of type may be, there is one danger, in my view, in the American approach: that is the tendency to base judgments of quality on public opinion. Of course, this is a very complicated problem, and I definitely do not say that Europe, as such, has the right answer. The drawback of the European approach is the abundance of expensive, individualistic novelties or even freaks."

Mr. van der Ploeg, in commenting on the possibilities of success for new type forms in the United States, wrote:

". . . Novelty types, bizarre scripts, or extremely wide letter forms do not last long despite the brilliance of their abbreviated careers in terms of tonnage sold. 'Radical departures' or novelties created for the sake of departing radically, burden the printer and lower standards of design for printing.

A responsible type foundry concerned with the broader aspects of type usage and its customers' real needs concentrates its design program on type faces of quality for which a need exists and which have a long-term potential use. Most type buyers are similarly motivated."

The following article, written for *Print Magazine* by Freeman Craw, vice president and art director of the Tri-Arts Press, is reprinted with the permission of *Print* and Mr. Craw. His treatise presents the viewpoint of a man who is a type designer, lettering artist and designer.

FREEMAN CRAW... Today's type designer must produce letters which are useful to the graphic designer. With so much literature today showing illustrations of machine-made products, it's certainly logical to use letter styles which relate to machine-age concepts rather than faces which don't relate to the form of these products.

But where did these faces come from, what makes these faces expressive of our times?

That there is a new art philosophy called "modern"—now largely accepted, even taken for granted—is probably due in large part to the public's wide exposure to all communication media, especially television.

But the origin of this new thinking, which has had profound effect on type and graphic design, has deep and branching roots. Perhaps the most important single force was the machine and intelligent design for it. Such a design meant understanding and taking visual advantage of a form natural to the machine. The result was a new appreciation of a new form, new proportion, a revised set of aesthetic standards. These standards were in harmony with timeless and universal design principles, but broke down the barriers of rigid Western architectural and book conventions.

Actually, influences on "modern" can be found throughout all history, particularly in the many primitive and Oriental arts. There were, however, several important groups of the post-World War I period which did much to explore, develop and define this new art philosophy; the de Stijl group in Holland, the Bauhaus in Germany, the Dadaists, all of which have had tremendous influence on all kinds of present-day design.

Too, various "schools" of modern painting have had strong bearing on present-day type and graphic design: Surrealism, Expressionism, and Cubism, most importantly.

Modern typography has been strongly affected, as is natural, by working in close harmony with all these important art styles. The result is that established types such as the Grotesques, the Moderns, and the Egyptians have been redesigned to fulfill a definite and current need: to serve as a strong but versatile design factor in combination with machine-age art—from Cubism to Surrealism.

These were some questions put to me by *Print* editors in a discussion of type styles, the designers, and the influences on them:

Q. How has the type designer's role changed through the years?

. . . His job has always been basically the same, of course: to sense the needs in letter styles and render such styles for general use. Type designers should also be good and experienced graphic designers so as to be acutely aware of the needs of graphic design and be in a position to keep pace with and understand graphic needs. This means a part-time activity in type design, and I think that's the best way. If a designer were to design type and nothing else, living in his ivory tower, probably he'd soon be out of touch with actual typographical needs.

Q. Is today's type designer meeting the graphic designer's typographic needs?

. . . It is believed by at least one progressive type founder (the founder commissions the type designer) that meeting the typographic needs of the modern graphic designer is at the same time meeting most other typographic needs. This is the reason for the many revivals and redesigns of basic nineteenth century styles in manufacture and use today . . . because they are so naturally suited to modern design.

Q. Does the graphic designer welcome the many type faces available to him today?

. . . Yes, but I think the graphic designer might be better off with fewer faces but ones that are of normal, well-cut design, with italics and a wide size and weight range—light, medium, bold; condensed, regular, expanded, etc. Bodoni is an example of such a flexible face: with a variety of weights in roman and italic, etc. It's important to add that old-style classic letters (Garamond, for example) do not lend themselves well to these bold weights, condensing and expanding.

Q. How has type design helped create an "American renaissance?"

. . . The nineteenth century faces have contributed much in making possible better visual expression in modern design by supplying letter styles related to, and therefore useful in, modern design. A few twentieth century recuttings have been done recently in order to render the original nineteenth century letter better suited to twentieth century needs. Important examples of this are the Grotesque and Clarendon styles being produced by founders today: new and improved renderings that still retain the identity and characteristics of the original nineteenth century fonts.

Q. What are the trends in letter design?

It is either to render letters well related to the forms inherent in modern design: familiar, anonymous, standard, established letter styles; or, on the other hand, to render natural, unaffected and completely free handwriting styles, one extreme or the other.

The logical prediction for a future trend is the development of sound current trends. This is especially applicable today. It's perhaps not too great an oversimplification to say that the basic principles of graphic and architectural design had remained as a tradition for several centuries or more, at least since the Italian Renaissance. The latter part of the nineteenth and early twentieth centuries saw the beginning, development, and, as I mentioned, the defining of what we call modern. It's surely not too much to predict and expect that this new kind of visual expression is here to stay for some time.

If there is any direction type design may take, it would logically continue to be from familiar nineteenth century designs which are naturally and inherently so well suited to modern shapes and textures—industrial, architectural, and graphic.

WARD RITCHIE . . . It has been for only a few centuries that we have had a combination of paper and ink that could be viewed through a design of letters to communicate ideas. And it may not be many more generations before it has found its own limbo. Already there are so many intrusions, by sight and sound, displacing the printed or written word in importance that we must expect a more scientific electronic and acoustic system to supplant our current and somewhat cumbersome alphabetical system of communication.

But while we are using it, let us enjoy the alphabet, in all its characters and many variations of style, to the utmost. The function of type through printing is, of course, to convey ideas. It should be completely subservient to that purpose. Any type that is recognizable can do this. But there are additional pragmatic requirements for a successful type face. The letters should so combine themselves as to lose their individuality in the unity of a word, in order to gain quick comprehension by the eye and brain without entanglement in aesthetics. And yet, aesthetically, a truly good type face arranged properly on a page can help to establish an unrealized communion with the reader. It is something we might call "warmth" for lack of a better word. This is the characteristic of a type which invites you to read, not to say "how beautiful" or "how interesting" or "how dull" this looks. Of course, in this we are thinking primarily in terms of books, the art of the printer which preserves knowledge.

In other phases, as in advertising, a more radical approach in the attention-provoking elements may be required, but when it gets to the basic selling copy there can be no substitute for a type face with the characteristics of warmth and readability. To professionally select a type with these qualities requires study, comparison and analysis. It is good to know what has come out of the past; it is wise to watch the contemporary trends; but it is basic to understand the form of letters and their relationship to the paper with which they eventually form a union.

Photo-lettering, or photo-process lettering as it is sometimes called, entered the graphic arts field in the early 1930's. This process offers headlines and sub-captions by photographing words which have been assembled from master alphabets. Within a few years after this new service began, several such organizations were formed. At present, while there are many companies producing captions by this method in most of our larger cities, the majority of work is done by a few large organizations that have offices or representatives in many areas.

The lettered alphabet styles employed for photo-lettering are drawn by staff artists or by professional lettering men, who either sell the alphabets outright or are paid on a royalty basis.

The larger companies have accumulated a great number of alphabet styles, which are converted into master negatives for use with the photo-lettering cameras. By using various camera lenses, the letters can be condensed or expanded without loss of letter height, or they can be italicized to any desired angle.

As in the fields of type design and hand lettering, the quality of the alphabets used for this process varies greatly, ranging from very bad to very good. The good letter designs face the danger of wearing out their welcome because of too much use over a short period of time, which causes the photo-lettering organizations to constantly seek new alphabet designs.

Although the advent of this new process has offered an additional outlet for the work of lettering men, it has also had some adverse effect on the lettering field. It has had no harmful effect on capable lettering specialists, but it has alerted them to the necessity of producing more objective expressions of letter styles. In all probability, it will not adversely affect the opportunities for the lettering specialist of the future.

As in all cases where a new process has affected an established craft, some antagonism to photo-lettering has occurred, especially from those whose careers have been disrupted.

I asked Mr. Robert M. Greve, president of Lettering Inc., Chicago, and Mr. Edward Rondthaler, director of Photo-Lettering, Inc., New York City, for their thoughts concerning the future of this process and its relationship to the lettering field. Their answers follow:

ROBERT M. GREVE . . . In an effort to defend and promote photo-process lettering, and discuss it from the lettering artist's viewpoint, I will consider it only as it would be done by one of the half-dozen leading photo-process lettering companies. I'm sure we all regard ourselves as part of the art business and not as typesetters. Our work is completely hand composed and is handled as a lettering artist would, but using pre-drawn letters. We are not discussing the various do-it-yourself methods such as paste-up type, cellophane letters, or the mechanical, machine-set, photo-process methods. Neither are we considering the relatively new photo-typesetting, which relates primarily to body copy.

Photo-process lettering is definitely here to stay. It is part of the American trend toward greater efficiency, speed, and production-line methods—even in the art business. It is part of the regrettable trend that inevitably eliminates the old-time guild worker, and some craftsmen, tradesmen, and artists.

The future will be determined greatly by the amount of money spent on advertising in print—newspapers, magazines, etc.—as opposed to TV and radio. It will also be determined by our own ability to produce creative new lettering styles which will convince the art director to use lettered headings in preference to typeset headings. Typeset headings recently have been doing a much better job than in the past. However, new photo-process styles are easier to produce, promote and market than new type faces.

The future for the *average* bread-and-butter lettering artist is somewhat bleak. He finds it difficult to compete with the quality, service and price of the good process-lettering houses. However, there is still a place for the real artist, the craftsman, the man who understands and can draw new and beautiful letter forms. Their earnings are excellent. Their numbers are few. They manage top-notch lettering studios or they design for the big process-lettering firms. We will never reach the saturation point of new lettering styles. So the future is not bleak for the man who can meet the exacting requirements of fine process-lettering alphabets.

And this alone has been instrumental in raising our lettering standards. To the art director in the many small cities throughout the country, process lettering is his only answer to a fine heading. These cities cannot support a good lettering specialist, but they do need fine lettered headings.

EDWARD RONDTHALER . . . As I see it, there will always be need for *good* lettering artists, just as there is need for *good* musicians. One would certainly not think of embarking on a musical career today unless one had real talent. Similarly, it can be said that the day is past when a man with too little talent can hope to earn a living doing second-rate finished lettering. He may, however, have enough imagination and facility to produce comprehensive lettering for art services, and there are ever-increasing opportunities in this area. Or, if he loves letters and wants to live with them, he can make his way if he will adapt to new tools—for example, the Protype machine, which is no machine at all in the mechanical sense, but rather a tool which enables the operator (in this case, the unsuccessful letterer), not only to reproduce finer letters than he could draw, but to apply his imagination in arranging them. I feel that there is a wide-open opportunity for young men interested in lettering, but with limited talent, to develop the skills compatible with the new photographic tools and to extend their possibilities.

Regarding his thoughts on the future of photo-lettering, Mr. Rondthaler referred to his article in the 1959 *Penrose Annual,* Volume 53.

In covering many facets of the potentials of photo-lettering, he speculates that "perhaps within no more than one generation, the era of metal type may be passing, replaced by some form or forms of photographic or 'cold' composition." The article contends that we are in a transitional period comparable to the fifteenth century transition from manuscript lettering to metal type.

Describing the work done in Photo-Lettering, Inc., mention is made of their alphabet laboratory, begun in 1936, in which experiments with new techniques for the development of letters are conducted. To quote from the article: "It appears likely that the findings of this alphabet laboratory, sharpened as they are on the steel of studio testing, will ultimately make a substantial contribution to the art of photographic type design."

 The art of lettering is an ancient one, but it is as vital and necessary today as in any preceding era. The growing business world, through its use of many forms of sales promotion, offers increasing opportunities for the use of skillfully drawn letter styles.

The modern lettering specialist is a comparative newcomer in the long history of the development of letter forms. In the early days of regional and national advertising, and up to the early part of this century, an artist in the advertising field was required to conceive and execute all the art work needed for an ad. The results, compared to current advertising art work, were generally of poor quality. There were, of course, some examples of good illustrations and lettering, presented in an acceptable format, but these were rare. The lettering was usually a crude copy of a type style or an inept attempt at inventing a style.

With the rapid growth of advertising agencies, and consequent recognition of the need for designers who specialized in planning layouts for advertisements, the old order soon changed. The art directors employed by agencies preferred to buy only the work that each artist was best qualified to do, and the day of the specialized commercial artist began. Some art schools, recognizing this fact, began to arrange courses in which, after general studies, specialized studies were available.

At first, the number of informed and competent lettering specialists was few, and their work was in great demand. This demand served the cause of the lettering field well, as the known specialists had to employ and train promising young men in order to provide faster service for clients. The importance of learning the history of the development of letters became apparent to sincere students of lettering, and the quality of their work improved as a result. Fortunately for the lettering field, some of the early specialists devoted some of their time to teaching, and within a few years many competent lettering artists could offer their services to the fast-growing advertising agencies.

Within this generation, package designing has become a multibillion dollar industry and, here again, the need for objectively designed lettering has grown steadily. Industrial designers, also, are increasingly aware that trade names, dials, meters, clocks, etc., should be designed and integrated with the complete unit. Only those with a fine knowledge of letter shapes can anticipate the end product when the lettering or numerals are to be reproduced by metal casting, stamping, or in plastics.

Only on occasion does one see good lettering used for television titles. However, I believe that the television industry will eventually recognize the psychological value of well-planned, interpretive letter styling for their show titles.

It cannot be said that all lettering being done today, or done in the past, is good, or even that a majority of the work is good. There are, and have been, lettering specialists whose work lacks the most necessary ingredient—artistry. The true lettering artist not only knows the "why" of letter shapes and how to manipulate his tools, but he has an inherent love for letter forms and the effect they create when combined into words and lines. He is an experimenter in the techniques produced by the use of various pens and brushes on different paper surfaces. He is a constant student of his craft, always searching for new approaches. In the face of increased competition from photo-lettering organizations and creative type designers, only men of this calibre will remain in the forefront of the field.

There is no doubt that photo-lettering has had its effect on lettering specialists. In the course of correspondence and personal talks with many of this country's top-rated men, a number have said that photo-lettering competes with their work to some degree, though largely on a price basis. The general consensus of opinion is that photo-lettering must be accepted as a permanent factor in the field. And, although it has hurt some of the less talented hand letterers, in the long run the status of the good lettering specialist is secure. Some say that there has been a lowering of lettering standards and that art directors rely too much upon photo-process specimen books for caption styling. Others claim that photo-lettering has made layout designers more lettering conscious and that the volume of their lettering work is as good as ever. The majority feel that there is too much sameness in the styles of photo-lettering being used, and that the lettering artist is needed to provide a distinctive change of pace.

Reactions have been generally healthy and confident, but one disturbing statement was made by several—that very few young men are entering the field. This should cause grave concern in the field of graphic arts. I personally cannot conceive of a time when lettering specialists will not be needed to contribute to the individual appearance of an advertisement, package or product. Without hand letterers, the entire field of letter designing would suffer. It is to be hoped that art instructors and art directors will encourage young students to train for this stimulating and rewarding form of art work.

The lettered interpretations of type forms shown in this section, and the lettering examples in Section 5, were done by able and successful artists. They do not cover the entire range of possible letter interpretations, which is limitless, but are shown as fine examples of the work of contemporary lettering specialists.

Apart from scripts, brush expressions, and various unusual styles, the majority of lettered captions today are individual interpretations of type forms. A skilled lettering artist usually retains the essential characteristics of a type style when drawing his version of the letters. Occasionally, some individual letters are designed in completely different form than that of the type design, but, generally, one can readily recognize the type style from which the lettered version was derived.

There are, of course, many occasions when well-selected and interestingly arranged typeset captions do the job so well that they could rarely be bettered by good lettering. Conversely, many lettered captions are so ably conceived and designed that their effectiveness could not be achieved by the use of type.

A lettering artist must not only know and appreciate the merits of well-designed type forms, but he must have the taste and good judgment to know how far afield he can go in his interpretation of them. Furthermore the ability to recognize good lettering cannot be confined to the lettering specialist alone. Art directors and other designers who use the services of lettering artists can get far better results from these men if their own knowledge of good letter styling is well developed.

An able lettering artist can find many opportunities for expression when his letter styles stem from standard type forms. The letters may be expanded or condensed, the weights changed to produce a desired tone, and the arc of the curved strokes altered. Serifs can be lengthened, shortened, thickened, or thinned. The letters can be drawn with less rigid strokes and used in a bouncing line when a layout calls for this treatment. At times, two type styles, which have some relationship in design, can be combined to produce a different effect.

At present, a rather small group of type alphabets are being used as source material for lettered captions. All of these alphabets were designed in the nineteenth century, or earlier, but some have been redesigned in recent times. Although this reference group is small, lettering men have devised many widely differing interpretations which give the impression that many more styles are being used.

The following type examples, which precede the lettered versions, comprise most of the styles on which lettered captions currently used in advertising are based. (Only partial type alphabets are shown to identify the styles, since this book deals with the applications of type and lettering and is not intended to be a reference for complete type alphabets. Instead, it must be assumed that professional artists and art students have, or should have, access to type specimen books which contain complete alphabets shown in display sizes and in text.) The lettered interpretations, done by skilled men, show some of the variations which spring from these type styles.

Other type designs are occasionally lettered. Often, these are styles that are used to recapture the feeling of a past era, such as the baroque forms of the eighteenth and nineteenth centuries and the Barnum, Playbill and Old Towne alphabets. Off-beat type interpretations, such as freely drawn Latin, are also used, but all these styles are naturally limited in application.

Bodoni type alphabets and lettered Bodonis are widely used. These type forms, considered to be the first modern styles, have a crisp, concise appearance, well-suited to many ad arrangements. Because of their symmetrical distribution of weights on the curved strokes, they can be lettered in many proportions, without letter distortions, in either a tightly condensed or widely expanded form. When lettered, the Bodoni serifs are sometimes bracketed on both the thick and thin strokes. Departures from the basic shape of the kerns are often made. Bodoni letters are used in bounced, free-style renderings, but the extreme difference between the thick and thin strokes calls for a restrained bounce or else legibility is lost.

ABCDEFGHIJKL MNOPQRSTUVW

ATF BODONI REGULAR

BAUER BODONI EXTRA BOLD

ABCDEFGHIJKLMNO

ABCDEFGHIJKLMNOPQRST

BAUER BODONI ITALICS

ABCDEFGHIJKLMNOPQRS

ATF BODONI ITALICS

abcdefghijklmnopqrs

BAUER BODONI EXTRA BOLD

abcdefghijklmnopq

BODONI REGULAR

abcdefghijklmnopqrstuvwxyz

BAUER BODONI ITALICS

abcdefghijklmnopqrstuvw

BODONI REGULAR ITALICS

NEW SUPPORT FOR YOUR BACK!

NEW BACK-CARE BY SIMMONS!

*First and only mattress
with a <u>built-in</u> <u>bedboard!</u>*

NEW FREEDOM
FOR
YOUR BACK!

Agency: Young & Rubicam, Inc. Client: Simmons Company
Art Director: Frederick Halpert. Lettering Artist: Sam Marsh Studios

Pond's exclusive formula the beauty oils that

Agency: J. Walter Thompson Company. Client: Chesebrough-Pond's, Inc.
Art Director: Kent Hansen. Lettering Artist: George Abrams

Emotional Tensions
*drain your skin
of beauty oils
— every day*

Agency: J. Walter Thompson Company. Client: Chesebrough-Pond's, Inc.
Art Director: Kent Hansen. Lettering Artist: George Abrams

People who enjoy
CORBY'S
...enjoy life!

Agency: Brooke, Smith, French & Dorrance, Inc. Client: Jas. Barclay & Co., Ltd.
Art Director: Charles Maricak. Lettering Artist: Lettering Inc. of Michigan

<u>replaces</u>

tension drains away

BOLD NEW PONTIAC

Agency: MacManus, John & Adams, Inc. Client: Pontiac Motor Division, General Motors Corp.
Art Director: George Kossman. Lettering Artist: Marley Hodgson

Known by the company it keeps

Agency: Warwick & Legler, Inc. Client: Joseph E. Seagram & Sons, Inc.
Art Director: Cle Kinney. Lettering Artist: William Yaris

Wake up Wonderful!

Agency: Young & Rubicam, Inc. Client: Simmons Company
Art Director: Frederick Halpert. Lettering Artist: Sam Marsh Studios

Simmons WONDERFUL *Beautyrest*

Agency: Young & Rubicam, Inc. Client: Simmons Company
Art Director: Frederick Halpert. Lettering Artist: Sam Marsh Studios

Acclaimed the

Agency: McCann-Erickson, Inc. Client: Chrysler Division, Chrysler Corporation
Art Director: Tom Heck. Lettering Artist: Sam Marsh Studios

see! the cleaner that walks on <u>air</u>!

Agency: Leo Burnett Company, Inc. Client: The Hoover Company
Art Director: Jack Dawson. Lettering Artist: Richard Kenyon—Stephens, Biondi, DeCicco

The Sparkle Corps

Corps

Agency: Young & Rubicam, Inc. Client: Union Oil Company of Calif.
Art Director: Ray Pederson. Lettering Artist: Mortimer Leach

new fine car style leader

The sturdy Clarendon forms have surged into prominence in this country since being redesigned for several type foundries. This style, originally designed in the nineteenth century, presents a strong but not overpowering effect that makes it highly useful for advertising captions. The close relationship between the weights of the strokes gives the letters a readable solidity that proves valuable when this style is used for outdoor displays. Clarendon is usually lettered in weights and proportions not available in the type forms, although the expanded forms of Fortune Bold, closely related to Clarendon, are valuable when wider type proportions are needed. Clarendon can be drawn effectively in bounced free-style form more easily than letters that contain thin hairlines. On the free-style renderings, the lettering artist often makes changes in some of the letter shapes, but the general characteristics of the Clarendon serifs and the ratio of the opposing weights are usually retained.

ABCDEFGHIJKLMNOPQ

RSTUVWXYZabcdefghij

klmnopqrstuvwxyz12345

67890.,-;:'!?$&

CLARENDON

DETERGENT

Agency: Compton Advertising, Inc. Client: The Procter & Gamble Co.
Art Director: Robert McDonnell. Lettering Artist: Morris Glickman

the Green Giant flavor

Agency: Leo Burnett Company, Inc. Client: Green Giant Company
Designer: Dr. Agha. Lettering Artist: Bill Ficho—Ficho & Corley, Inc.

It's unusual ale

Agency: Benton & Bowles, Inc. Client: Carling Brewing Co.
Art Director: James E. Clark. Lettering Artist: Frank P. Conley

Make
FRENCH'S
Crown o' gold
Meat Loaf

FRENCH'S MUSTARD

Agency: J. Walter Thompson Company. Client: The R. T. French Co.
Art Director: Frank Stephenson. Lettering Artist: Acey Cypress

The Cleaner with
the Automatic Shift!

Agency: Leo Burnett Company, Inc. Client: The Hoover Company
Art Director: Per Hogestad. Lettering Artist: Lettering Inc., Chicago

Clarendon serifs are sometimes used on single-weight letters, producing the effect of Stymie Light or Medium combined with Clarendon. When these letters are drawn in fairly bold faces, the relationship to Clarendon becomes more apparent.

ABCDEFGH
abcdefghijkl

STYMIE MEDIUM

You can <u>not</u> brush bad breath away... reach for Listerine!

Agency: Lambert & Feasley, Inc. Client: Listerine Antiseptic—Warner-Lambert Pharmaceutical Co.
Art Director: Walt Peters. Lettering Artist: Bill Reid

Just arrived

Agency: Young & Rubicam, Inc. Client: Simmons Company
Art Director: Frederick Halpert. Lettering Artist: Sam Marsh Studios

Make it a party!

Agency: J. Walter Thompson Company. Client: The R. T. French Co.
Art Director: Frank Stephenson. Lettering Artist: Sam Marsh Studios

Stymie Light can serve as the take-off point for other lettered single-weight styles that contain serifs. However, not much is gained by lettering these styles unless the letters are drawn in relaxed form. As a rule, free interpretations of Stymie Light and similar forms depart considerably from the design of the type, holding the relationship only by the use of serifs drawn in the same weight as the letter strokes.

the night before Christmas

put Packard-Bell all through your house

Agency: Robinson, Jensen, Fenwick & Haynes, Inc. Client: Packard-Bell Electronics Corp.
Art Director: Bix-Art. Lettering Artist: James L. Wood

the friendly "Pepper-Upper"

Agency: Grant Advertising, Inc. Client: Dr. Pepper Company
Art Director: F. M. Burt. Lettering Artist: Philip Peterson

The Caslon alphabets have served long and well in the field of graphic arts. These type forms, with their traditional feeling and air of dignity, are very effective when used for headlines in institutional ads, although their use is most assuredly not limited to this advertising category. These graceful type forms can contribute much to the physical appearance of many layout arrangements.

The use of lettered Caslons in advertising has not been continuous, but rather has maintained a pattern of recurring popularity. Lettered expressions rarely depart radically from the original letter shapes and weight distributions, but considered changes in proportion and general weights can produce pleasing interpretations. The off-center distribution of weights on the curved strokes does not allow for too much expanding or condensing, as these extremes tend to distort the delicate balance of the letters.

ABCDEFG
HIJKLMN

CASLON 540

abcdefghijk
lmnopqrstu

CASLON 540

abcdefghijkl
mnopqrstuv

CASLON ITALICS

Be Chewsy.

CHOOSE THE GUM THAT

Agency: Young & Rubicam, Inc. Client: Beech-Nut Gum
Art Director: Dana Cairns. Lettering Artist: Sam Marsh Studios

Only 'Love-Pat'...with its exclusive *creamy* foundation
...gives your skin this flawless, radiant look!

Agency: C. J. LaRoche & Co., Inc. Client: Revlon, Inc.
Art Director: Ralph G. Breswitz. Lettering Artist: Lettering Inc., N. Y.

Kodak Retina IIIc —
the camera with an eye to your future

Agency: J. Walter Thompson Company. Client: Eastman Kodak Company
Art Director: John Cook. Lettering Artist: Rio Studios

YOUR FIRST TASTE
WILL TELL YOU
it's <u>real</u> whipped cream

Agency: D'Arcy Advertising Company. Client: Reddi-Wip, Inc.
Art Director: Kenneth Kemp. Lettering Artist: Mortimer Leach

No more roadside tire changing!

Agency: Young & Rubicam, Inc. Client: The Goodyear Tire & Rubber Co.
Art Director: Frederick Halpert. Lettering Artist: Sam Marsh Studios

BELONGS !

The simplicity of the Gothic forms allows for their logical use in practically all forms of advertising. A check through current space advertising, outdoor displays and mailing pieces will show that their use is widespread, covering a great range of diversified products. In the type styles, these single-weight (or near single-weight) letters are available in numerous weights and proportions, and are identified by many names. In many cases, the changes of design in these differently named alphabets are quite minor and can be noted only by the trained eye of professionals in the graphic arts field.

On some occasions, Gothic forms are lettered because exacting requirements, which govern the width of line or several lines, call for proportion and spacing adjustments that could not be accomplished by the use of type. Lettering artists who are aware that single-weight letters are the skeletons of letter forms can produce many variations when drawing these letters. The rigid strokes can be relaxed by drawing them with minutely concave sides or by flaring the endings. Sharp corners, which occur within the letters where vertical, horizontal, or diagonal strokes are joined, can be reduced by a gentle rounding at their meeting point. Gothics are truly elastic letters and can be drawn in innumerable weights and proportions.

ABCDEFGHIJKLMN

FUTURA DEMI BOLD

abcdefghijklmnopqr

FUTURA DEMI BOLD

abcdefghijklmnopqrst

FUTURA DEMI BOLD ITALIC

ABCDEFGHIJKLMN

FUTURA BOLD CONDENSED

abcdefghijklmnopq

FUTURA BOLD CONDENSED

ABCDEFGHIJKL

NEWS GOTHIC

abcdefghijklmno

NEWS GOTHIC

ABCDEFGHIJKLMNOPQR

ALTERNATE GOTHIC

abcdefghijklmnopqrstuv

ALTERNATE GOTHIC

ABCDEFGHIJK

VENUS BOLD EXTENDED

abcdefghijklm

VENUS EXTRA BOLD EXTENDED

ABCDEFGHIJKLMNOPQR

VENUS MEDIUM EXTENDED

abcdefghijklmnopqrstuvwx

VENUS MEDIUM EXTENDED

ABCDEFGHIJKLMNOPQRSTU

FRANKLIN GOTHIC CONDENSED

abcdcdefghijklmnopqrstuvwx

FRANKLIN GOTHIC CONDENSED

TWO GREAT NEW LUXURY LINERS

Agency: Young & Rubicam, Inc. Client: Moore-McCormack Lines, Inc.
Art Director: Arthur Harris. Lettering Artist: Sam Marsh Studios

This is the one that's delicious for drinking

Carnation Instant

Agency: Erwin Wasey, Ruthrauff & Ryan. Client: Carnation Company
Art Director: George Labadie. Lettering Artist: James L. Wood

4 Fishermen Fishsticks

Agency: Doherty, Clifford, Steers & Shenfield, Inc. Client: Fulham Bros.
Art Director: Shirley Starbuck. Lettering Artist: Frank P. Conley

A TERRIFIC NEW CAR POLISH!

Agency: Young & Rubicam, Inc. Client: Simoniz Company
Art Director: David Wylie. Lettering Artist: Walter Wencel—Bundy Freiday Studio

New kind of deodorant dri-mist sprays on dry...keeps you dry!

YOU MAY BE PAYING $32 TOO MUCH FOR YOUR AUTOMOBILE INSURANCE!

Agency: Needham, Louis & Brorby, Inc. Client: State Farm Insurance Co.
Art Director: C. Franklin Johnson. Lettering Artist: Lettering Inc., Chicago

New Super Sea-Horse 35-quiet as the night!

Agency: J. Walter Thompson Company. Client: Johnson Motors
Art Director: William Silet. Lettering Artist: Carl Corley—Whitaker Guernsey Studio, Inc.

THE LITTLE TRAVELERS

Lettering Inc. Specimen Book

You can telephone Hawaii as clearly as you call across town

Agency: N. W. Ayer & Son, Inc. Client: American Telephone and Telegraph Co.
Art Director: Howard Henry. Lettering Artist: Horace Paul

THE SWITCH IS ON

Agency: McCann-Erickson, Inc. Client: Chrysler Corporation
Art Director: Robert Pliskin. Lettering Artist: Bob Shaw

FACTS ABOUT CANNED PINEAPPLE

Agency: J. Walter Thompson Company. Client: Pineapple Growers Association
Art Director: Preston Philhower. Lettering Artist: William A. Coppock

SEAMLESS NYLONS
3 PAIRS ONLY $2⁰⁰

Agency: Needham, Louis & Brorby, Inc. Client: Kraft Parkay—Kraft Foods
Art Director: Harold L. McVeigh. Lettering Artist: Harry Kasvin

Hit Parade has <u>all</u> you want!

the tobacco...
the tip...
and the taste!

Agency: Batten, Barton, Durstine & Osborn, Inc. Client: Hit Parade Cigarettes—The American Tobacco Company
Art Director: George Sanders. Lettering Artist: Richard Bickel

DRY SKIN CLEANSER

Agency: McCann-Erickson, Inc. Client: Dorothy Gray, Ltd.
Art Director: Tom Heck. Lettering Artist: Irving Bogen

SIESTA SLEEPER SEAT

Agency: Foote, Cone & Belding. Client: TWA (Trans World Airlines, Inc.)
Art Director: G. Kirkpatrick. Alphabet designed by G. Kirkpatrick, executed by Peter Dom

Newest...

finest in the skies!

Agency: Foote, Cone & Belding. Client: TWA (Trans World Airlines, Inc.)
Art Director: G. Kirkpatrick. Lettering Artist: Peter Dom

"We paid rent on our house before we built it"

Agency: McCann-Erickson, Inc. Client: The Savings & Loan Foundation, Inc.
Art Director: John Murray. Lettering Artist: Robert Evans—The Headliners, Inc., New York

NEW
LIQUID
BODY
SHEEN ®
by SIMONIZ

Agency: Young & Rubicam, Inc. Client: Simoniz Company
Art Director: David Wylie. Lettering Artist: Emil Klumpp

New Simoniz Floor Wax - childproof because there's vinyl in it!

Agency: Young & Rubicam, Inc. Client: Simoniz Company
Art Director: David Wylie. Lettering Artist: Bill Ficho—Ficho & Corley, Inc.

The Century alphabets are also extensively used in display sizes for advertising captions. These well-balanced forms are among the easiest to read letters employed today. This assured readability has, at times, brought about some over-use; but when the style is *right* for presenting the copy in an advertisement, Century is extremely effective. Type styles in weights and proportions that fulfill the needs of the layout preclude the need for lettering. Therefore, lettering artists are called upon to draw these letters in weights and proportions that are not available in type forms. When they are lettered in the type proportions, this is usually done in order to adjust the letter spacing so as to contain the lines within a specified width or to produce a less rigid caption. Century Schoolbook is most often used as reference by lettering artists, but interpretations of Century Expanded are also lettered, especially the italics. When regular Century forms are lettered, the thinner hairlines sometimes give the letters a near-Bodoni feeling, but the bracketed serifs with flat endings retain the Century characteristics.

ABCDEFGHIJKLMNOP

CENTURY SCHOOLBOOK

abcdefghijklmnopqrstuv

CENTURY SCHOOLBOOK

abcdefghijklmnopqrstuv

CENTURY SCHOOLBOOK ITALICS

ABCDEFGHIJKLMNOPQSRT

CENTURY EXPANDED

abcdefghijklmnopqrstuvwxyz

CENTURY EXPANDED

abcdefghijklmnopqrstuvwxyz

CENTURY EXPANDED ITALICS

Because the gift tells so much about the giver...

Agency: Warwick & Legler, Inc. Client: Joseph E. Seagram & Sons, Inc.
Art Director: Ed Bright. Lettering Artist: William Yaris

SYLVANIA *cuts the cabinet in half!*

Agency: J. Walter Thompson Company. Client: Sylvania Electric Products, Inc.
Art Director: Charles Ziegler. Lettering Artist: Ad-Let Studios

–the exciting look and feel of the future!

Agency: Batten, Barton, Durstine & Osborn, Inc. Client: DeSoto Division, Chrysler Corporation
Art Director: Gene Foster. Lettering Artist: Tony Violino—KV Studios

RED CARLING CAP ALE

Toast the Winners with Red Cap

Agency: Benton & Bowles, Inc. Client: Carling Brewing Company
Art Director: Louis Menna. Lettering Artist: Frank P. Conley

Proclamation!

Agency: Young & Rubicam, Inc. Client: Four Roses Distillers Company
Art Director: Arthur Seller. Lettering Artist: George Abrams

a great drink begins with a great whiskey

Agency: Warwick & Legler, Inc. Client: Joseph E. Seagram & Sons, Inc.
Art Director: Edward Cottingham. Lettering Artist: Julian Mansfield

mcgregor
pepperell

Agency: Benton & Bowles, Inc. Client: McGregor Pepperell
Art Director: Henry Eastland. Lettering Artist: Frank P. Conley

performance out of this world...

smart fishermen

have all
the luck!

Agency: The Cramer-Krasselt Company. Client: Evinrude Motors
Art Director: Alfred H. Biermann. Lettering Artist: Lettering, Inc.

The type faces shown on these pages are being used for display captions, but are rarely lettered. Occasionally, one sees lettered expressions of Corvinus, Onyx, Bulmer, Hellenic, Baskerville, and variations of Old Towne. These renderings either are done in different weights and proportions from those of the type or are done in modified relaxed forms.

ABCDEFGHKRS abcdefghkrs

CORVINUS

ABCDEFGHKRS abcdefghkrs

MADEMOISELLE

ABCDEFGHKRS abcdefghkrs

MODERN #20

AbcdEfghkrS

TANGO

ABCDEFGHIJK MNOPQRSTUV

BASKERVILLE

ABCDEFGHIJKLMNOPQRSTUVWXYZABCDEFGHI

ONYX

ABCDEFGHIJKLMNOP

BULMER

ABCDEFGHIJ abcdef

CHISEL

ABCDEFGHI

HELLENIC WIDE

ABCDEFGHIJKL

LYDIAN

ABCDEFGHIJKLMNOPQRSTUVWX

OLD TOWNE

ABCDEFGHIJKLMNOPQ

STYMIE EXTRA BOLD

The problems I encountered in designing an alphabet family planned for exclusive use in Chevrolet advertisements are similar to the kinds of problems that confront other lettering artists, type designers, and designers of alphabets for photo-process organizations. In each of these related fields, the designers deal with the development of letter styles that differ in some way from existing forms. The description below details the problems of a specific assignment and how they were carried out.

A few years ago, Mr. James Hastings, vice president and creative director for art of Campbell-Ewald Company, Mr. George Guido, the art director on the Chevrolet account, and Mr. William Tara, consultant to Campbell-Ewald, decided that one alphabet family should be used throughout the 1957 Chevrolet advertising campaign in newspapers. Noting that, at that time, competitive car advertisements tended to change lettering styles frequently, they felt that the consistent use of one alphabet family would be helpful in product identification.

I was asked by Mr. Tara to experiment with some letter styles for consideration by Campbell-Ewald. The requirements were that the forms be conservative and yet maintain an individual personality, and that they be designed for use in a wide range of sizes.

The work began with the drawing of several sets of letter styles on tracing tissue. In most cases, I attempted to combine some of the characteristics of two or more different letter styles. One early run-through was based on a lettered interpretation of Bodoni italics, but subsequent changes began to eliminate most of the Bodoni characteristics. The corners were softened and the hairlines rolled smoothly into elongated oval kerns. The f, g, i, k, y, and z were radically changed and the serifs were eliminated on the p and q strokes. Thinking that I might be on the right track, I drew a complete lower-case

a b c d e f g h i j k l m n

o p q r s t u v w x y z

A B C D E F G H I J K L M

N O P Q R S T U V W X Y Z

Fig. 1

alphabet in pencil and ran through the capital italics also. After testing the letters in word form, I decided that the letters were too soft for the intended purpose and that more brisk forms should be used for introducing a new car. Therefore these run-throughs were discarded (Figure 1).

Eventually, a combination of Bodoni, Century Schoolbook, and Century Expanded began to show definite possibilities. Taking into consideration that the letters would also be used in fairly small sizes, the thin strokes were drawn heavier than Bodoni hairlines but a bit thinner than those of Century Schoolbook. The roman letters were drawn with briskly bracketed serifs. A minor departure was taken from the parent forms in that the curves were drawn in more balanced shapes. The small "points" on the outside of the Bodoni curves, which occur on both romans and italics, were softened (Figure 2).

atn hu

Fig. 2

The up-swinging hairlines on the italics were drawn as leaning U shapes, which, while eliminating the Bodoni "point," also modified the sharper swing of Century italics. The right-hand strokes on the h, m, n, and the left strokes on the v and y retained more of the relaxed shapes of Century Expanded but were drawn with modified swelling strokes. This swelling, however, was considerably more restrained than that found on the strokes used in cursive italics (Figure 3).

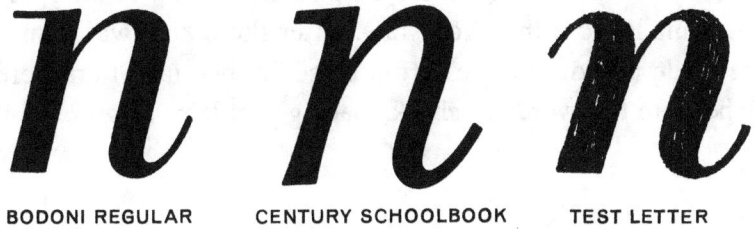

BODONI REGULAR   CENTURY SCHOOLBOOK   TEST LETTER

Fig. 3

Several key letters, both roman and italic, were drawn on tracing tissue in various weights and sent to Campbell-Ewald (Figure 4). I only sent lower-case letters, as I felt that the capitals would not be too difficult to do once the lower-case forms were okayed. Mr. Hastings and Mr. Guido checked the tissues in Detroit. These were returned to me with noted suggestions for adjustments. The weight most suitable for the letters was also decided upon, and the go-ahead was given for drawing the finished alphabets.

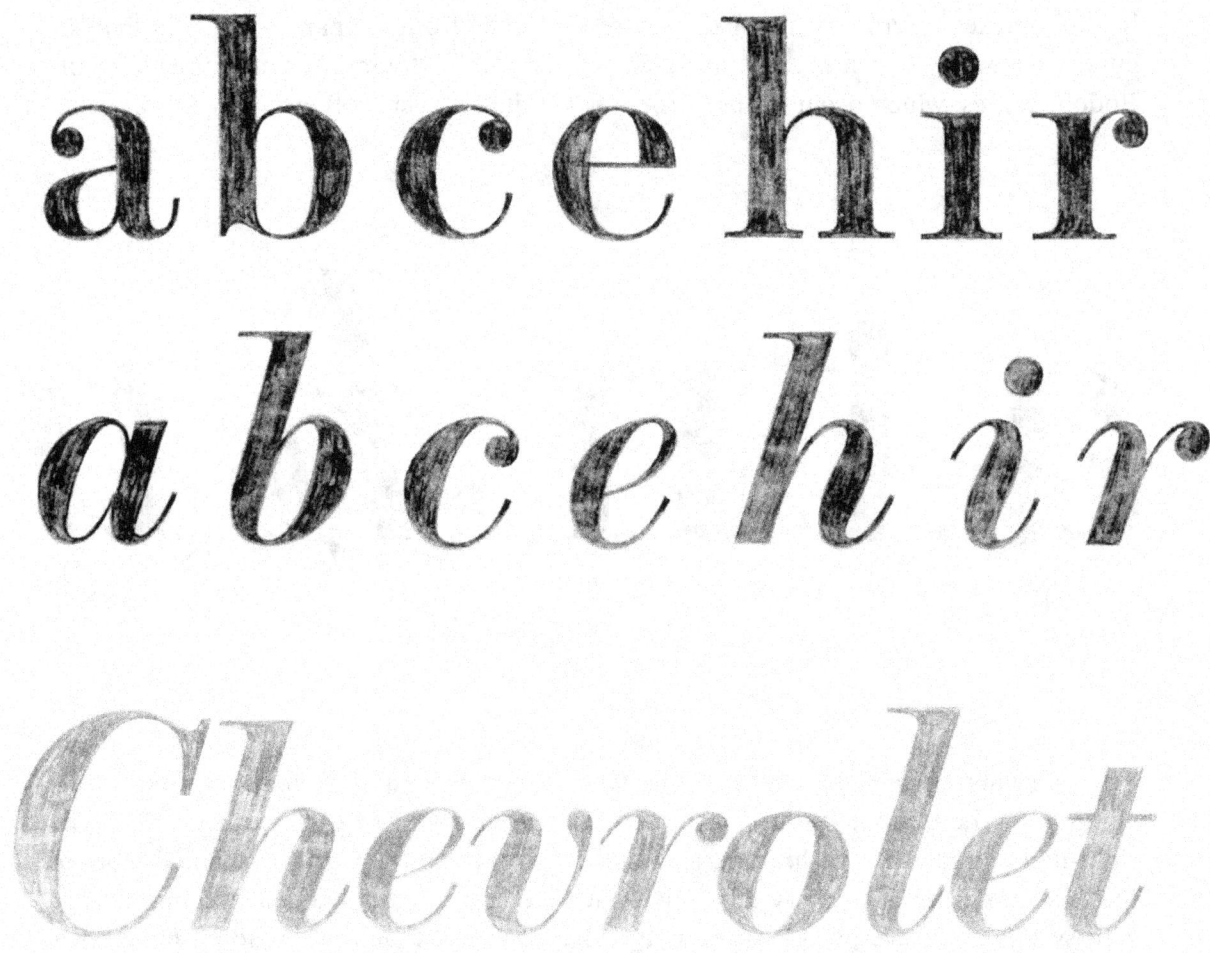

Fig. 4

The letters were drawn fairly small on the first tissues so that the relationship of the thick and thin strokes as they would appear in an average-size reproduction could be seen more clearly. These tissues were then photostated up to a larger size, and the final tracings were made from the photostats. After the inking was completed, several photostats were made in reduced size. From these, individual letters were cut out and cemented on paper into test words to check spacing problems (Figures 5–10).

a b c d e f g
h i j k l m n
o p q r s t u
v w x y z ! ? $

Fig. 5

Chevrolet Performance!

Fig. 6

a b c d e f g
h i j k l m n
o p q r s t u
v w x y z-j p

Fig. 7

A B C D E F G
H I J K L M N
O P Q R S T U
V W X Y Z
1 2 3 4 5 6 7 8 9 0 O

Fig. 8

ABCDEFG

HIJKLMN

OPQRSTU

VWXY !?$

1234567890

Fig. 9

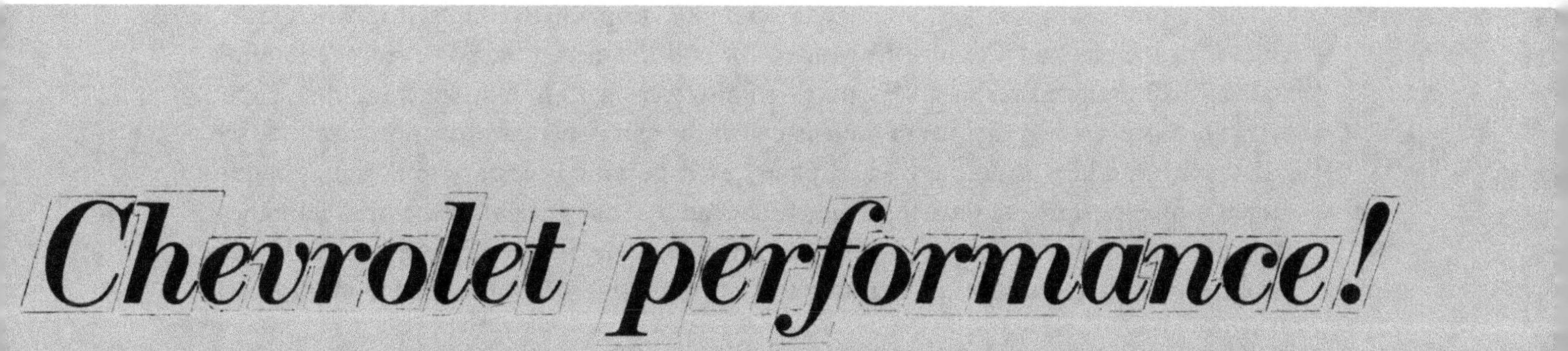

Chevrolet performance!

Fig. 10

After some letter adjustments, the completed alphabets and test words were mailed to Campbell-Ewald. From there, Mr. Guido sent the alphabet plates to Fitzgerald-Calvillo Studio where the individual letters were printed on small cards that could be assembled into words in much the same fashion that type is set in the typesetter's stick. Next, these test-word assemblies were photostated in lines of test copy (Figure 11). Additional words, containing many combinations of letters were also assembled. These prints were checked by Mr. Guido, who noted the need for further adjustments in the proportions of some letters. The prints with his notations were returned to me, and final adjustments were made.

the quick brown chevrolet fox jumped over the lazy dog's back

the quick brown chevrolet fox jumped over the lazy dog's back

Fig. 11

After acceptance of the completed alphabet family, it was decided that a condensed version of the lower-case italics was also needed to cover those situations where an advertisement called for longer copy than layout space would normally permit. These condensed italics, and the accompanying capitals, were drawn in the same weight as the original italics.

Although the alphabets were originally created for use in newspaper advertising, the italic forms were adopted for magazine advertisements. Eventually, in order to maintain the similarity of caption styling throughout the 1957 campaign, the italics also became the predominant form used in the newspapers.

In the following year's Chevrolet campaign, Campbell-Ewald used Lining Gothic type for captions and Century Expanded for sub-heads. Later, however, the lettered italics I had designed for the 1957 campaign also were used in magazine and newspaper ads. Then, since many layouts of the ads called for extremely large caption displays (see "that purr you hear is no pussy cat," page 62), it became necessary to design an additional alphabet with less bulk than that produced by enlargement of the original italics. The new set of letters, drawn in a lighter, taller form and containing thinner hairlines, dropped the characteristics of Century and assumed the form of refined Bodoni italics (Figure 12).

The original italic alphabet, in a slightly heavier form, and the later version of the italics—together with other heading styles—were continued in use for three years in Chevrolet advertising, under the direction of Mr. Guido.

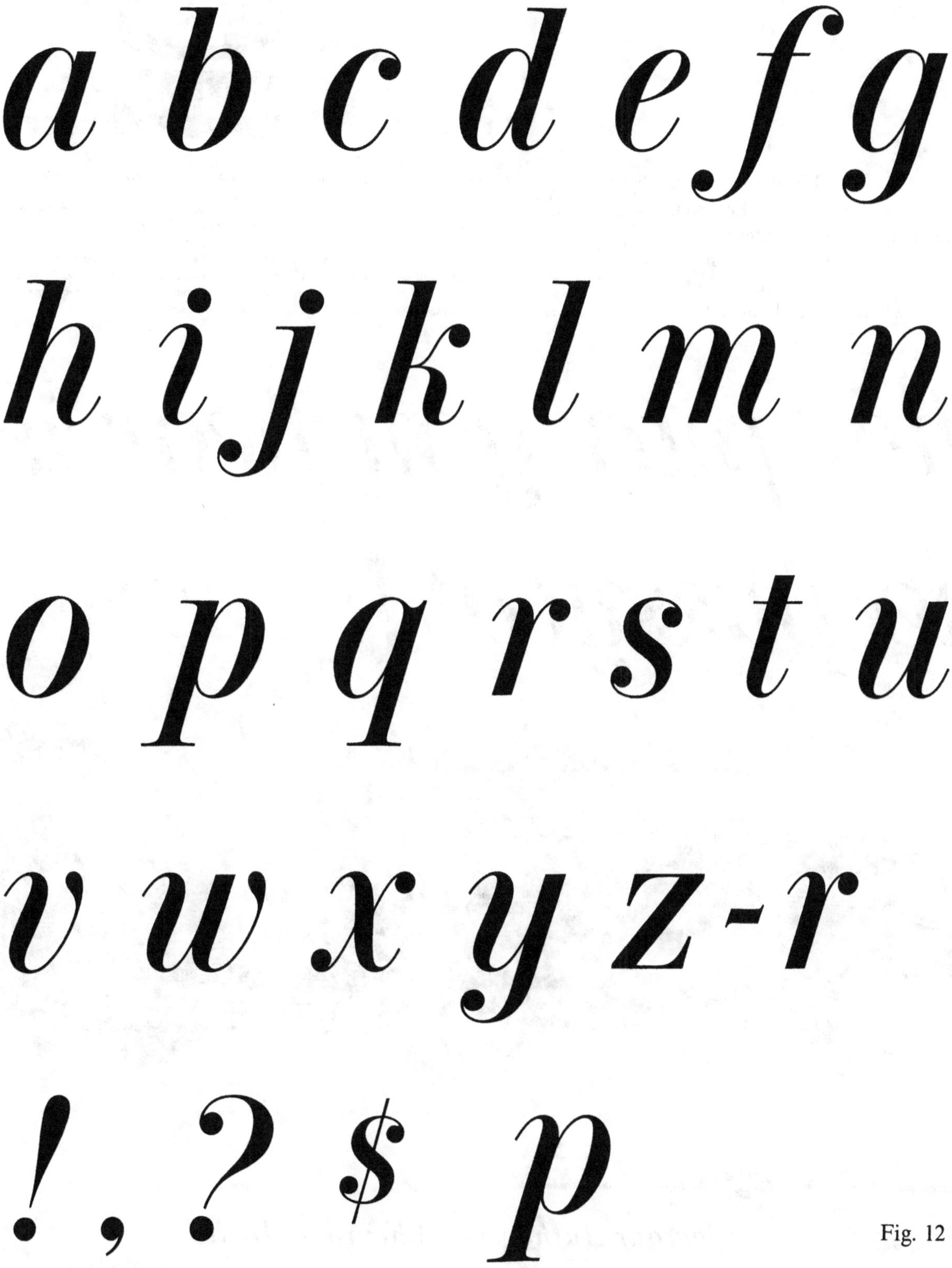

a b c d e f g

h i j k l m n

o p q r s t u

v w x y z-r

! , ? $ p

Fig. 12

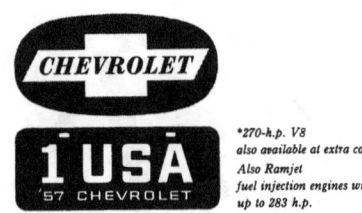

*270-h.p. V8
also available at extra cost.
Also Ramjet
fuel injection engines with
up to 283 h.p.

It's that new V8
in the '57 Chevrolet.
It's as quiet as a contented cat
and as smooth as cream . . .
and it's cat-quick in response
when you call for action!

No household tabby sitting in a sunny window ever purred more softly than Chevy's new V8 engine. It's so kitten-quiet and cream-smooth that you can scarcely even tell when it's idling.

But when you nudge the accelerator, you know it's there, all right! It pours out the kind of velvety action that helps you be a surer, safer driver. Its right-now response keeps you out of highway emergencies. It overpowers steep hills with such ease they seem like level landscape.

This new Chevrolet V8 puts up to 245 high-compression horse-

power* under your command! With 283 cubic inches of displacement, this beautifully designed V8 is a new, bigger and better edition of the engines that have put Chevrolet at the top of the performance ladder. It's sassy, sure—but as tame to your touch as a purring pussycat.

Come try the smoothest V8 you ever put a toe to, and all the good things that go with it. Like new Turboglide—the first and only triple-turbine automatic drive (an extra-cost option). And Chevy's own special sweet and solid way of going.

that purr you hear is no pussycat!

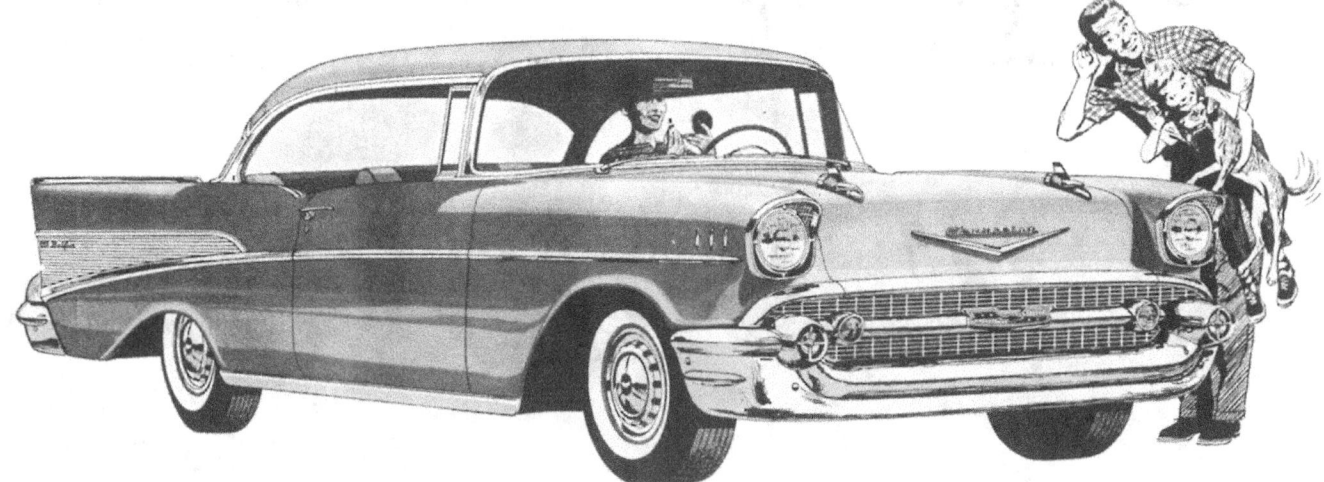

Sweet, smooth and sassy! The Bel Air Sport Coupe. Body by Fisher, of course, with all that means in extra fineness of construction, materials and details.

Only franchised Chevrolet dealers CHEVROLET *display this famous trademark*

See Your Authorized Chevrolet Dealer

Agency: Campbell-Ewald Company. Client: Chevrolet Motor Division, General Motors Corp.
Art Director: George Guido. Lettering Artist: Mortimer Leach

Reduced from full-page newspaper advertisement

Nothing without wings climbs like a Chevrolet!

Chevy wagons!

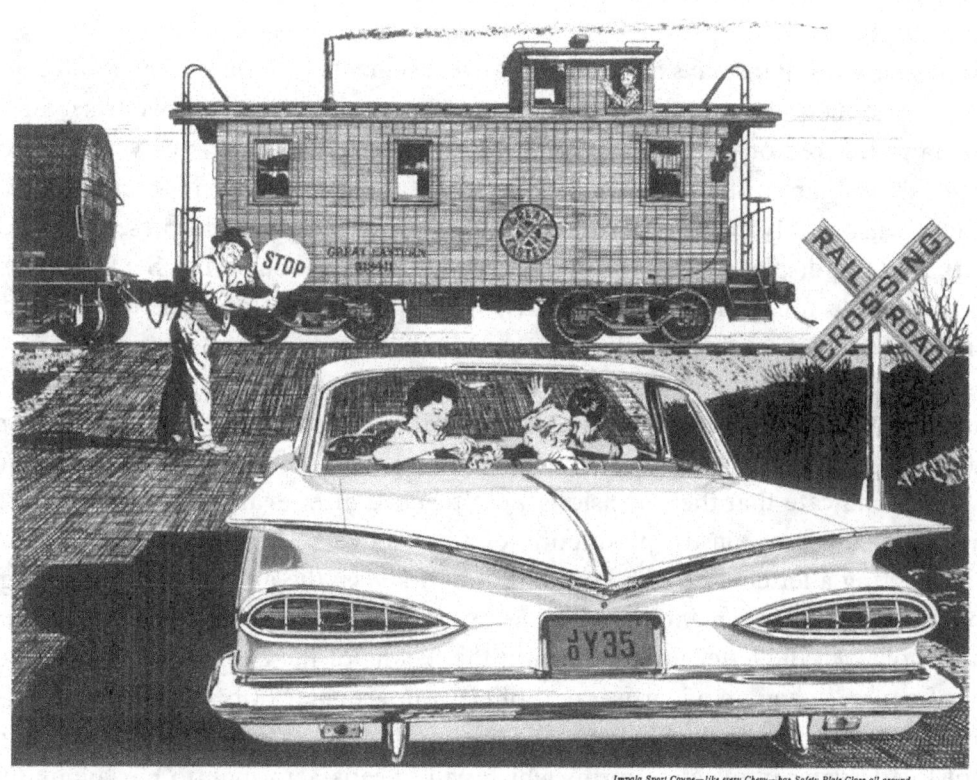

Impala Sport Coupe—like every Chevy—has Safety Plate Glass all around.

Chevy stops quickest... goes farthest on a gallon!

Chevy showed the best brakes of the leading low-priced three in a test of repeated stops at highway speeds conducted and certified by NASCAR. Chevy also won over the other two in a NASCAR economy run—getting the most miles per gallon for 6's and V8's at normal cruising speeds of just over 55 miles an hour.*

Fresh as this new Chevy is to look at, it's inherited more than its share of those long familiar Chevrolet traits—economy and dependability.

Whether you prefer a 6 or V8, you know you're getting the kind of engine that gets the most out of a gallon. And Chevrolet alone in its field brings you hydraulic valve lifters in all popular engines—6 and V8. This mark of a modern engine means smoother, quieter performance for you.

Greater-than-ever dependability is evident in Chevy's surer stopping, longer wearing Safety-Master brakes—with more lining area than any other low-priced car. There are many more advances just as funda-mental, but why not stop at your dealer's and let Chevy do its own sweet talking!

*National Association for Stock Car Advancement and Research

CHEVROLET

see your local authorized Chevrolet dealer for quick appraisal—early delivery!

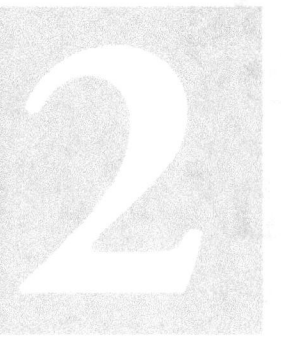

SPACE ADVERTISING

The following section displays a number of advertisements that were prepared for a wide variety of products. Some of the captions in these advertisements were set in type, others hand lettered or produced by photo-process methods. The ads were selected in order to show many different forms of lettered and typeset expressions. There are, of course, considerably more lettered and typeset forms being used in present-day advertising than those displayed here. Many additional styles are shown in Sections 1 and 5.

In all of the following advertisements, the captions play an essential part in the physical presentation of the layouts. In some instances, their role is secondary; in others the caption dominates the page. But in all cases, the styles were selected and arranged into captions by the art directors in order to fulfill the needs of their individual layouts. The accompanying statements by the art directors, giving their reasons for the choice of letter styles, indicate that their decisions were reached after evaluating all of the factors that must be considered in the production of an effective advertisement.

In selecting a letter style or a combination of styles, the art director must judge its compatibility to the design and mood of the layout, and, in many instances, he must also evaluate how well the letter forms interpret the feeling of the copy's message. There are times, of course, when an advertisement offers no particular opportunity for the use of interpretive forms. On these occasions, the choice of letter styles depends upon the good taste of the designer in selecting forms which will fit satisfactorily into his layout. Often, the type of product being advertised can influence his decision.

To a skilled designer, the interpretation of mood and feeling does not call for the use of time-worn clichés, such as snow resting atop letters, flames rising from them, or wriggling forms suggesting agitation or fear, etc. At his command are numerous letter styles that can subtly or strongly convey the desired feeling.

The great variety of products being advertised today necessarily calls for many different layout arrangements and copy approaches. While there are some standard formats that have proven to be effective in selling advertised products, the opportunities for new page arrangements are unlimited.

A particular kind of advertisement can influence the art director's choice of lettering or type styles. For example, dignified institutional ads require far more stable forms (usually, traditional "old-styles") than sophisticated "designed" pages or gay or humorous presentations demand. The letter styles employed in an advertisement for cosmetics would be strongly dissimilar from those used in an advertisement for trucks. Copy statements may require forms which imply such diverse ideas as quality, stability, lightheartedness, vitality, or excitement.

While a particular letter style may automatically suggest itself as the solution to a problem, there are often alternative designs which may work as well, or better. A well-designed style that differs from those too commonly used can be found if the advertising designer will take the time to consider other forms before making his decision. However, popularly used styles should not be eliminated from consideration just because of their popularity. If one of these forms is *right* for an advertisement, that is when it is most effectively used.

All too often, a new or recut type form, surging into popularity, is employed by layout men just because it is new, with complete disregard for its fitness in a particular ad. A survey of type and lettered styles used in ads during the past years shows that many art directors have played this game of "follow the leader." As was the case with the tremendous over-use of brushscripts and brush letters a few years ago (now fortunately reduced to a more logical ratio), the current over-use of such popular styles as Venus, Century and Clarendon has caused many ads to lose their individuality because of the sameness of their letter styles. Along this line, I have seen, in a single magazine, two or more advertisements, each promoting a similar and highly competitive product, in which the type or lettered styles were exactly the same—in some cases, the same size and weight! Such unfortunate occurrences can hardly be helpful to product identification.

A thoughtfully planned caption is an essential element within the advertisement. Although the reader is seldom aware of why he is attracted by an ad, properly selected lettering and type do their part in gaining his attention and thereby help to sell the product.

Although Mr. Sekiguchi has used the word "intuitive" regarding his selection of these lettered expressions, I feel strongly that, in any creative work, intuition can only be relied upon when the designer has a sufficiently solid background and sense of good taste to enable him to recognize when his ideas are practical. Many designs for ads are developed intuitively by an art director, but knowledge and experience are the controlling factors. I believe that these ads are fine examples of the necessary combination of talent and knowledge.

The feminine handwritten style used in the talcum powder ad gives the intended impression that the lady is saying the words. The combination of Copperplate capitals with free-flowing script is pleasantly arranged in this ad and in the lipstick ad on the following page.

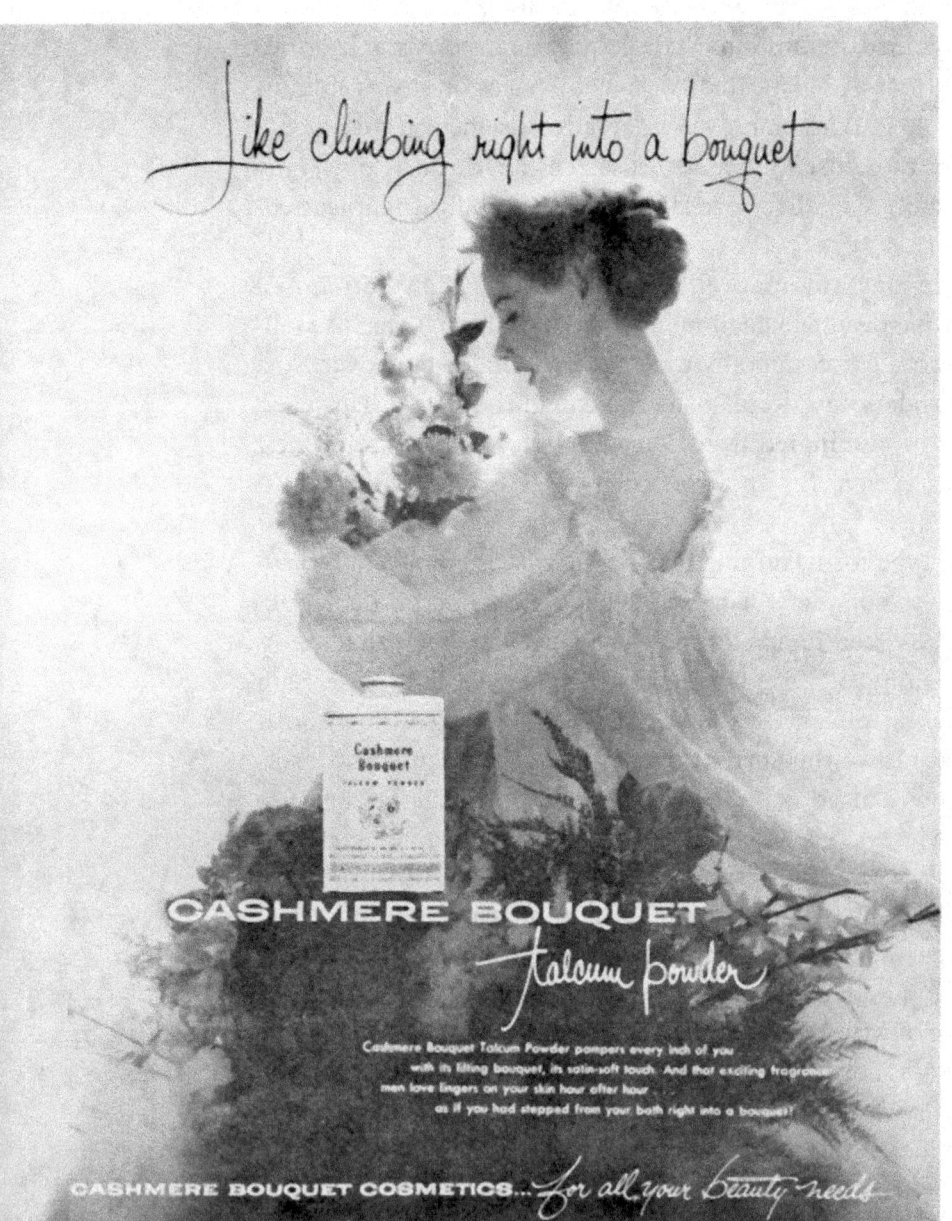

Agency: Bryan Houston, Inc.
Client: Cashmere Bouquet Cosmetics—Colgate-Palmolive Co.
Art Director: Kenichiro Sekiguchi
Lettering Artist: Larry Ottino

KENICHI**KO** SEKIGUCHI: *Graduate of Pratt Institute's School of Advertising Design, New York. Seven years with Kudner Agency as art director on several Goodyear Tire and Rubber Company industrial accounts, and associate art director on accounts for National Distillers, Schick Electric Shaver, and United States Tobacco Company. One year at Biow, Beirn and Toigo as art director on Whitehall Pharmacal Company, and Bond Clothing accounts. From there to Bryan Houston, Inc. as art director on accounts for J. P. Stevens, Cashmere Bouquet Cosmetics, and Gunther Beer. Presently with the G. M. Basford Company where he is responsible for approximately ten accounts.*

like climbing right into a bouquet

CASHMERE BOUQUET

talcum powder

CASHMERE BOUQUET COSMETICS... *for all your beauty needs*

KENICHIRO SEKIGUCHI: "My choice of letter styles on both the Cashmere advertisements was rather intuitive. Each ad called for the use of styles light enough to hold a feminine quality and yet strong enough to maintain readability when used over the varying tones of a photographic background. After running through several experimental roughs, I felt that these selections were right.

"Once this matter was settled in my mind, it was merely a case of selecting the right lettering artist to go with the job and giving him as much of a free hand as possible, while still seeing that he kept the spirit I had in mind."

On the Inner Glow Lipstick ad, the hairlines of the Bodoni letters, running in reverse on a color photograph, have been drawn thicker to protect against possible disappearance should there be any off-registry on the color printing; while the Bodoni line beneath the illustration, running on a white background, returns to the thin hairlines usually found in these forms. The combination of the light Bodoni lower case with the free brush letters produces an attractive change of pace.

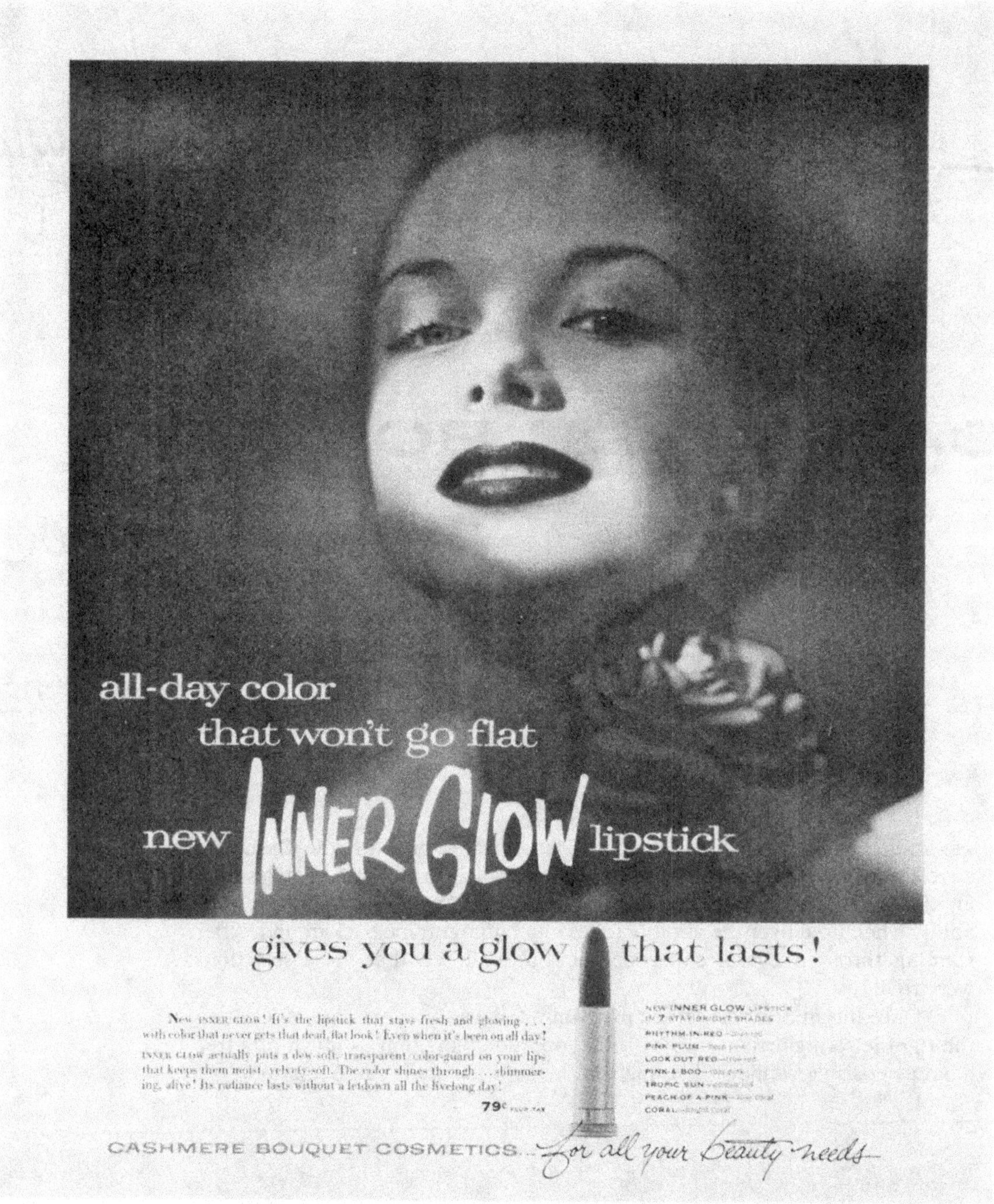

all-day color
that won't go flat

new INNER GLOW lipstick

gives you a glow   that lasts!

Agency: Bryan Houston, Inc.
Client: Cashmere Bouquet Cosmetics—Colgate-Palmolive Co.
Art Director: Kenichiro Sekiguchi
Lettering Artist: George Abrams

Among its many uses, Caslon type has long been employed for the headlines of institutional advertisements and for the titles of scholarly articles and stories. The Caslon alphabets have an air of stability, dignity and dependability, attained by only a few type faces. Because of their excellent readability, they have also served well in various forms of advertising, both in type and lettered forms.

I can imagine no better choice of type for the titles of the "Adventures of the Mind" series in *The Saturday Evening Post*.

Art and Human Dignity

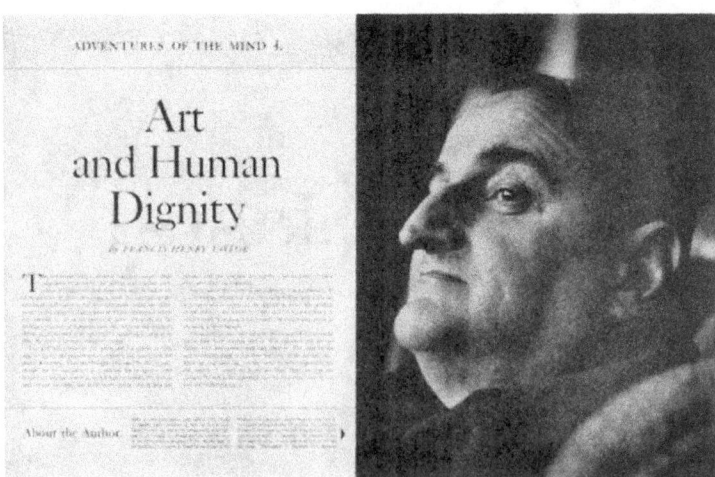

Reprinted by special permission of "The Saturday Evening Post." Copyright 1958 by The Curtis Publishing Company.

Art and Human Dignity

By FRANCIS HENRY TAYLOR

The art world today is divided into two camps—those who wish to preserve the ageless and guiding principles of humanism and those who seek to find in art an expression of their own groping with the mechanical determinism of the present day. The humanities today are understood by the masses as that residue of human experience which has proved to be of no practical value whatever in the ordinary conduct of contemporary life, whereas the sciences, bereft of philosophical or speculative significance, appear to offer the answer to every maiden's prayer.

The gulf lying between the artist and his public is wide and deep; it is the more serious because it has lasted now for nearly a century. Thus the thoughts provoked by this inquiry should not be considered as a polemic for or against contemporary art, but rather as an attempt to explore the terrain and climate in which the artist works today—for at best the painter and the sculptor are merely representative of their time and their environment.

The modern movement is not a theory; it is a condition. It is a condition arising out of a series of historical facts and consequences which center on the dignity of man—his position in the universe, his search for truth, and his constant desire to render truth in sensible form so that other men may grasp its meaning and its beauty.

Artists and laymen have become the victims of the scientific world they have created, and in their common fear for the future have lost contact with one another. The crisis in the arts is nothing more or less than the crisis of the human race. How far, one may ask, can the artist be held responsible for the society of which he is the product? How far can the *Zeitgeist* be laid at his doorstep? Are we to assume that he has sold his birthright for a

About the Author

Both as conversationalist and author (The Taste of Angels; Fifty Centuries of Art) the late Francis Henry Taylor was one of the wittiest and most perceptive in his field. For fifteen years he was Director of the Metropolitan Museum of Art. At the time of his death last November he filled the same post at the Worcester Art Museum, whose superb collection he was largely instrumental in developing. The article beginning on this page is excerpted from material which appeared originally in Daedalus, the Journal of the American Academy of Arts and Sciences. It was his last work.   Photograph by Elizabeth G. C. Menzies

As Mr. Hamilton states, the word "Venice" used as a heading on a travel poster logically calls for the use of traditional letter forms. In this ad, the ragged texture of the letters, which are drawn in a relaxed form, makes for an admirable integration of the word with the illustration. Despite the deliberately loose rendering, the letters retain the essence of Classic Roman forms.

The decorative, "old-time" letter style chosen for the words "San Francisco" is an example of the valuable function that this style, and its contemporaries, can perform when an ad seeks to retain the flavor of a past era. Many of the poster letter styles that were used in the eighteenth and nineteenth centuries are too bizarre and hard to read, by our present standards, but among them one can find several styles, which, if used sparingly and in the proper situations, can still be employed effectively in present-day advertisements.

The standard base line of these ads combines a square Gothic form with Copperplate. The horizontal bands, produced by the use of letters with flats replacing curves, form a solid foundation for the rectangular ads.

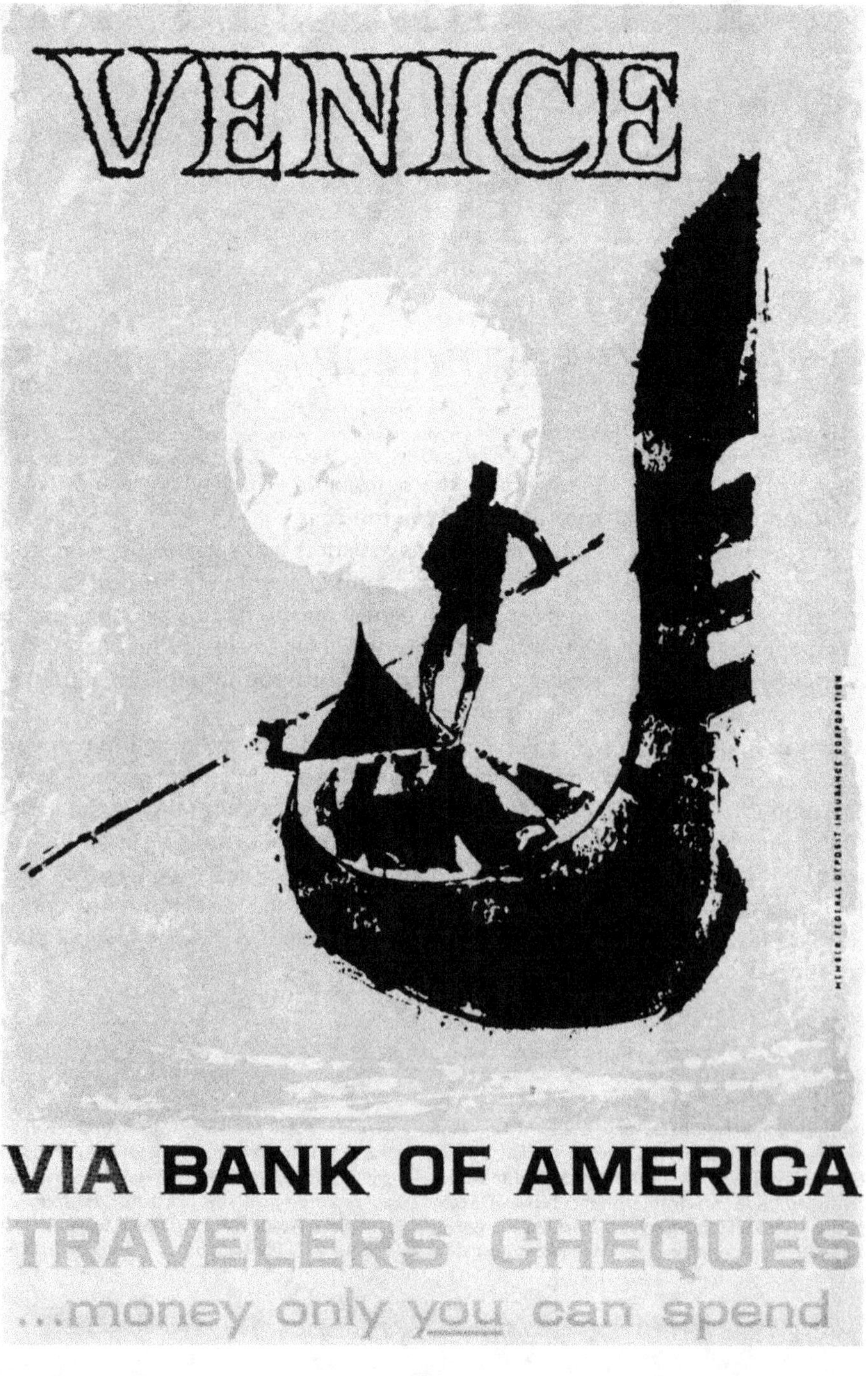

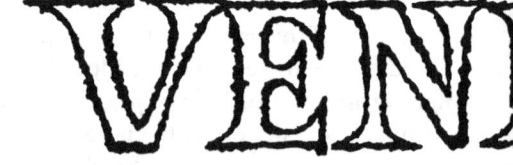

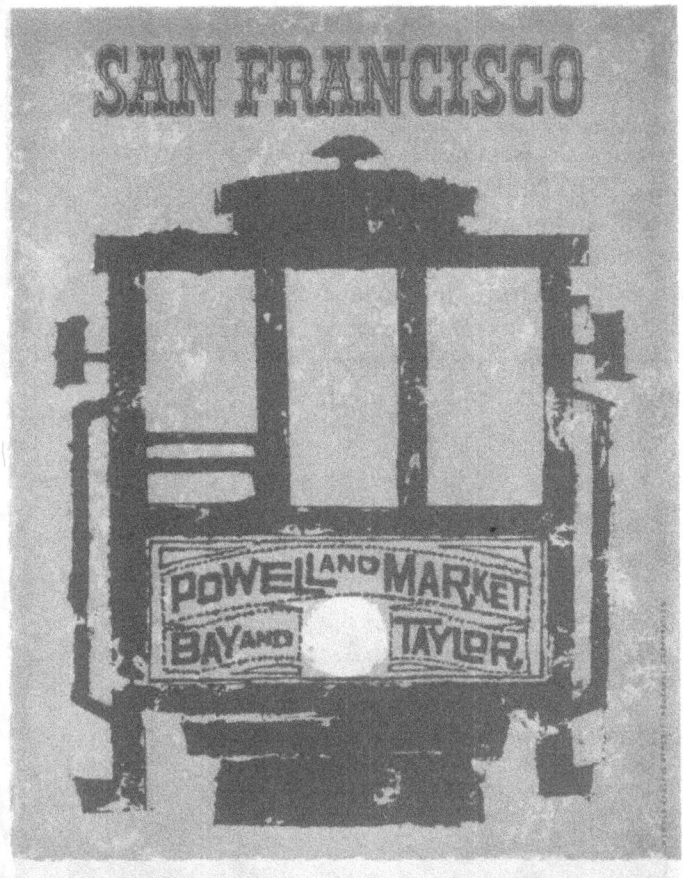

ED HAMILTON: *Attended Los Angeles art schools and had several years of art-service and agency experience in that city. Five years as an art director with one of New York City's larger agencies preceded his position with Johnson & Lewis Advertising, Inc. of San Francisco, where he is art director on the Bank of America account.*

NICHOLAS SIDJAKOV: *Studied art in Berlin and at the Beaux Arts in Paris before beginning his career as an artist, first in Switzerland and later in Paris. In 1955, Mr. Sidjakov came to San Francisco where he soon gained recognition as an outstanding designer and illustrator. He lives in nearby Sausalito with his wife and son.*

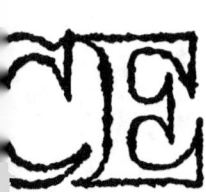

ED HAMILTON: "The series of two-color Travelers Cheque ads have proven successful and owe much of their excellent design and technique to Nick Sidjakov. The serif style of the Venice ad heading seemed to reflect Venice's tradition of beauty and culture. However, the conventional form of the letters appeared out of character with the technique employed in the illustration, hence, the modification of the letter form to bring the two into harmony.

"Lettering based on old type forms was considered a logical choice to reflect the colorful history of San Francisco and still be in complete harmony with the illustration of the cable car.

"The lettering on the base of the ads, stemming from Copperplate forms, seemed to offer a 'corporate' feeling compatible with the strength and dignity of a large financial institution such as Bank of America. And the firm structure of the letters offered a 'solid' base on which to support the dominating illustration."

This caption was not lettered specifically for the BOAC ad but was assembled from an alphabet designed by Robert Evans, president of The Headliners, Inc., New York. The alphabet is called "Catalina Light" and is one of 48, drawn in different weights and proportions, that were done by Mr. Evans. The alphabet from which this caption was produced was drawn with a flat-sided pen. A water-color sable brush was used to build up most of the others in this alphabet family.

The softening of corners where the various strokes meet—such as on the crossbar of the "t," the diagonals on the "k," and on other joinings—gives the letters a smooth, flowing effect, which makes them useful in many layouts where the kind of letters needed to express the "feel" of a statement precludes the use of crisp Gothic forms.

She speaks with a quiet British accent!

JOHN E. RUSSELL: *Studied at Cooper Union in New York City. Joined Federal Advertising Agency, New York City in 1937. Worked for Morey Humm and Warwick as associate art director from 1941 to 1956, interrupted by service in the Air Force during World War II. After V-J Day, was transferred from combat flight crew duty to public relations as staff artist. Joined the Victor A. Bennett Company in 1956 as senior art director. Now employed as art director for Ketchum, MacLeod and Grove in Pittsburgh, assigned to the Alcoa account.*

JOHN E. RUSSELL: "After working on several layout ideas for the BOAC ad, I decided that this one had the dignity required by the message and made its point quickly without being blatant. For the headline, I wanted a letter style that was both simple and distinctive. I decided that the 'Catalina Light' alphabet would serve well in interpreting the copy statement."

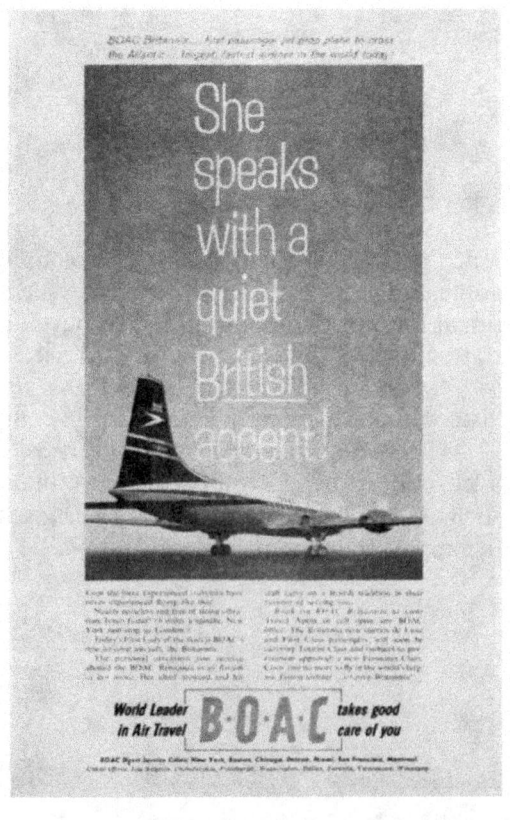

Agency: Victor A. Bennett Company, Inc.
Client: BOAC (British Overseas Airways Corp.)
Art Director: John E. Russell
Lettering Artist: Robert Evans—the Headliners, Inc.

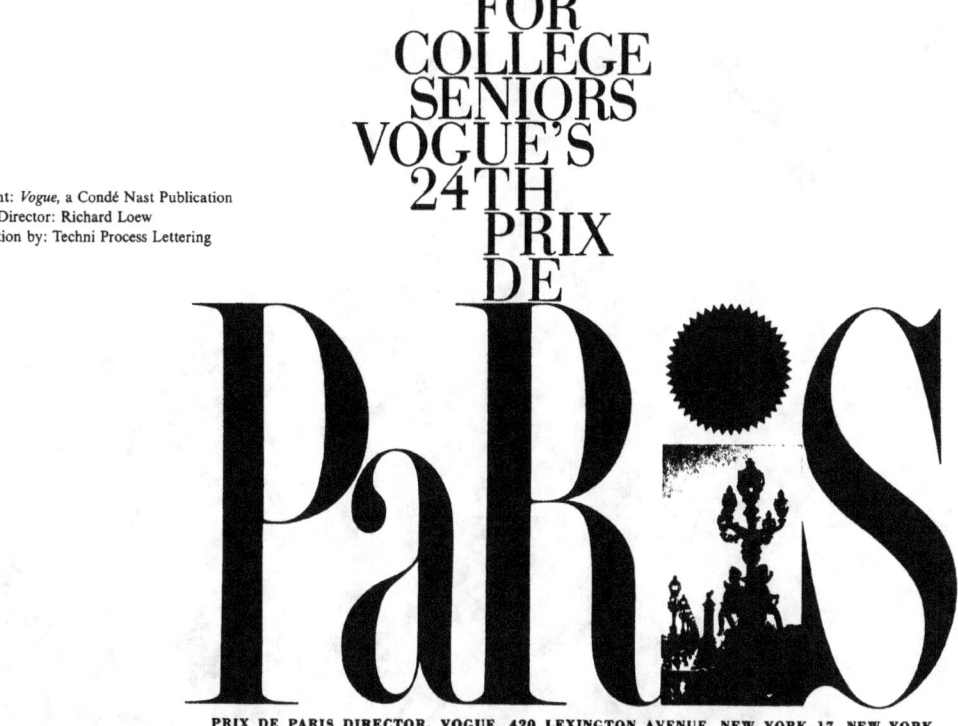

FIRST PRIZE PARIS...Like to be Paris-bound for two wonderful weeks? Like to win a thousand dollars in cash? Like to open a career for yourself in fashion, writing, advertising, merchandising, decorating or publishing?

Are you a college senior working towards a bachelor's degree? If you are, enter VOGUE's famous Prix de Paris competition. Enroll now through October 20, 1958.

1st PRIZE: two exciting weeks in Paris, flying both ways, all expenses paid, or **$1000** in cash (winner's choice). **2nd PRIZE:** $500 cash. 10 Honourable Mention Winners will each receive $25 cash prizes.

In addition, all winners will receive top consideration for positions on VOGUE, GLAMOUR, HOUSE & GARDEN, VOGUE PATTERN BOOK, VOGUE KNITTING BOOK. Other top contestants will be recommended for jobs to stores, advertising agencies and other magazines.

It's VOGUE's annual search for editorial talent. You use VOGUE to complete two quizzes of four questions each, based on actual editorial problems. If answered satisfactorily, you will be eligible to write a 1500-word thesis on a topic in the February 1, 1959 issue.

Use the entry blank below . . . before October 20, 1958.

Client: *Vogue,* a Condé Nast Publication
Art Director: Richard Loew
Caption by: Techni Process Lettering

FOR COLLEGE SENIORS VOGUE'S 24TH PRIX DE PaRiS

PRIX DE PARIS DIRECTOR, VOGUE, 420 LEXINGTON AVENUE, NEW YORK 17, NEW YORK
Please enroll me as an entrant in VOGUE's 24th Prix de Paris.

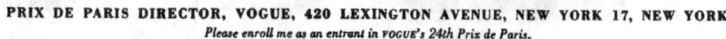

 The stacked lines on this ad help to make the caption a complete design unit. Although the words are staggered on both sides of the stack, a set of letters under the "f" in the word "for" are placed in a near-vertical line, which gives some stability to the free setting.

The majority of stacked captions in current use are generally set or lettered in Gothic forms, but here the use of Bauer Bodoni presents a sparkling yet readable caption. The alternating capitals and lower cases in "Paris" are tall and condensed but hold their family relationship to the letters of normal proportion. As Mr. Loew writes, "The word 'Paris' is easily recognized," thus allowing for the device used for the letter "i," which enhances the caption design.

RICHARD LOEW: *35 years old and a native New Yorker, he has been "Vogue's" promotion art director for four years, as well as a free-lance graphic designer. Before joining "Vogue," he was an agency art director and a promotion designer for "Time." His work has received awards from the Art Directors' Club, the AIGA, and the Type Directors' Club, as well as recognition in "Graphis." He is also a free-lance furniture designer.*

RICHARD LOEW: "This advertisement, announcing *Vogue's* annual competition for college seniors, presented us with the problem of suggesting two conflicting ideas: the academic image of college and the gay, exciting image of a Paris vacation. Since few graphic symbols suggest both ideas (a champagne bottle might suggest Paris, for instance, but would be objectionable to many college administrators in relation to college), we decided to solve the problem abstractly by doing a type advertisement. It was also necessary to maintain the *Vogue* image; therefore the particular type style was chosen because of its simple, elegant, and feminine qualities. We felt that stacking the type gave the design a European feel. Since the word 'Paris' is common and easily recognized, we felt that we could introduce a slight innovation without sacrificing legibility. Thus the decorative 'i' which graphically reinforces the ideas of college and Paris."

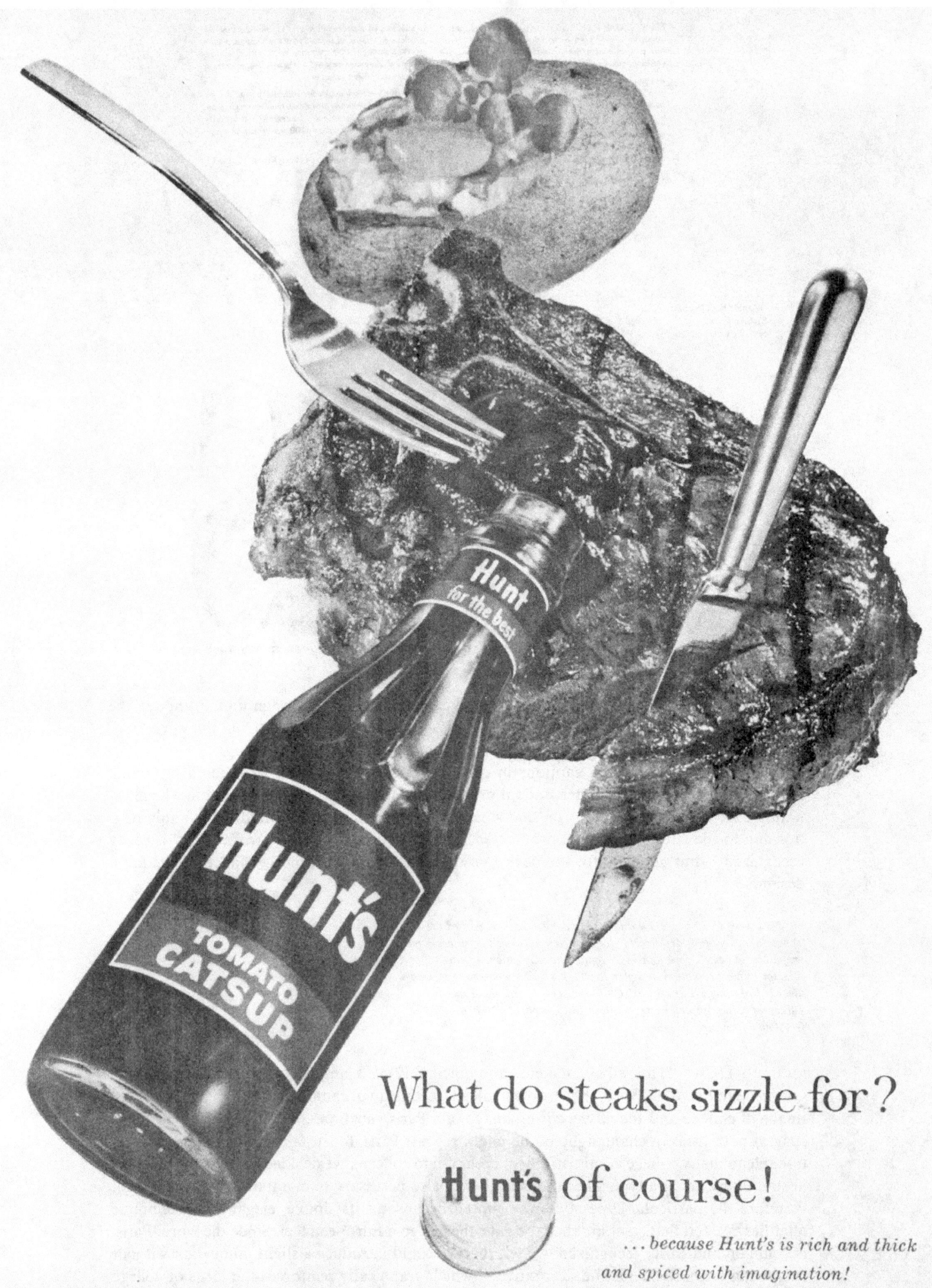

What do steaks sizzle for?

Hunt's of course!

...because Hunt's is rich and thick
and spiced with imagination!

Mr. Silverman and I discussed the style of letter forms for this series at some length. I ran through a test tissue which was photostated down to reproduction size so that it could be judged in relationship to the other elements in the layout. The reduction made the letters appear to be in the Bodoni classification and a bit too light in tone for the needs of the layout. Therefore, it was decided that the hairlines should be drawn a bit thicker than they had been to hold more closely to Century. A bounced caption of this sort naturally allowed for some departure from the true Century forms, but the degree of tumble and bounce had to be restrained for the sake of readability.

What do steaks sizzle for?

of course!

HAL SILVERMAN: *Born in New York City, but received his formal education in Los Angeles. Attended UCLA and was graduated from Art Center School. Started work for Young & Rubicam in New York City. Served two years in the Army and then resumed work at Young & Rubicam, Los Angeles. Has served as A. D. on several accounts, Hunt Foods being the most recent. Currently employed by Erwin Wasey, Ruthrauff & Ryan, Los Angeles.*

HAL SILVERMAN: "The caption copy on this ad was one of a series of playful puns about the combination of a particular food with Hunt's Catsup: 'What do eggs scramble for?' 'What do cold cuts warm up to?' 'What do steaks sizzle for?'

"The words almost styled themselves. They had to bounce—nothing 'rock-and-roll,' but just enough to let the lightheartedness of the idea come through.

"The classroom question-and-answer feeling of the phrase called for the ease and familiarity of Century Schoolbook. In the finished lettering, the characters were modified for more grace and legibility and then jostled into a slight bounce.

"The words now *looked* like what they said."

Agency: Young & Rubicam, Inc.
Client: Hunt Foods and Industries, Inc.
Art Director: Hal Silverman
Lettering Artist: Mortimer Leach

It should be noted that while the captions shown in these ads seem to be quite unrestrained, the letters are clearly defined and the words are easy to read. This would indicate that in many forms of advertising more liberties can be taken in the interpretation of letters than is being done at the present time. Facing the competition of improved type designs and photo-process lettering, lettering artists will inevitably be required to produce more objective and interpretive letter forms.

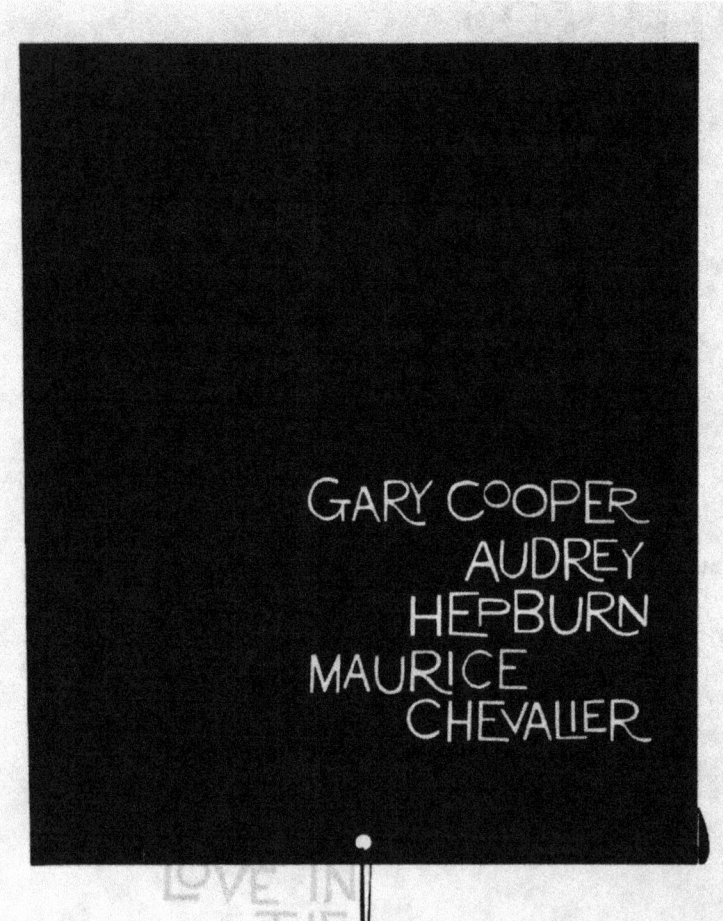

SAUL BASS: *New York born, he has been designing on the West Coast since 1946. While regional in residence, he has received international recognition. In the past ten years, his work has won more than 40 national awards. Best known by the public is his work for the motion-picture industry, notably the titles for "Around the World in 80 Days," and his design for "The Man with the Golden Arm." Winner of the National Society of Art Directors' 1957 award of "Art Director of the Year."*

Client: Allied Artists
Designer: Saul Bass
Lettering Artist: Art Goodman

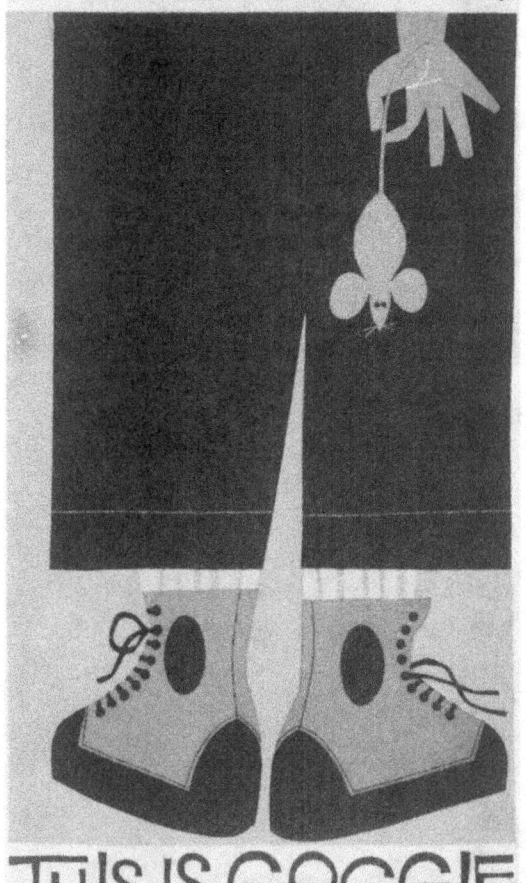

SAUL BASS: "The lettering used in this group of advertisements had no dependence upon traditional forms. The style was based on the needs of the all-over design and mood of the presentation.

"On the advertisements for 'This is Goggle' and 'Love in the Afternoon' the uninhibited bounce and interlocking of the letters that vary in size were planned to give the effect of naive gaiety.

"The stark and distorted forms used in the 'Vertigo' ad were chosen in order to integrate the caption within the general design of the layout.

"While the lettering for the San Francisco International Film Festival has more obviously been designed to form a pattern complete in itself, the lettering for the movie ads was also planned with this in mind—to use the caption styles for an illustrative effect."

Client: Otto Preminger
Designer: Saul Bass
Lettering Artist: Art Goodman

Client: San Francisco Film Festival
Designer: Saul Bass
Lettering Artist: Art Goodman

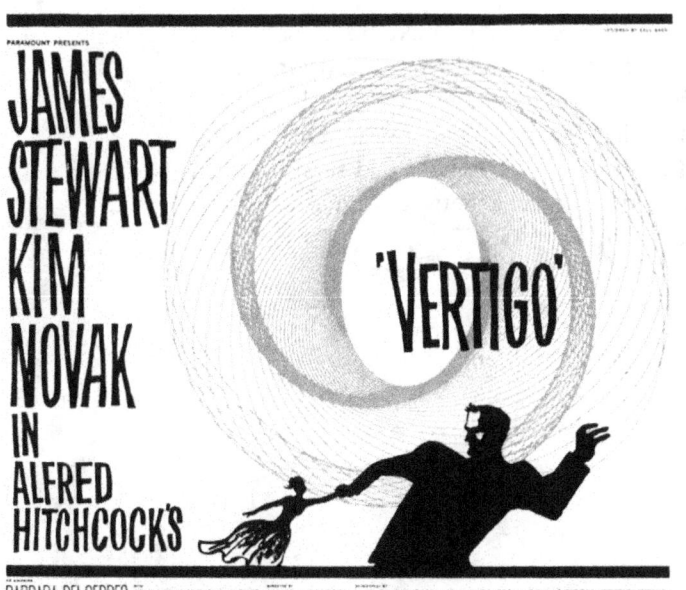

Client: Vista Vision
Designer: Saul Bass
Lettering Artist: Dave Nagata

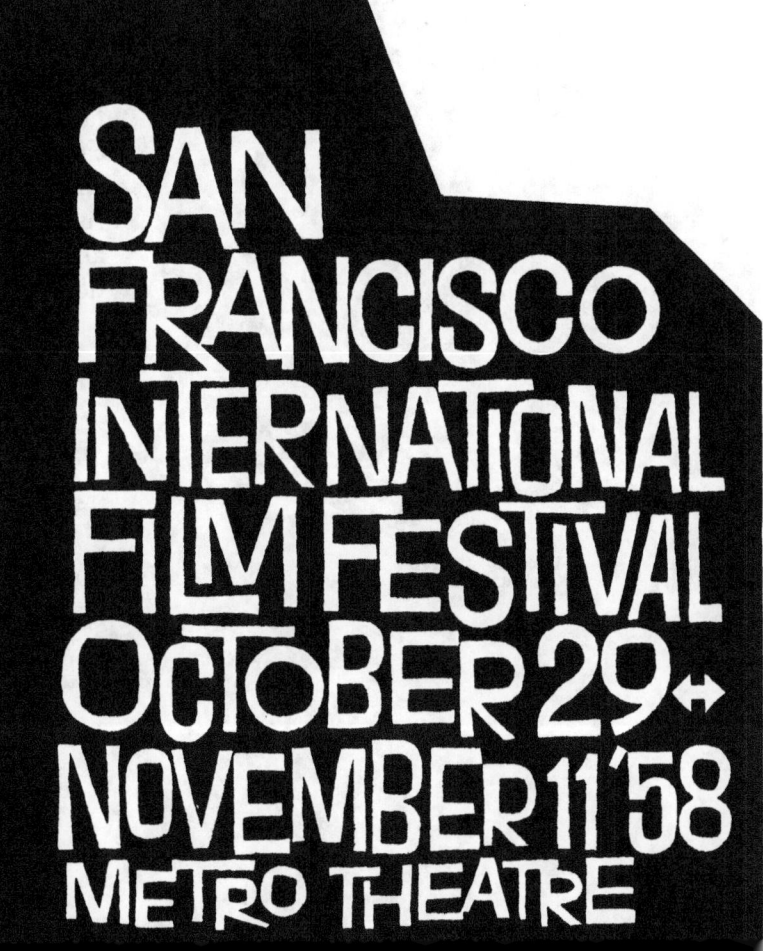

In this Life Saver ad, we have a good example of the use of a caption as part of the all-over page design. The curve of the caption continues the rhythm produced by the placement of the change purse, the Life Savers, and the package. The simplicity of the light sans-serif letters produces an easy-reading line despite the deep swing of the caption. The letters are drawn with a slight flare at the end of the strokes, which adds an air of informality to the line, in a pleasantly informal ad.

Delicious flavor "change"...Butter-Rum

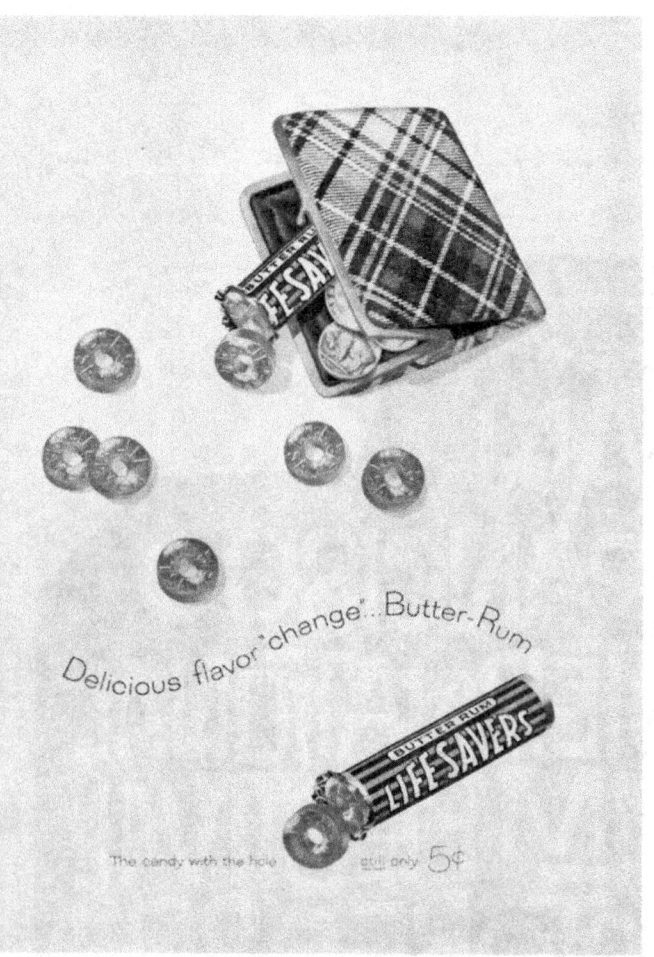

FRAZIER PURDY: *Born in New York City, 1929. Completed high school but had no formal art training—studied under his father, Leavitt Purdy. First job: mount room at Lennen & Newell, 1952. From there to a studio, doing comps. Back to Lennen & Newell as assistant art director on Old Golds. Thence to Young & Rubicam in 1954 as assistant art director until he was made an art director in May of 1957. Spends his spare time woodworking and sailing.*

FRAZIER PURDY: "I used a light, extended, sans-serif face on the Life Saver Butter Rum advertisement because I felt that it would be in keeping with the general all-over light feeling of the page. I also felt that by running the headline in a curve it would serve to form an effective and pleasant link between the central portion of the ad and the product."

Agency: Young & Rubicam, Inc.
Client: Life Savers—Beech-Nut Life Savers, Inc.
Art Director: Frazier Purdy
Lettering Artist: Sam Marsh Studios

While Nicholas Cochin type is rarely used as a display face in current advertisements, its effective use in the Bermuda ad proves a point: type designs that reflect the feeling of Old-World tradition can serve a double purpose; when the mood of the ad suggests the use of a traditional form, these designs can supply it, and they also offer the opportunity to display letter forms other than those in current favor. During any period in which certain type or lettered forms are in extremely popular use (or over-use, in some cases), this change of pace can be advantageous.

BERMUDA

Another world awaits you in these lovely little islands

JULES L. MENGHETTI: *After studying art in Philadelphia and New York schools, his first three years in the advertising business were spent with N. W. Ayer & Son in Philadelphia. When J. M. Mathes, Inc. was founded in New York in 1933, he was invited to join them under the direction of Mr. Lester J. Loh, who at present is executive vice president in charge of all creative departments.*

Agency: J. M. Mathes, Incorporated
Client: Bermuda Trade Development Board
Art Director: Jules L. Menghetti

JULES L. MENGHETTI: "The use of Nicholas Cochin type, designed by Peignot in 1912, was decided upon for the headline because its grace and feeling of Old-World tradition seemed to express best the copy statement and the atmosphere of Bermuda. The body copy was set in Caledonia, which was designed by W. A. Dwiggins. This type has a widespread acceptance. Its basic design seems equally appropriate for institutional or commercial work, and for book, periodical, or advertising composition."

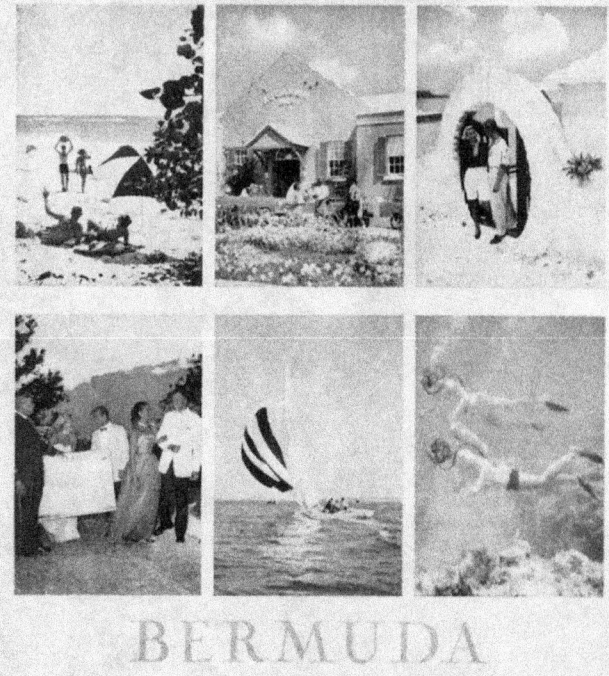

Brushscripts can be employed to express many moods, depending upon their weights, degree of bounce, and rhythmic or angular strokes. The texture of the letter edges can also produce a planned effect.

The light and carefree rendering of the caption, "Resort at Sea," is a fine choice for an ad such as this. Freely rendered scripts call for rapid brush strokes and are usually written out many times before the desired effect is achieved. In many cases, individual words or segments of words are selected and pasted into a line, after which any necessary retouching is added.

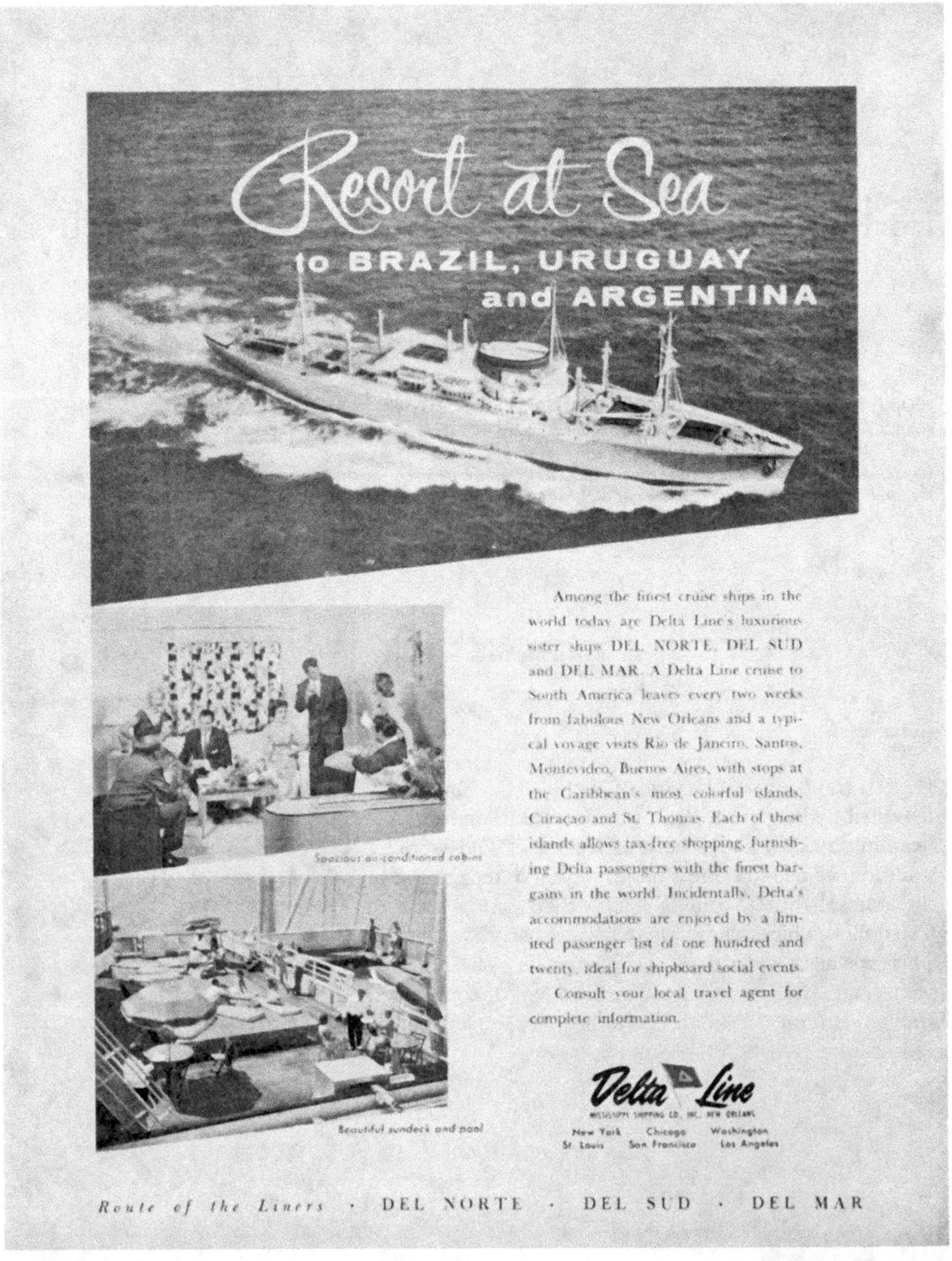

R. C. BRANDT: *Started his career in Chicago—being schooled there at the Art Institute, Fred Mizen Academy, and the American Academy, where he specialized in layout under Frank Young. His first art directorship was with the Carter, Jones and Taylor Agency in South Bend, Indiana, in 1939. National recognition has included having material selected for hanging in the Art Directors' Club show and the STA exhibits in Chicago. His layouts secured the Socrates Award for the Public Service account and the Joshua Award for a hotel client. His experience with lettering started with show-card writing in 1931 at the age of 17.*

Resort at Sea

to BRAZIL, URUGUAY and ARGENTINA

R. C. BRANDT: "Hand lettering in this particular style was chosen to suggest a carefree, relaxed, vacationy feeling, and to take the curse off the 'square,' realistic photographs. (This was also the reason for cropping and arranging the photographs like 'flags' on a lanyard.) Also, since we used the phrase 'Resort at Sea' as a slogan, the lettering style makes it individual, like a signature."

Agency: Bauerlein, Inc.
Client: Delta Line, Inc. (Division of Mississippi Shipping Company, Inc.)
Art Director: R. C. Brandt
Lettering Artist: Lloyd G. Reedy

While the design of the letters for "THE CAR" gives the words the vigorous and fresh look that Mr. Shure desired, an air of dignity has also been effected. The letters, which contain characteristics of the Classic Roman forms, have an attractive crispness resulting from the use of paper cutouts. This, as the art director planned, produces a contemporary effect while maintaining a feeling of quality.

DON SHURE: *Senior art director, McCann-Erickson, Inc. Formerly art director in Detroit, Chicago, Mexico City, and New York with MacManus, John & Adams, Inc., and Kenyon & Eckhardt, among others. Studied at New School for Social Research, Cranbrook Academy, Wayne University, Toledo Museum School of Design, Theodore Keane's Art School. Exhibited at Art Institute of Detroit, Toledo Museum of Art, and Art Directors' Club. Works reproduced in Art Directors' "Annual," "Modern Publicity," "Art News." Jury: Art Directors' Club, New York and Detroit; A.I.G.A., New York; "National Scholastic." Major accounts worked on: Buick, Coca Cola, National Biscuit, Chrysler, Imperial Chrysler, American Rayon Institute, Dorothy Gray, Nestle, Talon, CBS Radio, Stetson Hats, Manhattan Shirts, Dow Chemical, and others.*

DON SHURE: "'THE CAR' lettering was originally a paper cutout—a derivation from the Matisse 'Jazz' book. Of a different character, our objective was that of achieving a new vitality and of creating a new image for Buick that would reflect the contemporary design and new look of the car."

Agency: McCann-Erickson, Inc.
Client: Buick Motor Division, General Motors Corp.
Art Director: Don Shure
Lettering Artist: Irving Bogen

FROM BUICK FOR 1959 COMES

THE CAR

A new class of fine cars within reach of 2 out of 3 new car buyers ▶

Mr. Thompson is among the group of designers who try to devise ways of using type in interesting and unusual arrangements. In a sense, these men use type forms as source material and employ them to compose units of design, either integrated with other elements on the page or as a counterbalance.

There are, unfortunately, still too many layout men who lack the imagination and inventiveness to use standard type forms as a decorative part of a layout.

HARVEY THOMPSON: *Art training: Art Center School, Los Angeles. Art director, Abbott Kimball, New York. War service: Training Aids Division, Signal Corps. After the war returned to Los Angeles as a free-lance art director. Art director, Silverwoods Department Stores and "Telefilms Magazine." Presently, director of advertising design department at Art Center School, art director for "Wisdom" magazine, and consulting art director.*

HARVEY THOMPSON: "With a low art budget, the use of type often becomes a necessity. For my own taste, type frequently leaves much to be desired, but it does force the designer to try to use type in a more creative way. I have tried to put this particular philosophy to work in this single page of a two-page spread. Alternate Gothic #2 was selected as a note of contrast in style to the ornate qualities of the Michelangelo sculpture. The type, when set, seemed very hard and black to me, so the gray benday was used on some words and letters to give a more decorative, softer effect."

Client: *Wisdom* Magazine
Art Director: Harvey Thompson

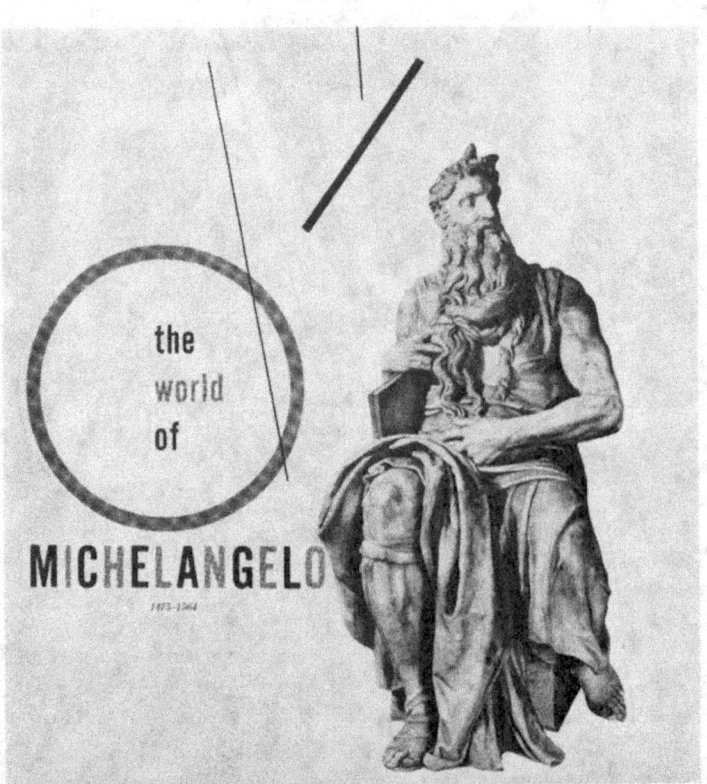

the world of

MICHELANGELO

1475 - 1564

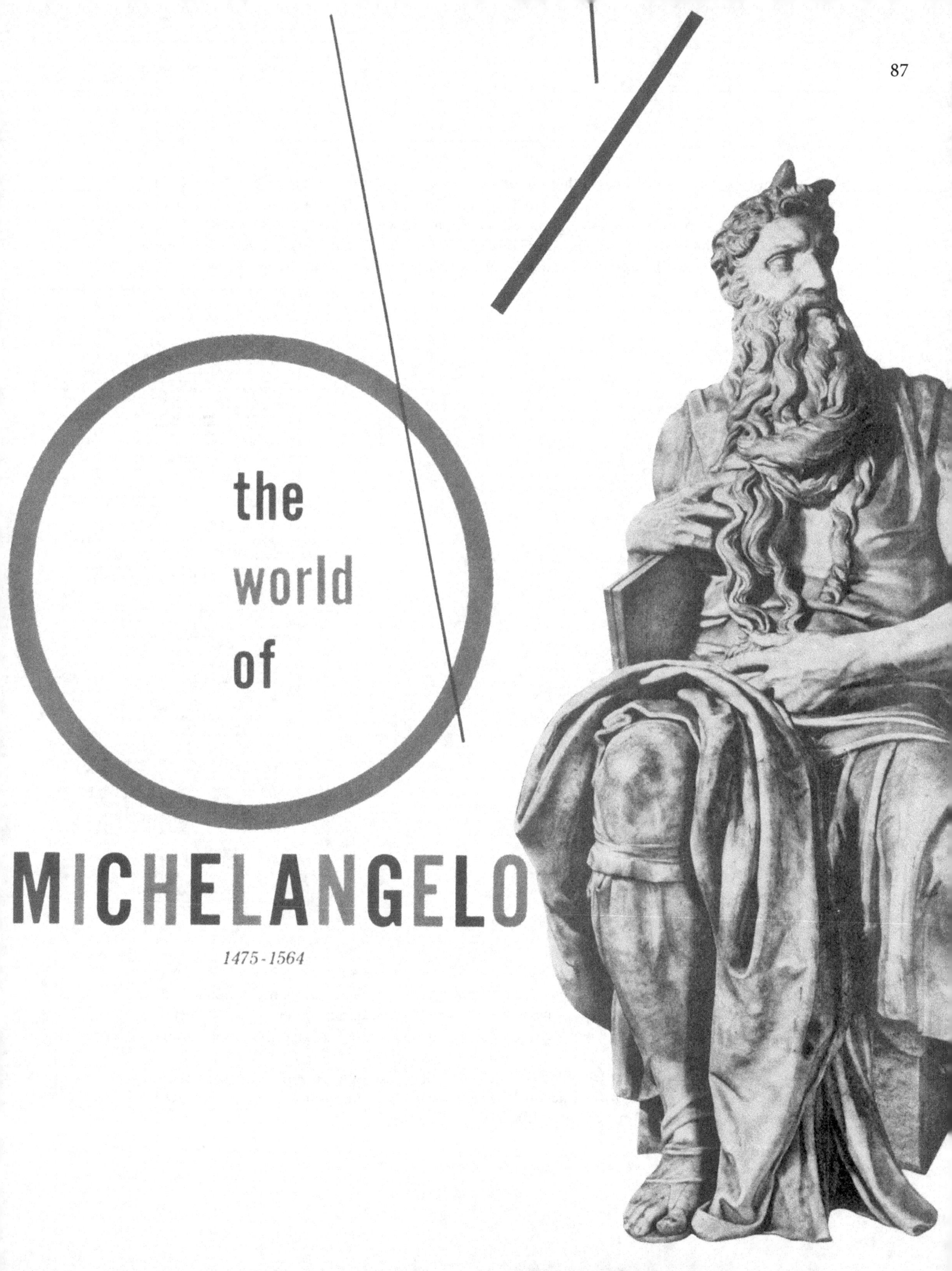

In my opinion, the breaking of the caption on this title page into separate reverse blocks, rather than detracting from the caption's readability, is more likely to attract the reader's attention than if it had been set on a straight line. The eye moves easily from panel to panel, while the staccato feeling adds to the excitement of the statement. Although I may be carrying symbolism too far, I like the use of expanded letter forms in an article about life extension.

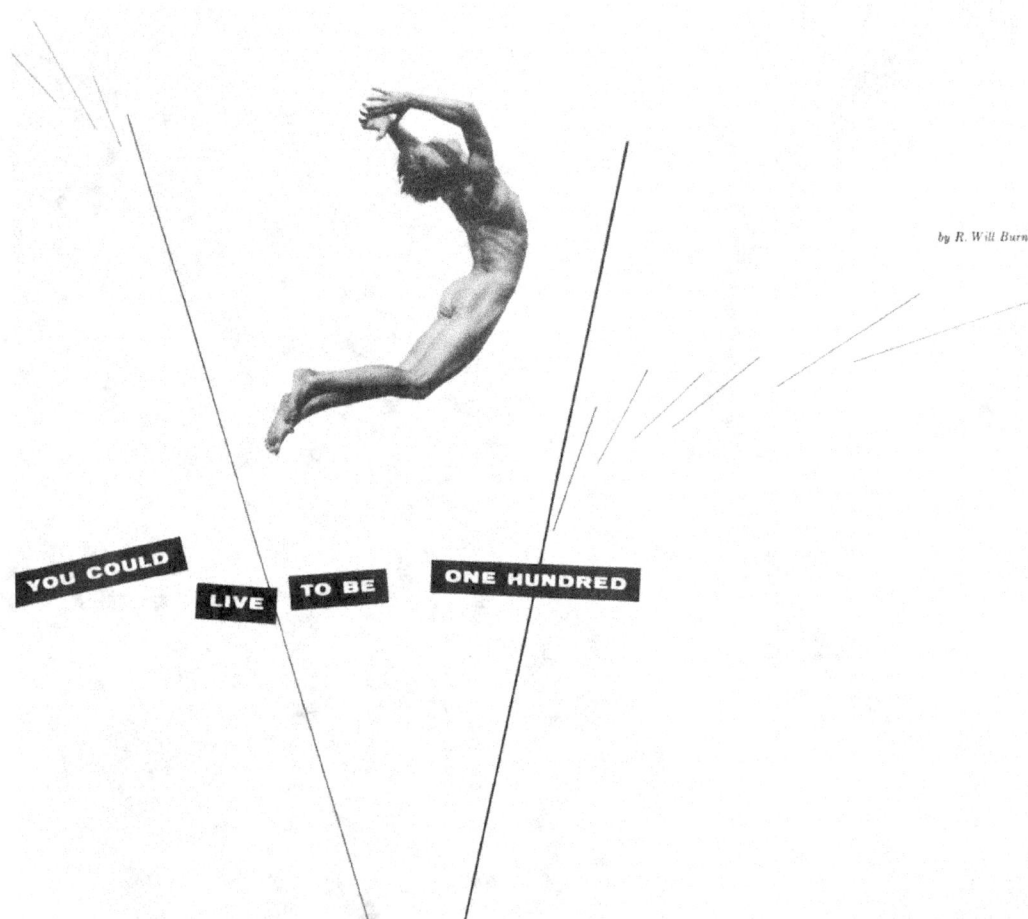

HARVEY THOMPSON: "This particular article seemed to call for a more symbolic treatment than could be obtained with the obvious portrait type of picture. I felt a certain emotional 'wallop' could be achieved in this way. The photo of the youth leaping in the air was selected as a symbol of vitality. The lines were used as an aid in helping to give the whole format a feeling of movement.

"Venus Extra Bold Extended was selected for the heading to give a contrast to the white space and the fineness of the line work. The irregular placement of the panels was used to enhance the feeling of movement, but still retain legibility."

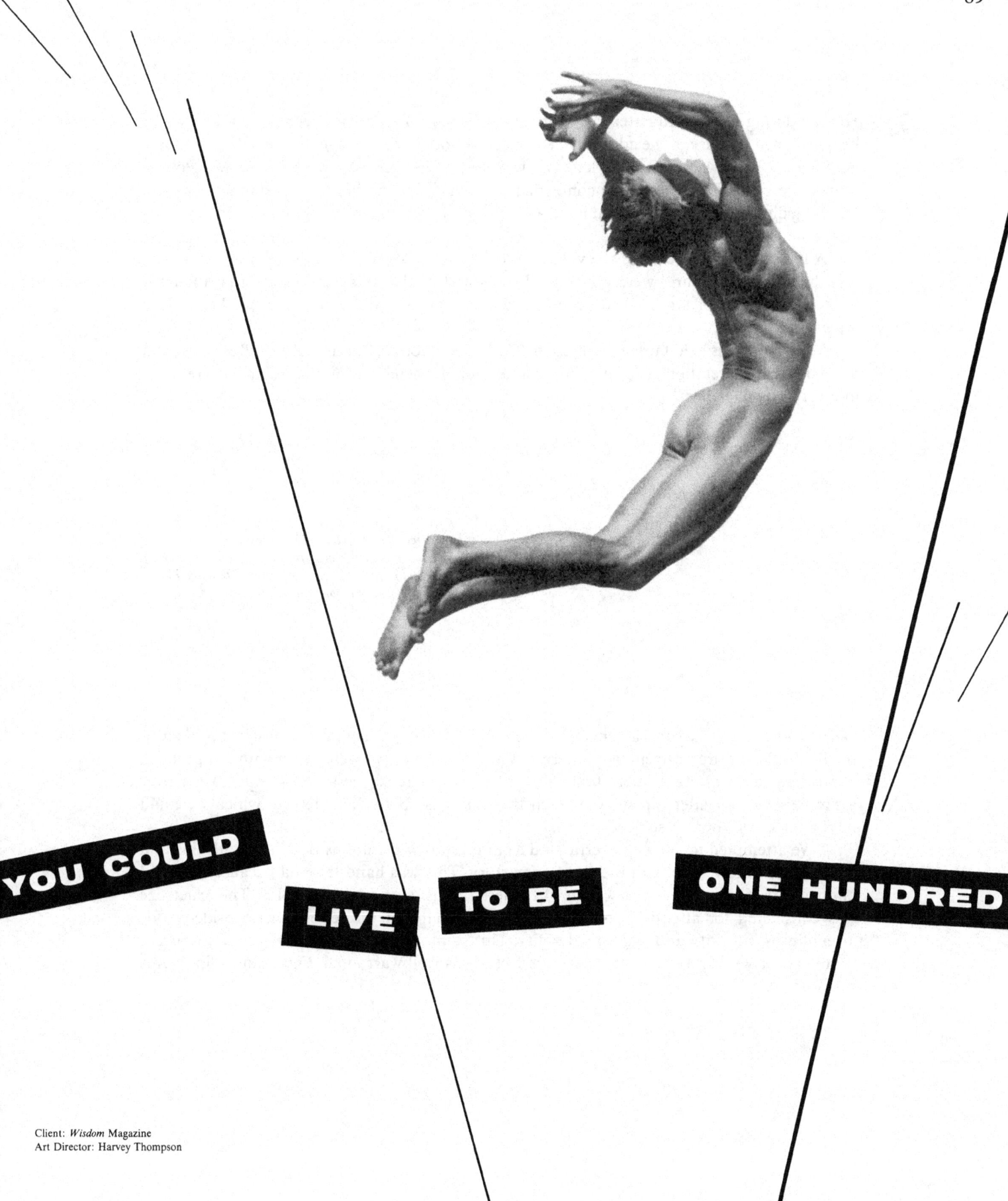

YOU COULD LIVE TO BE ONE HUNDRED

Client: *Wisdom* Magazine
Art Director: Harvey Thompson

Hand lettering a standard letter form for the major text of an advertisement could very well be questioned because of the additional expense. Although the average reader of the ad shown here may not be aware that hand lettering was used, it has served a purpose. As Mr. Powers writes, the general color *could* be controlled, and this, plus the familiar Caslon letters used, undoubtedly makes for easy readability. As Mr. Powers states, readership figures have proved this to be true.

A few years ago, I lettered the voluminous text for a Mobilgas newspaper ad, and, here too, the readership figures were very high. It may well be that this occasional departure from the tonal qualities of typeset text produces just enough of a difference to hold the reader's attention.

Mr. Mullen has held fairly closely to the Caslon type forms, but the subtle differences from them in his interpretation of the individual letters and his sensitive letter spacing have resulted in a very pleasing effect.

FENTON POWERS: *Started with J. Walter Thompson Company in their San Francisco office and was later transferred to the New York office, where he has been for many years. Over this period of time, he has worked on many of the accounts handled in that office.*

FENTON POWERS: "As you can imagine, the subject of a spark plug is a tough problem to publicize. People are not generally interested in them. Thus, we were faced with the problem of making the subject as interesting as possible with a terse message of copy to get over a simple idea—a leadership story. We felt that this was about the extent to which we could hold an audience on our subject.

"We attempted to get as powerful and as interesting a picture as possible. With this as a stopper, we followed up with the short copy story. This was hand lettered because we could control it perfectly. The exact weight of the letters was considered for color. The exact size was considered for attention and readability. The shape of the letters was considered for friendliness, sincerity and again readability. This cannot be matched with type. Lettering is more expensive than type. In this case, we feel it was well warranted. Our readership figures prove this also."

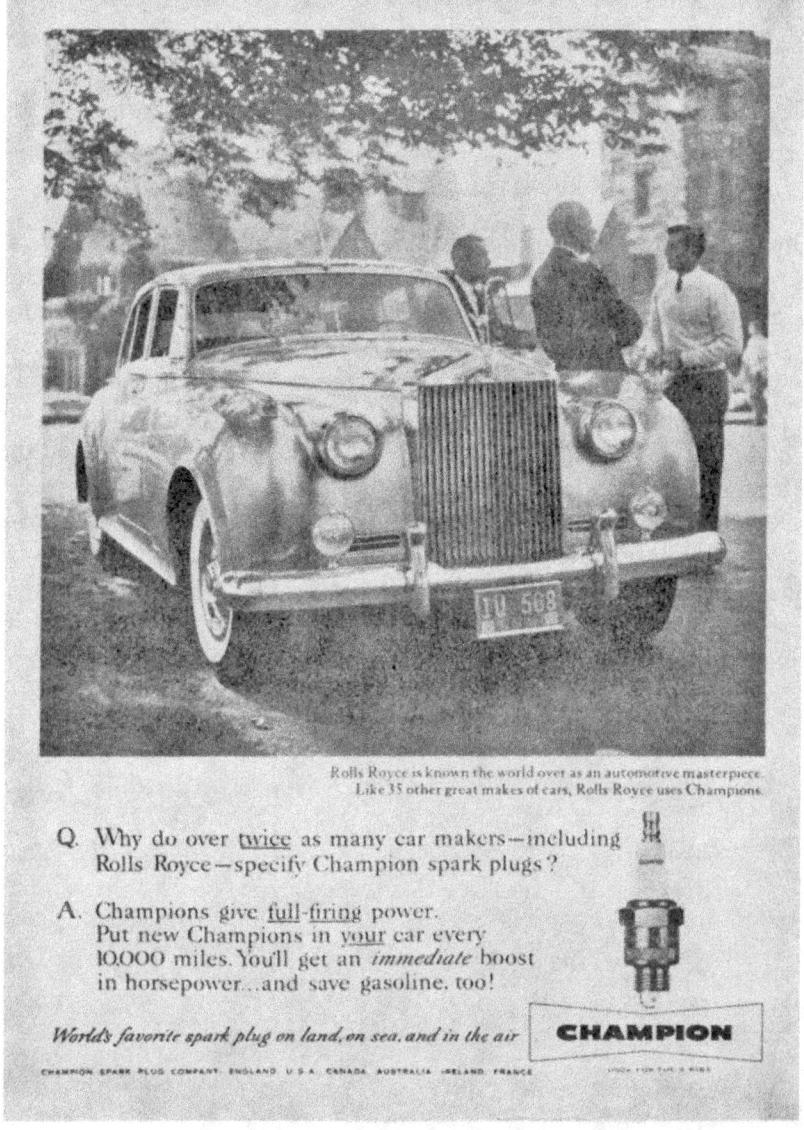

Agency: J. Walter Thompson Company
Client: Champion Spark Plug Company
Art Director: Fenton Powers
Lettering Artist: Jerry Mullen

Q. Why are nearly <u>twice</u> as many police cars in the U.S.A. powered by Champion spark plugs?

A. Champions give <u>full-firing</u> power.
Put new Champions in <u>your</u> car every 10,000 miles. You'll get an *immediate* boost in horsepower...and save gasoline, too!

92

 Keeping a family relationship among the types or lettering used in an extensive advertising campaign is, in my opinion, very important. Readers are subconsciously conditioned to the caption styling and to its relationship with the product. And this must surely increase the "seen-associated" score in readership surveys.

The Futura Medium Condensed forms, which were used throughout the Edsel campaign, are concise, simple forms and, as Mr. Groen writes, easy to read. Despite their simplicity of design (in fact, quite likely because of it), the constant use of these forms in all media made them a definite form of product identification.

Only a limited number of letter styles can be used successfully in a three-line major caption. If an art director anticipates this possible requirement when working on layouts that are part of a particular advertising campaign, he should avoid the use of ornate styles, and he should not use any forms which contain a sharp variation between the thick and thin strokes. Letters containing extremely thin hairlines tend to vibrate when used in a caption of more than two lines.

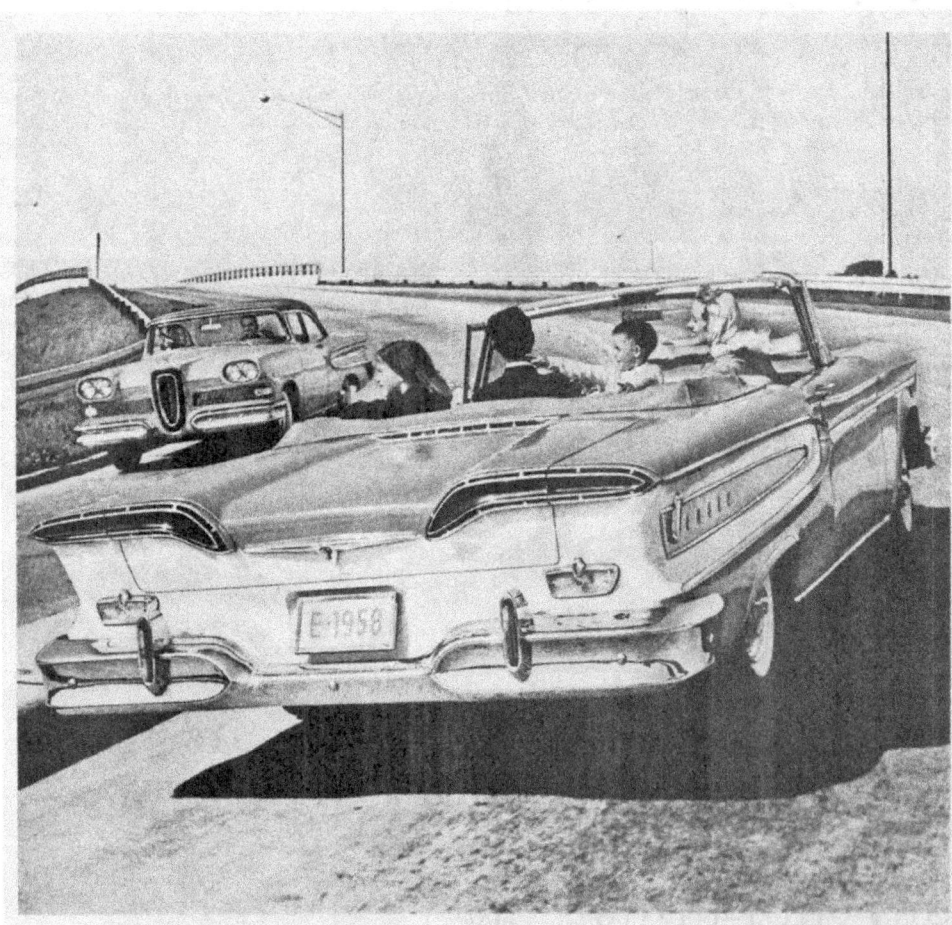

Agency: Foote, Cone & Belding
Client: Edsel Division, Ford Motor Company
Art Director: John Groen

JOHN GROEN: "a. The condensed version of this face is easy to read.

"b. We were using a good deal of white space, especially in newspapers, and the weight of the face added the right amount of color within the headline area when related to the illustration and the body text, etc.

"c. It is difficult to control, at all times, the lengths of headlines and subheads. This variable was another factor in the choice of a type face which would be easily read when set in one short line and which would not discourage reading when the headline length extended to two or possibly three display lines.

"d. With all possible uses considered, such as national magazine and newspaper ads, dealer ads, collateral material, etc., a family relationship of all print material was achieved through the basic use of the same type faces, even though the print material was handled through two offices of Foote, Cone & Belding in different cities."

JOHN GROEN: *Studied at Art Center School in Los Angeles, and worked on department-store advertising and in art studios in that city. After some free-lance work, specializing in lettering and layouts, joined the Los Angeles office of Foote, Cone & Belding as an art director. Three years ago, after 12 years in the Los Angeles office, was transferred to their Chicago office. Some of the accounts on which he has worked as art director are: Lockheed Aircraft Corporation; Hughes Aircraft Company; Hughes Tool Company; All-Year Club of Southern California; Cole Swimwear; Catalina Swimwear; Bullock's; Edsel Division, Ford Motor Company; and S. C. Johnson & Son, Inc.*

DRAMATIC EDSEL STYLING leads the way

Less than fifty dollars difference between Edsel and V-8's in the Low-Priced Three

By going directly to ancient letter forms for inspiration, this personal interpretation by the lettering artist in designing the individual letters used for the CHEF BOY-AR-DEE advertisements has resulted in an interesting and highly readable letter style. While the lower-case forms show a relationship to Nicholas Jenson, they are drawn with considerably more calligraphic action, thereby adding a distinctive flavor to the headline.

Agency: Young & Rubicam, Inc.
Client: American Home Foods, Inc.
Art Director: Arthur Cady
Lettering Artist: George Abrams

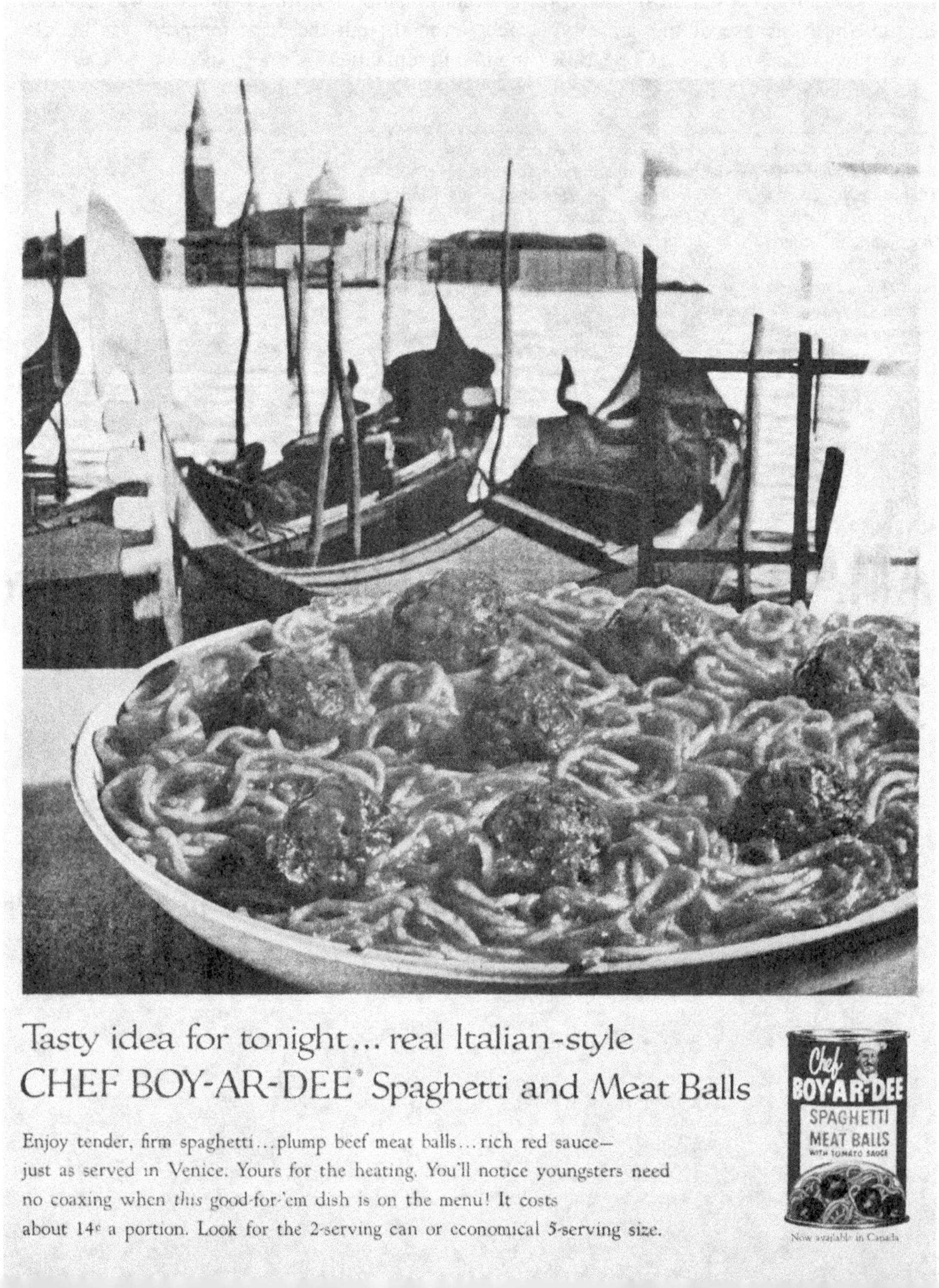

Tasty idea for tonight... real Italian-style
CHEF BOY-AR-DEE® Spaghetti and Meat Balls

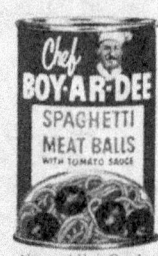

Enjoy tender, firm spaghetti...plump beef meat balls...rich red sauce—
just as served in Venice. Yours for the heating. You'll notice youngsters need
no coaxing when *this* good-for-'em dish is on the menu! It costs
about 14¢ a portion. Look for the 2-serving can or economical 5-serving size.

real Italian-style

ARTHUR CADY: *Was born in Buffalo, N. Y., and grew up in Canada. He received his education at Antioch College and the Art Students League. Has been with Young & Rubicam for more than ten years, working in two installments. Married, he has two children but still has time for "do-it-yourself-ing," water-color painting, drawing, gardening, studying foreign languages, travel, amateur writing, antiqueing, reading and commuting.*

CHEF BOY-AR-DEE®

ARTHUR CADY: "The aim: to create very simple, readable, conservative lettering, yet in a style that would be fresh and possibly unique in modern advertising, to be used over a long period of time in CHEF BOY-AR-DEE advertisements.

"The method: the obvious source, considering our Italian-style product and subject, was Roman stone cuttings. The designer, George Abrams, worked directly from photos of rubbings and drawings of the originals in the Roman Forum. Since the Forum provided no lower case, he observed and was influenced by the great Italian typographers of the post-Rennaissance, specifically Nicholas Jenson.

"Quoting from Stanley Morrison's 'Four Centuries of Fine Printing' about Nicholas Jenson: 'Jenson's associate and successor, Herbort, issued a catalogue of books for sale which, after the manner of advertisers, contained a lengthy commendation of Jenson's types, wherein exaggeration was certainly not lacking. After speaking of the correctness of the Jenson editions, he proceeds to claim that: "The quality and value of his types is another marvel to relate, for it ought to be ascribed rather to divine inspiration than human wit." The panegyrist is, however, well within the mark when he claims that: "The characters are so methodically and carefully finished by that famous man that the letters are not smaller or larger or thicker than reason demands or than may afford pleasure."'

"This was exactly what Abrams and I were about, though we had completed the job long before we saw the quote. Mrs. Lydia Carter, the typographer at Young & Rubicam, brought to our attention this apt description of what we ourselves were trying to do.

"It is also interesting that the completed lettering has strong similarities to, and compatibility with, Goudy's Kennerley Old Style (again designed by the same methods and in the same spirit), which Mrs. Carter recommended for the body text in preference to popular cuttings of Jenson because it has more width and color."

I agree completely with Mr. Stone when he writes that "there is no more readable type face" than Century Schoolbook. As a high percentage of the public in this country learned to read from textbooks set in Century, these forms draw their attention subconsciously.

The freely drawn capital "I's" leading into the caption and body text on this ad, relating as they do to the technique of the illustrations, add to the compatibility of the printed message with the drawings.

In any case, wouldn't <u>you</u> say ONE is enough?

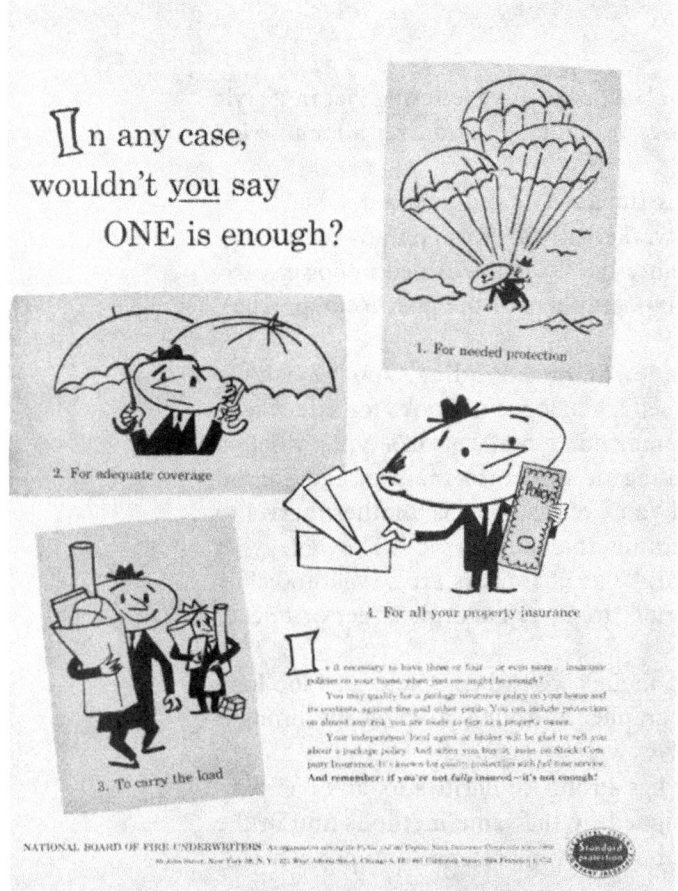

ROBERT STONE: *Studied at Toledo Museum of Art, followed by five years of art-studio experience. He has been with J. M. Mathes, Incorporated since 1942 where he has served as art director on accounts in such diverse fields as insurance, cosmetics, beverages, plastics, food, travel, and home furnishings. Mr. Stone, a former instructor at Pratt Institute, is a member of the Art Directors' Club of New York, National Society of Art Directors, and Westport Artists.*

ROBERT STONE: "Because we were trying to achieve a simple, primer-type feeling in this ad, Century Schoolbook was the obvious selection for headlines. In my opinion, there is no more readable type face."

Agency: J. M. Mathes, Incorporated
Client: National Board of Fire Underwriters
Art Director: Robert Stone

The individual letters of these light single-weight forms have been gently relaxed, and the lines have been subtly bounced, thus giving a "warmer" feeling to the copy statement than could be accomplished with similar type forms. The simplicity of the letter forms has maintained easy readability in a three-line caption.

CARL LINS: *With N. W. Ayer & Son for six years and since then, for the past 34 years, he has been with Young & Rubicam, Inc. Most of his work as art director and supervisor has been on food accounts. These include General Foods, Borden's, Lipton, and International Milling in Canada. Work has received many awards from the Art Directors' Club. Introduced toned water-color lettering (finished by Pete Dom) for Swan's Down Cake Flour in 1941.*

CARL LINS: "The problem in this ad was to use a headline, eminently legible and yet sufficiently subordinate to the appetite-appeal of the illustration. I felt, also, that the style should combine well with the other elements in the ad in suggesting quality. This light, sans-serif line resulted.

HOME-COOKED TASTE

Agency: Young & Rubicam, Inc.
Client: Lipton Soup
Art Director: Carl Lins
Lettering Artist: Peter Dom

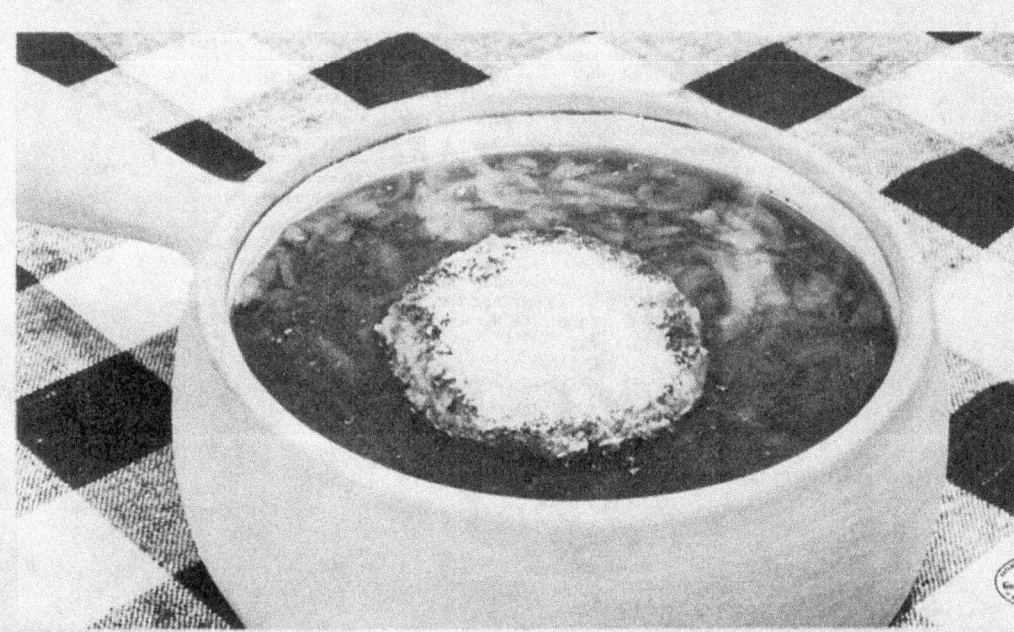

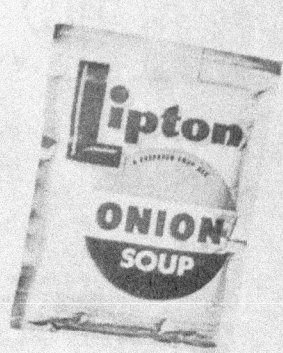

SO ELEGANT! THIS LIPTON SOUP WITH FRESH
HOME-COOKED TASTE
plenty of hearty nourishment, too!

Just sniff that fragrance . . . Lively onions simmering slowly in rich beef broth. *Lipton Onion Soup!*

So nourishing. Lipton uses the kind of ingredients a real French chef would choose to make this special treat.

Lipton Soups are delicious. And you can fix them in minutes.

• • • •

There's so much good in Lipton Soup Mixes . . . body-building proteins, carbohydrates for energy, minerals and vitamins essential to good nutrition.

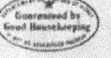

CHICKEN NOODLE • ONION
GREEN PEA • TOMATO VEGETABLE
BEEF VEGETABLE

To those unfamiliar with the subtleties in the design of letter forms, the sentence in the statement from Mr. Hurd, "These adaptations were tiny—some of them can only be seen under a magnifying glass . . ." may seem to be baffling. They might question why the changes were made at all if they can be seen only by enlargement.

Here, however, is the difference between "good" and "excellent." Great type designs and outstanding lettered expressions all contain minute elements of design that make for true artistry.

Although the average reader may not be aware of the beauty of the letter forms, he is favorably affected by them. This is all that the artist or advertiser would desire.

THE WORLD'S MOST BEAUTIFULLY PROPORTIONED CARS

The newest word in cars is *proportion*—the classic measurement in the fine art of automotive design and styling.

Proportion makes the beautiful difference in the Fords for 1959. You'll see it in every new shining inch of finely designed steel. It flows the whole clean length of these brand-new cars. You'll see it in the new thin-line roof, in the fresh, straight-through look of its big picture windows, and in the long glittering accents of chrome.

So elegant is the new Ford that it received the Gold Medal of the Comité Français de l'Elégance —awarded at the Brussels World's Fair. The citation in French: *"Pour proportions exceptionnelles et la ligne élégante."*

Proportion is a matter of power and motion, too. In Ford's new Thunderbird V-8 engines for 1959, the power is proportioned for increased responsiveness. You will get more responsive power at the speeds you actually drive—30 to 70 miles per hour. The new Fords are proportioned for new economy with new Fordomatic savings, new thrift in gas and oil that's easy on the pocketbook every smiling mile. These cars act new, look new, *are* new in every gleaming inch!

AWARDED THE GOLD MEDAL AT THE BRUSSELS WORLD'S FAIR
by the Comité Français de l'Elégance—for beautiful proportions

The new features are tailored together to give you a rewarding feeling that until now has only been available in the Thunderbird. See for yourself the 1959 Ford's Thunderbird elegance.

And all this Thunderbird sort of sweet-moving action . . . all this new performance and economy . . . will come to you at traditionally sensible Ford prices, which means the most possible value for the fewest possible dollars. You'll get more car per dollar than ever before!

There is a special feeling in these 1959 Fords— and you can get that New Ford Feeling in the World's Most Beautifully Proportioned Cars starting soon. That's when your Ford Dealer puts the newest of all Fords on display.

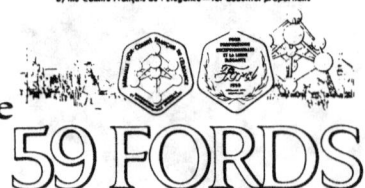

the 59 FORDS

Altogether new in everything you see, feel or touch

RICHARD HURD: "After the phrase, 'The World's Most Beautifully Proportioned Cars,' was first approved at the Ford Division, we began the serious study of how best to present these words.

"From the first, it seemed obvious that these words suggested a deeper and richer meaning than ordinary type, no matter how elegant, could illuminate. The words seemed to call for something classical, beautiful, symbolic, for an inscription treatment of some sort.

"At this point, we consulted Sam Marsh, one of New York's finest designers of lettering. He went, quite simply, to the source: the incised kinds of letterings and type faces developed from the original Trajan Roman Capitals. Most of these were somehow lacking—either one letter or another seemed weak or would not 'go together' with the next.

"So he went all the way back to Trajan, to be brief, and began making tiny but necessary changes in the ancient Roman Capitals so that each of the words of our phrase would 'stand up,' as it were. These adaptations were tiny—some of them can only be seen under a magnifying glass—but the result is unique.

"What we have is what seems to be an open-face type face but actually is an *incised* letter. Somehow this has a peculiarly satisfying feeling. And it has a further advantage—this lettering in itself is uniquely Ford's; it has never been achieved in just this way, and with just this result before.

"It makes, we believe, a magnificently appropriate background for the beautifully proportioned 1959 Fords."

Agency: J. Walter Thompson Company
Client: Ford Division, Ford Motor Company
Art Director: Richard Hurd
Lettering Artist: Sam Marsh Studios

WORLD'S
MOST
BEAUTIFULLY

Advertisements in which the complete text has been lettered are rarely seen in present-day advertising. When this interesting device is employed, there should be (and usually is) a sound reason for so doing. In regard to the General Electric advertisement, Mr. Ruben has given a clear explanation of the thinking that preceded his decision to have the entire text lettered.

Regardless of the weight of the letters, and whether they are drawn freely or conservatively, a pleasing tonal quality for the body text is of paramount importance.

When the layout calls for a line-up of the text on both the left and right sides (as in this advertisement), the lettering artist must make careful changes in the letter proportions and spacing in order to reach the required width of a line, while still maintaining the same "color" relationship to the other lines. When too much squeezing or opening of letters and words becomes apparent to the eye, the line will tend to separate itself from the pattern of the text. Although the text of the General Electric ad presents the casual effect that was required, one may be sure that Mr. Rockwell gave considerable thought to the balance of the gently bounced letters on each line and to the relative bounce of all the lines. Bounced letters can make the problem of justifying the lines somewhat easier to solve because the proportion and spacing changes are easier to conceal, but the problem of retaining even color becomes more difficult.

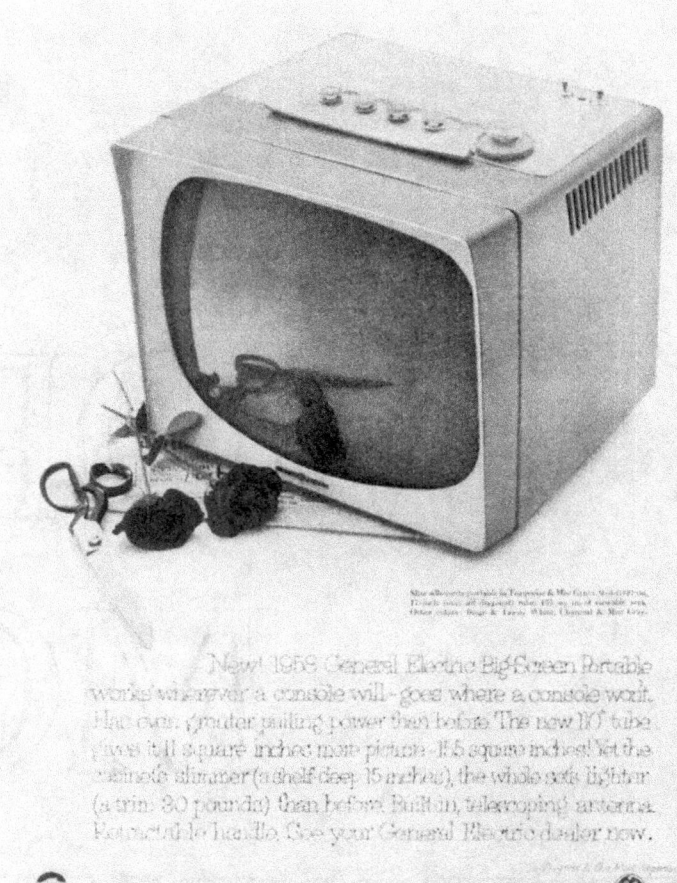

Agency: Young & Rubicam, Inc.
Client: General Electric Company
Art Director: Leonard Ruben
Lettering Artist: Harlow Rockwell

LEONARD RUBEN: *Born 1921 in St. Paul, Minn. Entered the Army in October, 1940, as private in the 105th Field Artillery, 27th Division. Ended service January, 1946, as 1st lieutenant. Received B. F. A. in 1952 from Pratt. Working for M. A. at Columbia. Joined Young & Rubicam in 1955 as an art director. Married in 1949 and has four children; two and two. He says his only hobby is making money.*

LEONARD RUBEN: "The TV set is the star, but a cold star. The words themselves are technical. Plain, cold type might make this ad look like a dealer's specifications sheet.

"To use an analogy, the body copy is like someone who has been called upon to deliver an extemporaneous speech. It has all the casual qualities, the imperfections, the warm human charm of an unrehearsed talk.

"The lettering itself is layout lettering done with a soft lead pencil, screened in two colors. It acts as a foil and counterpoint to the photo. The ad, which is strong product sell, doesn't have the curse of too much 'ad-iness'."

New! 1958 General Electric Big-Screen Portable works wherever a console will – goes where a console won't. Has even greater pulling power than before. The new 110° tube gives it 11 square inches more picture – 155 square inches! Yet the cabinet's slimmer (a shelf-deep 15 inches), the whole set's lighter (a trim 30 pounds) than before. Built-in, telescoping antenna. Retractable handle. See your General Electric dealer now.

Progress Is Our Most Important Product

GENERAL   ELECTRIC

Formal scripts are always useful when an advertising statement or a trademark calls for an air of dignity, quality and prestige.

Because of the elegance and beauty of these scripts, their use is limited, which becomes an advantage to the designer who has a valid reason for using them. When any letter styles are too commonly used for captions, the ads in which they are used lose individuality.

The caption shown here is an example of lettering taken from a comprehensive layout. Over the years, I have seen several such reproductions of lettering taken from comprehensive layouts, including some of my own work. A decision to forego the use of finished lettering is often made in order to hold a spontaneous feeling, sometimes lost in the finished work. At other times, a tight publication deadline makes the use of a retouched line of comprehensive lettering necessary.

On the Formal script caption displayed here, the lettering artist has maintained a grace and evenness of tone rarely seen on comprehensive layouts.

Agency: The Aitkin-Kynett Company, Inc.
Client: The Penn Mutual Life Insurance Company
Art Director: Michael R. Lombardo
Lettering Artist: Willie Martino—Martino Studios

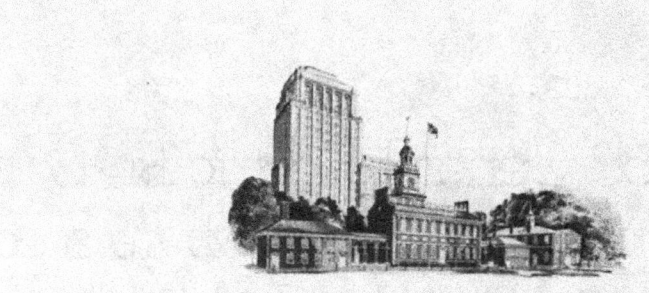

The Measure of Achievement

We are proud of the outstanding achievements of the members of the Penn Mutual "Million Club" shown on the following pages. Last year, each man helped his clients translate their plans for the future into more than a million dollars worth of present security, independence and peace of mind.

The scope of their accomplishment cannot be measured merely in figures, however. In bringing the full versatility of life insurance to bear upon the varied range of individual problems and ambitions, each underwriter was helping determine the shape of countless tomorrows for individuals and their families . . . people like you . . . like your friends and neighbors. Viewed in this way, the achievements of the Penn Mutual "Million Club" members add up to a sum total of *more than 000 million dollars worth of secure, happy tomorrows!*

The characteristic that distinguishes every Penn Mutual underwriter is his dedication to client service of the highest calibre. Thorough training plus broad and extensive experience makes each Penn Mutual man a specialist in translating future plans into present realities.

. . . find your "Million Club" Member on next pages.

THE PENN MUTUAL LIFE INSURANCE COMPANY · INDEPENDENCE SQUARE, PHILADELPHIA, PA.

MICHAEL R. LOMBARDO: *A graduate of the Philadelphia Museum of Art school, he has worked in several Philadelphia advertising agencies doing layout work and art directing for both trade and consumer advertising over the past 20 years. For the past six years, he has been associated with The Aitkin-Kynett Company, in Philadelphia, as associate art director.*

Measure

The Measure of Achievement

Achievement

MICHAEL R. LOMBARDO: "The reason for hand lettering in this advertisement was to counterbalance the square finish halftones in the spread which followed this title page, thus accomplishing movement and freedom. This choice of Formal script lettering reflects the prestige and character of the insurance men whose photographs appeared in this advertisement. Incidentally, the hand lettering we used was from the comprehensive layout made up by the Martino Studios. The reason for using the comprehensive lettering was to keep the freshness and freedom."

The signature on this Hunt's Catsup advertisement served as the only copy used in this series. Because the signature was planned to run in quite small sizes, it was necessary to letter it in a weight that would imprint clearly and yet not appear fragile. The hairlines were drawn thin, but strong enough to avoid breakage in the reproduction process.

Hunt...for the best

ROBERT WHEELER: *A native of Tennessee, he was raised in Texas. He has worked in newspaper art departments, free lanced in New York and Chicago, and worked as an art director in Milwaukee and New York. Since 1940, war years excepted, Bob Wheeler has been an art director with Young & Rubicam, first in New York and now in Los Angeles. In addition to Art Directors' Club awards, he has received awards from A.I.G.A. and from poster competitions. In the Y & R New York office, he worked on the Jello, American Tobacco, Cannon Mills, Singer Sewing Machine, and Four Roses accounts, among others. Since 1946—in the Los Angeles office of Young & Rubicam—he has worked on the Hunt Foods account, Bireley's, Consolidated Aircraft, American Home Foods, Union Oil, Snider, Capitol Records, and Goodyear Tire and Rubber Company.*

ROBERT WHEELER: "Type faces, like types of people, have their individual characteristics. I chose Bodoni to express the 'Hunt . . . for the best' signature in the Hunt's Catsup advertising in *Vogue* and *Harper's Bazaar* because I believed it was *in character*—not stuffy and not off-beat. Having chosen the style, I decided to have the signature hand lettered in order to hold the weight and letter proportions established on the layout. Mort Leach, who designed the label on the bottle shown in this ad, did the finished lettering."

Agency: Young & Rubicam, Inc.
Client: Hunt Foods and Industries, Inc
Art Director: Robert Wheeler
Lettering Artist: Mortimer Leach

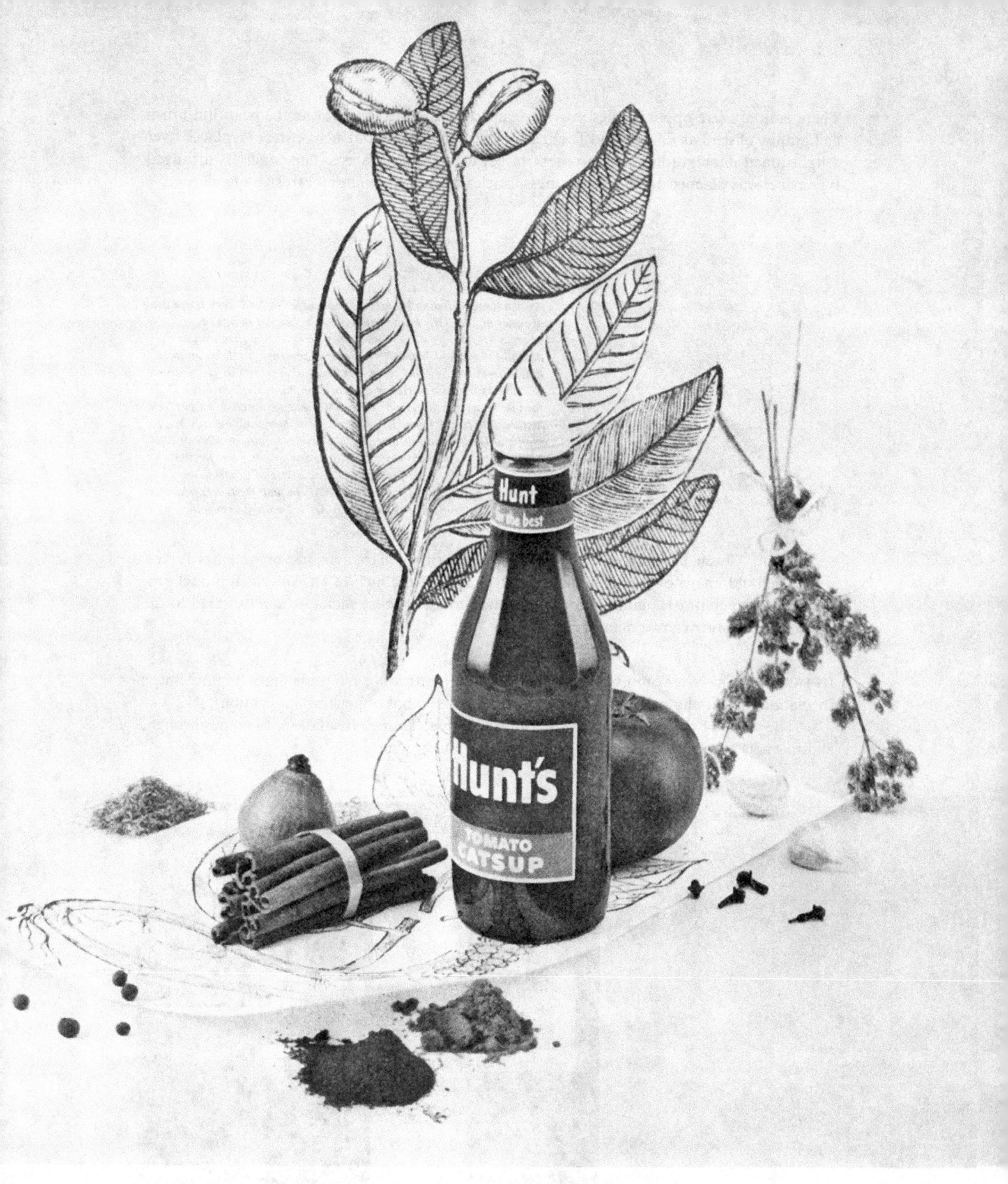

Hunt...for the best

There are only rare opportunities in American advertising to incorporate the beautiful brush calligraphy of the Far East. In the Teishi advertisement, these bold, active strokes, placed over a light-toned photograph, make a potent target for the reader's eye. The concisely arranged type panel was planned to deliver the message clearly and yet in an inobtrusive manner.

HY FARBER: *Beginning his professional career in New York advertising agencies in 1937, Hy Farber assisted in the format design of Marshall Field's New York newspaper "PM." Other publication designs followed, including "Air Force Magazine," while on military duty with the U. S. Army Air Force, Second World War. He returned to civilian life and advertising art work for Paramount Pictures; then he became art director of West Marquis Advertising. In 1947, he turned to free lancing. His work has won numerous awards in National Design competitions. He has been a faculty member of UCLA's art department since 1952, a consultant on color for the U. S. Navy, founder and president of the Society of Contemporary Designers, president of the Association of Graphic Designers, and vice president for the Southern California Art Education Association.*

HY FARBER: "Teishi, as represented by the Japanese written characters, means Imperial Prince.

"The bold image of the Oriental characters against the face of an American model produces a sharp contrast, planned to call attention to a Japanese facial product offered to the sophisticated American woman."

HY FARBER: "The cover of this brochure is designed to introduce the trade mark 'ti' for Thorpe Insulation, plus a photo of a tank within the 't,' as a symbol of general application.

"The circle of the 'i' is die cut to permit the name, Thorpe Insulation, to come through, and this acts as a lead-in to the following pages of the brochure."

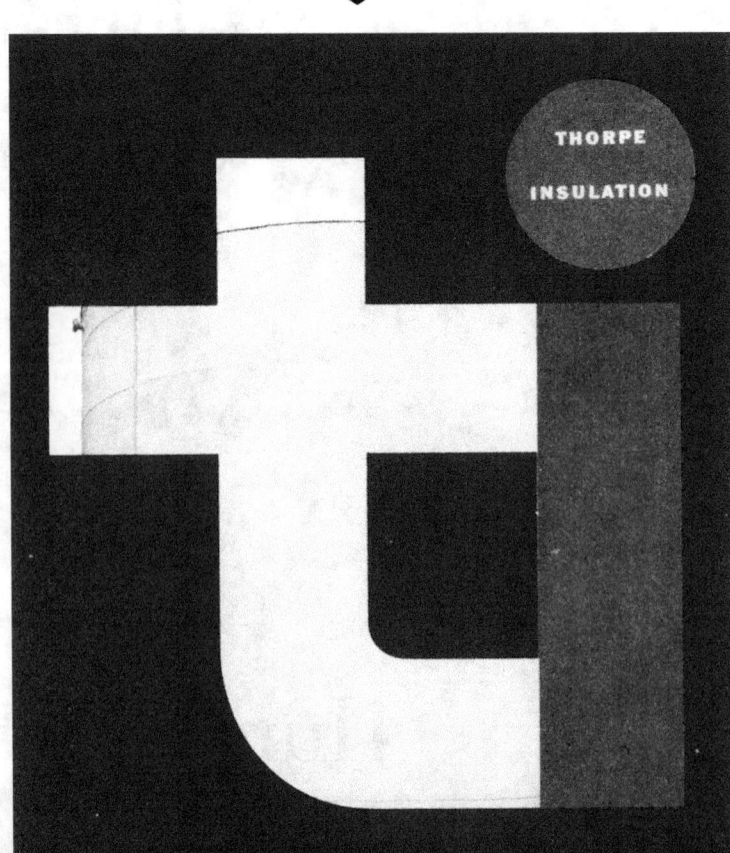

Client: Thorpe Insulation
Designer: Hy Farber

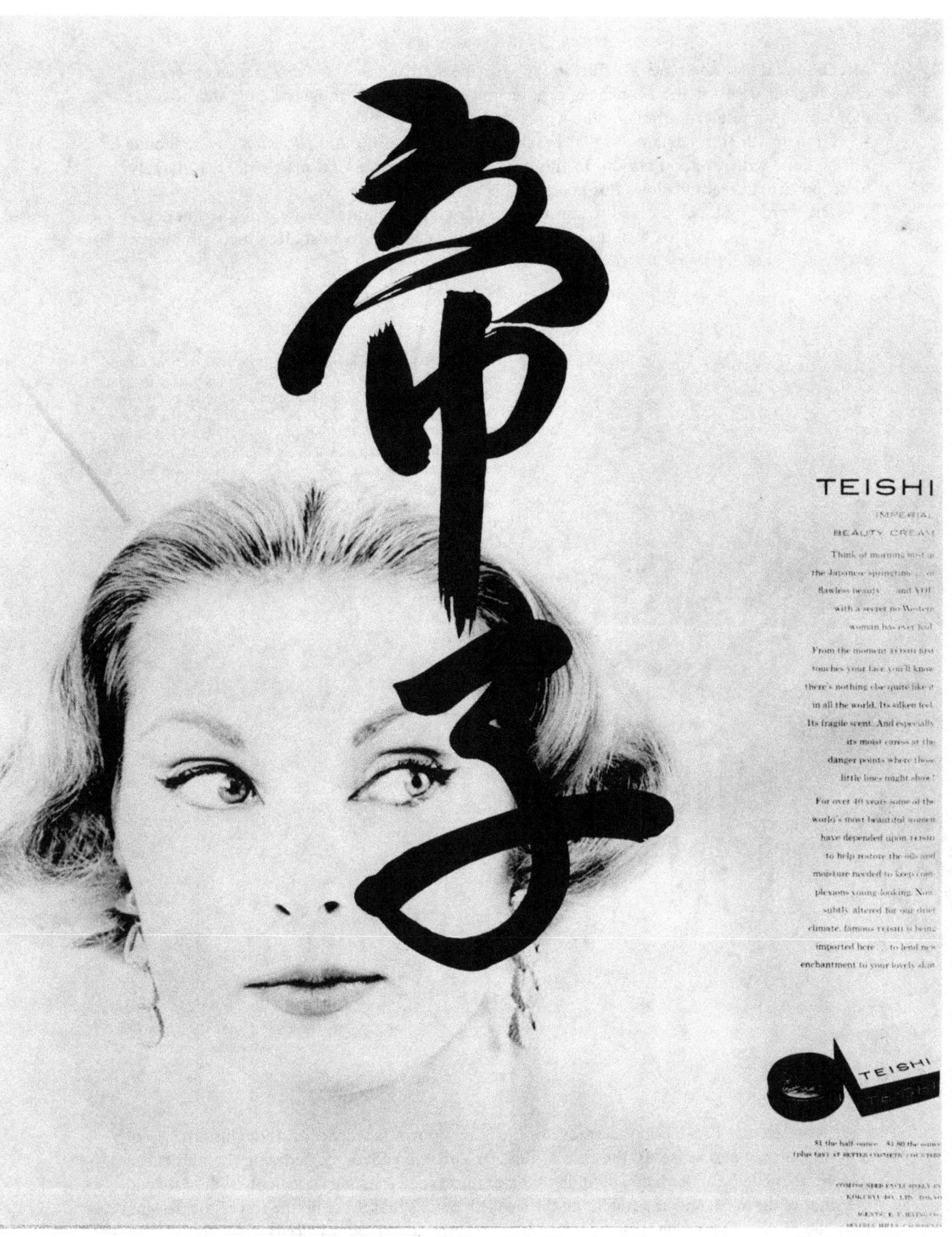

TEISHI

IMPERIAL
BEAUTY CREAM

Think of morning mist of
the Japanese springtime, of
flawless beauty — and YOU
with a secret no Western
woman has ever had.

From the moment TEISHI first
touches your face you'll know
there's nothing else quite like it
in all the world. Its silken feel.
Its fragile scent. And especially
its moist caress at the
danger points where those
little lines might show.

For over 40 years some of the
world's most beautiful women
have depended upon TEISHI
to help restore the oils and
moisture needed to keep com-
plexions young-looking. Now
subtly altered for our drier
climate, famous TEISHI is being
imported here to lend new
enchantment to your lovely skin.

TEISHI

$1 the half-ounce, $1.80 the ounce
(plus tax) AT BETTER COSMETIC COUNTERS

COMPOUNDED EXCLUSIVELY BY
KOKURYU-DO, LTD., TOKYO, JAPAN

AGENCY: E. T. BEING CO.

Agency: Dentsu Advertising, Ltd., Tokyo, Japan
Client: Kokuryu-Do, Ltd., Tokyo, Japan
Designer: Hy Farber

Mr. Diamond has used type tastefully in the Mobilheat ad and on the *Art Direction* cover. The crisp Bodoni used for the Mobilheat caption ran in two colors, thus avoiding any possible monotony as a result of arranging the words in five lines.

I agree with Harry Diamond that breaking words, as on the *Art Direction* cover, should not be done without good reason. In this case, the cover design of a magazine, read largely by fellow artists, readily allows this liberty.

The word "oysters," lettered within the line drawing, integrates easily with the line technique. Off-beat letter styles, forming part of an unusual design, are most often successful when executed by the illustrator, as was done here.

HARRY O. DIAMOND: *A native of Los Angeles, he received his early training in Los Angeles City College and Chouinard Art Institute. Worked many years in New York as an art director and illustrator. Served with the O.W.I. in the China-Burma-India Theatre during World War II. Returned to Los Angeles in 1947, where he works as an all-around advertising designer and illustrator. He is widely known for his zestful, humorous illustrations for newspaper and magazine advertisements and features, and for cook books. He heads the advertising art department and illustration department at Chouinard Art Institute. He has received honors from the Art Directors' Clubs of Los Angeles, San Francisco, and New York.*

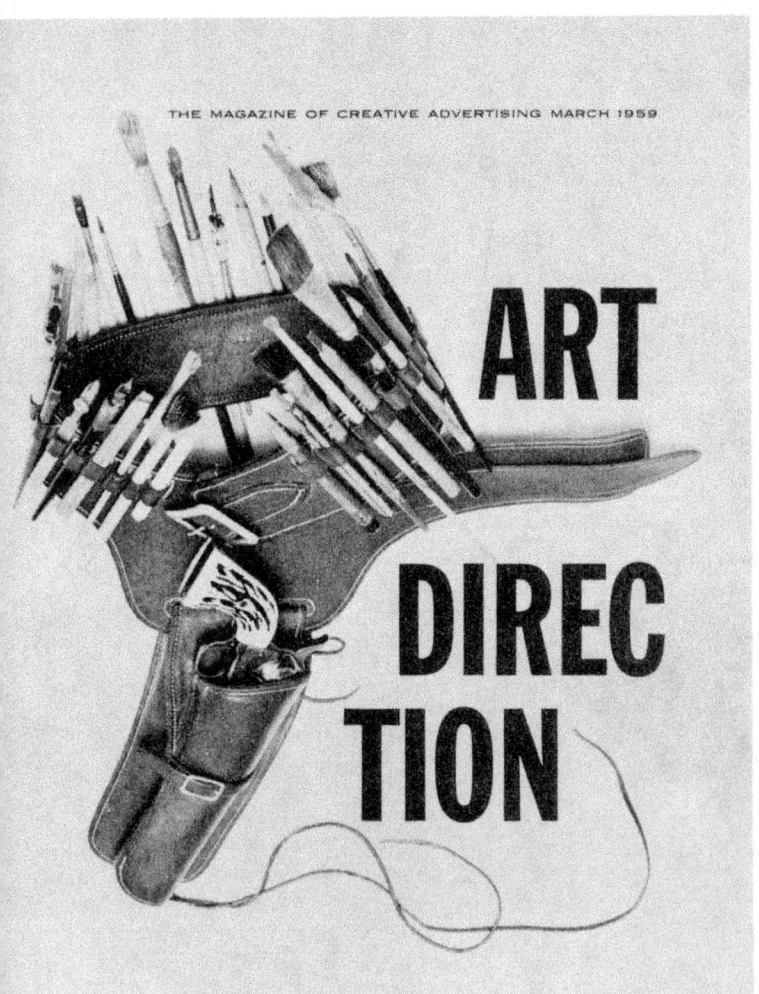

THE MAGAZINE OF CREATIVE ADVERTISING MARCH 1959

ART DIREC TION

Client: *Art Direction*
Art Director: Harry Diamond

HARRY DIAMOND: "I really don't approve of breaking up words willy-nilly, though I have seen it done with wit and sense. In the case of this *Art Direction* cover, considering the audience, it seems to me to be about half willy-nilly. I felt that I needed a strong statement, both to reflect the vigor of the West, and as a foil for all the smallish details that make up the rest of the design. Franklin Gothic Extra Condensed, along with Copperplate, served my needs—quickly!"

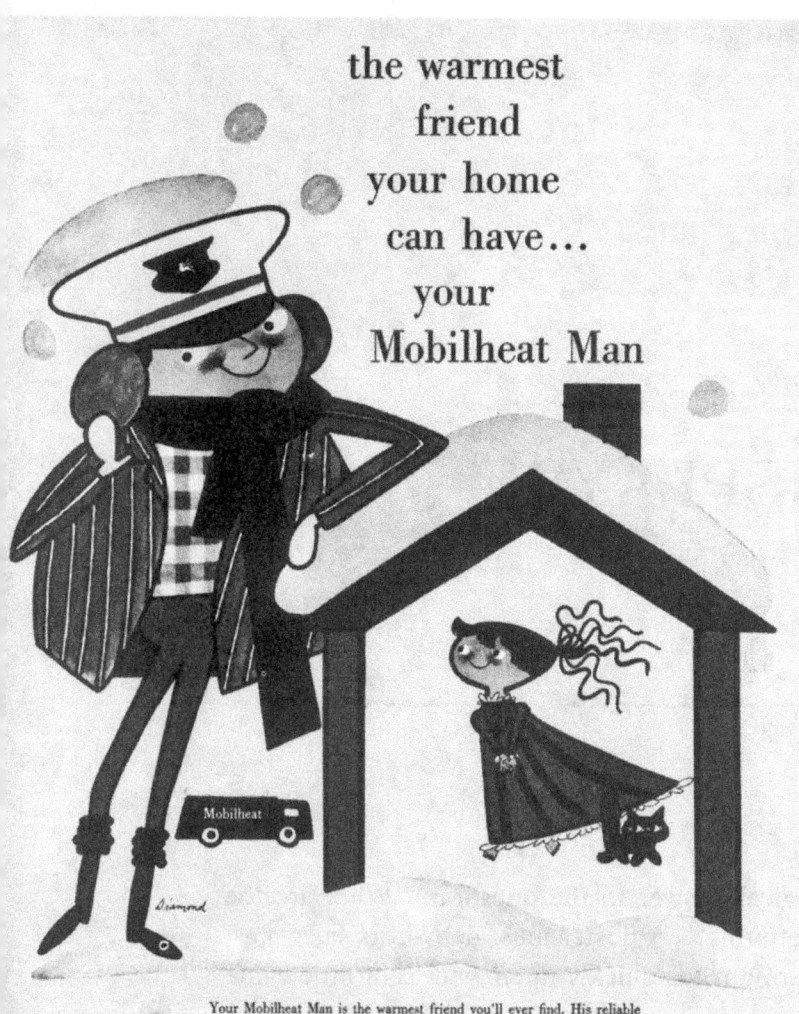

the warmest
friend
your home
can have...
your
Mobilheat Man

Your Mobilheat Man is the warmest friend you'll ever find. His reliable
service means worry-free comfort for you and your family regardless of
the weather. Prompt and automatic deliveries assure you that your tank will be amply supplied
without a second thought on your part.   Mobilheat is made in Ferndale
especially for the homes in the Northwest. This golden oil is made clean,
delivered clean, burns clean and
puts out maximum heat. **Mobilheat**

Be sure, be safe, be smart... call your Mobilheat Man now and you will be cozy all winter long.

Agency: Stromberger, LaVene, McKenzie
Client: General Petroleum Corp.
Art Directors: Harry Diamond, Joe Franz

HARRY DIAMOND: "Bodoni seemed right for the Mobilheat series for several reasons: looks fresh and clean, very easy to read, and not too self-conscious. Then too, it feels warm, friendly, and seems to me to reflect integrity. At least, these were the qualities I hoped for, as did the advertiser. The letter weights are the same thickness as those used in my drawing, and that, considered along with the fact that the vertical feeling of Bodoni suited the vertical workings of the design, also helped in the selection."

HARRY DIAMOND: "This nonsense drawing served as an introduction to some fine fish cookery. The lettering should be regarded as just another part of the drawing. If one doesn't know what oysters look like in a line drawing, the word helps! On the other hand, the greyness of the word helps to establish the black accents."

Client: Little, Brown and Company, Inc.
(illustration from: "James Beard's Fish Cookery")
Art Director: Harry Diamond

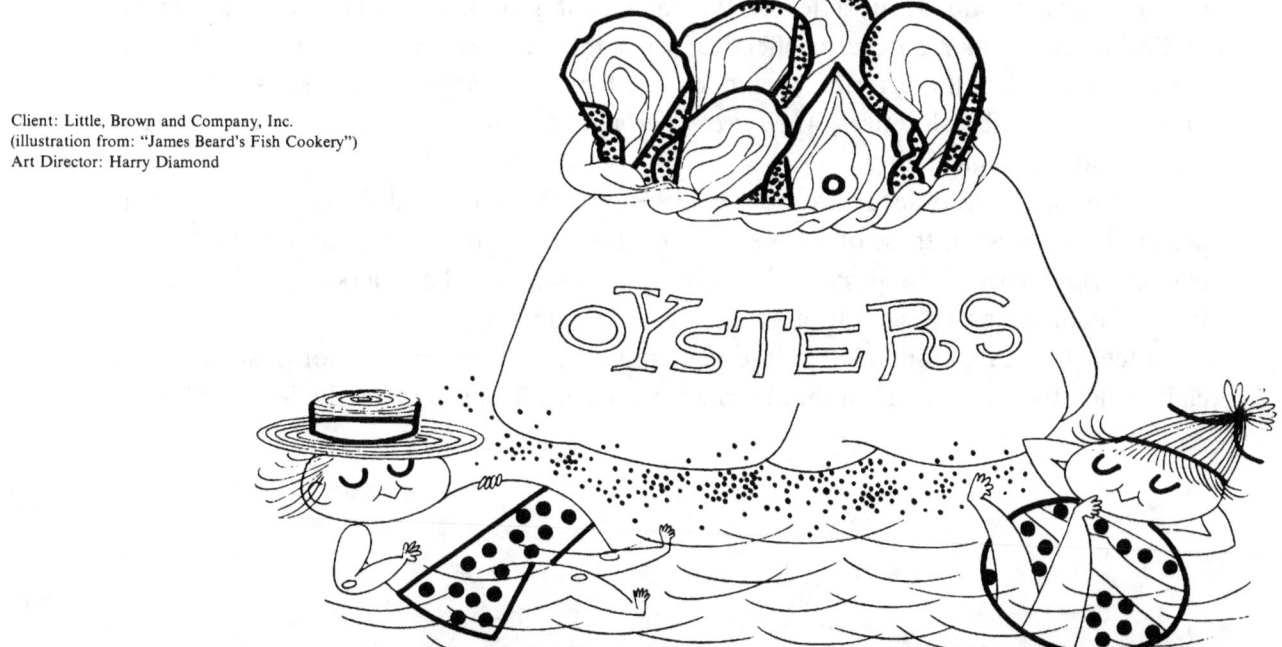

3 OUTDOOR DISPLAYS

Simplicity and readability is the most logical answer to the question: "What are the most important requirements for poster lettering?" A poster must deliver its sales message within a few seconds. Unless the lettering reads quickly, the poster is of little value to the advertiser.

This fact, of course, has been known to poster designers for a long time. It is natural, therefore, that simple, single-weight forms are most often used. The majority of today's posters employ variations of these styles, changing only their weights and proportions. At times, the rigidity of Gothic forms is relaxed by drawing the letters a bit loosely, which then allows slightly bounced lines. These free renderings necessarily must be more restrained on a poster than they would have to be in captions for magazine and newspaper advertisements where greater latitude is offered.

However, the workability of single-weight forms does not preclude the use of other styles with equal success. Century and Clarendon, long familiar to the public, are good poster letters, as are other styles in the thick-serif group. Some classic forms, such as Caslon and Bodoni, are also effective when the thin strokes and serifs are drawn more sturdily; but these forms should be used only in large display sizes. Modified brushscripts and brush letters, *when used sparingly,* can also produce an interesting effect and still retain legibility.

At times, a radical departure from conventional forms can aid the effectiveness of a poster. The success of these off-beat styles depends largely upon the skill of the designer and lettering artist. If the poster colors are well chosen and the letters large, the attraction value of the poster can offset a minor loss in legibility.

I feel that slim, refined letters are generally impractical for outdoor posters, especially when the letters contain thin hairlines which are likely to make the letters vibrate.

Only on rare occasions do light-face letters work out reasonably well. They are most likely to be successful when the words spell out a well-known brand name or familiar advertising slogan. But even then, strong contrast between the color of the letters and the background is necessary.

Conversely, letters can be "bolded" beyond readability. Evidently based on the supposition that if bold letters have impact then bolder ones have even more, some posters have displayed elephantine letter forms which are barely readable from the average viewing distance. In all cases, the degree of letter spacing must be considered carefully. Viewed from a distance, letters tend to close up. While wide letter spacing is not mandatory, enough space should be allowed between the letters to avoid massing of the forms. Experienced lettering artists always evaluate the spacing problems by examining their penciled lettering from a distance, or by using a reducing glass, before making the final adjustments on a trace-down tissue.

In recent years, some posters have presented adaptations of magazine or newspaper advertisements. Some have failed because not enough consideration was given to the transition into another medium. The success of these adaptations depends upon several factors. If the poster follows a lengthy advertising campaign in newspapers and magazines, or is displayed concurrently with such a campaign, the public is conditioned to recognize the advertising format and associate the ad with the product. However, the illustrations usually need simplifying, the copy must be reduced to a minimum, and the letter forms must be strengthened to poster requirements. Posters in this category sometimes contain "throw-away" lines, usually sub-captions that were used on the page ads but which cannot be sufficiently enlarged to be easily read on a poster.

It is extremely fortunate that in recent years advertising men have learned the value of brevity in the sales message of an outdoor display. While one still sees posters which are cluttered with copy, these are now very much in the minority. Also in the minority, but unfortunately still being posted, are displays in which the lettering is so small that it cannot be read more than a few yards away from the poster. Our fast-moving public does not have the time or the inclination to try to absorb a wordy message or to concentrate on deciphering obscure lettering.

The essences of a selling poster are an attractive illustration or design, minimum copy, and a clear display of the trade name. In some successful posters, the illustration serves as the attention getter; in others, the style, size, arrangement and color of the lettered message must perform this function. But in either case, all of the elements in the poster must speak clearly and quickly.

Since this is a book on applied lettering and type, the posters which appear on the following pages were selected in order to show displays in which the lettering plays a distinct part in the design arrangement. The letter styles vary, but all speak clearly. Some of these posters have won awards in advertising exhibitions, and all were successful in achieving high readership figures.

Agency: Young & Rubicam, Inc.
Client: Bireley's Division, General Foods Corp.
Art Director: Alex Mendoza
Lettering Artist: Mortimer Leach

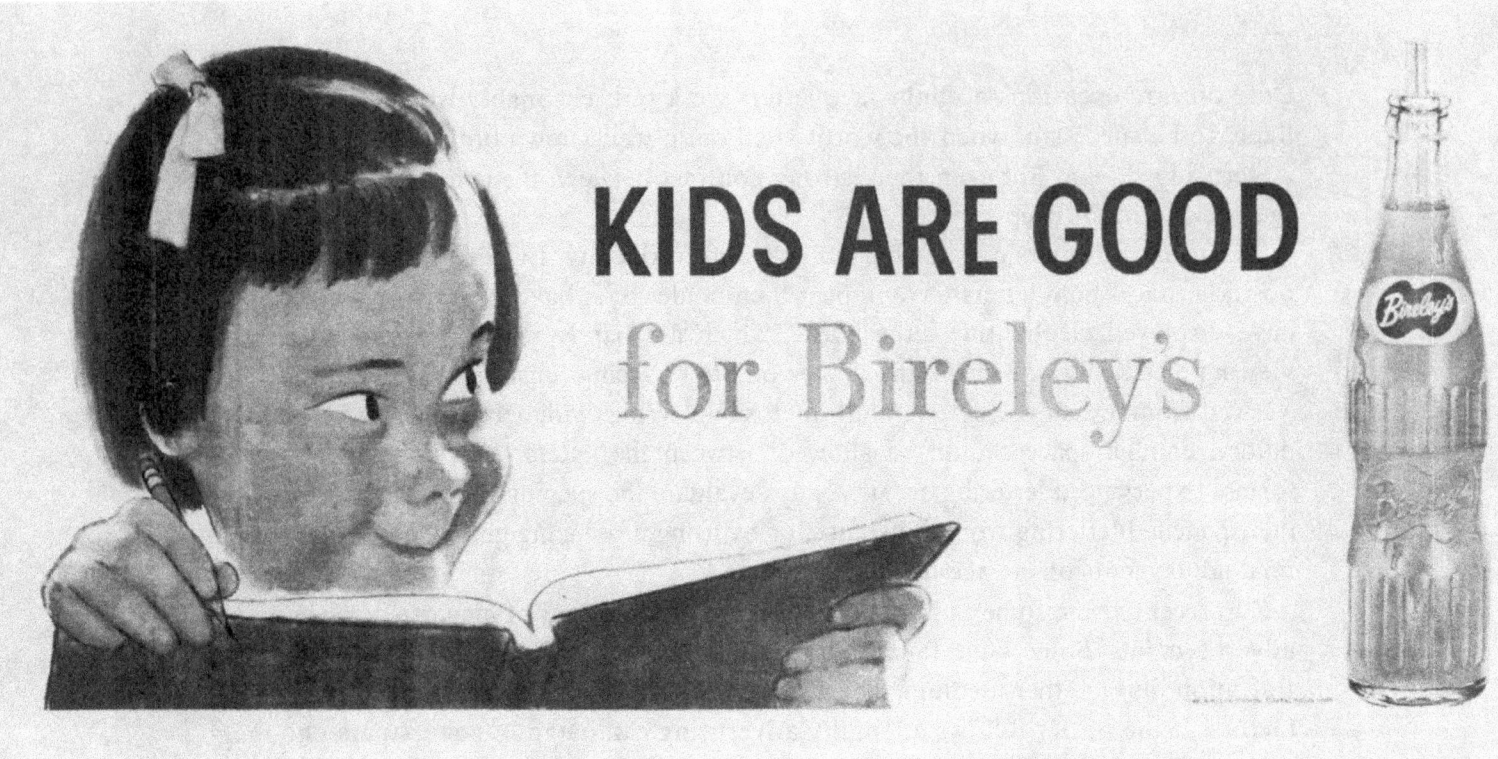

The letter proportion of the Gothic letters used for "kids are good" was controlled by the area between the child's head and the Bireley bottle. To get taller display, the letters had to be somewhat condensed. As a change of pace, the words "for Bireley's" were lettered in the same style and color in which "Bireley's" appears on the container pack.

KIDS

Bireley's

Deluxe

 Familiar Century Schoolbook forms have been used in this Walker's DeLuxe poster. The letters used here are an interpretation of these forms by Lettering Inc. They are a slightly more expanded and weightier version of the actual type forms, giving the letters a more sturdy quality. While retaining basic Century Schoolbook design, minor changes have been made in the design of some letters which appear here: notably the capital "D's" and the lower-case "a," "e," "k," "r," and "s."

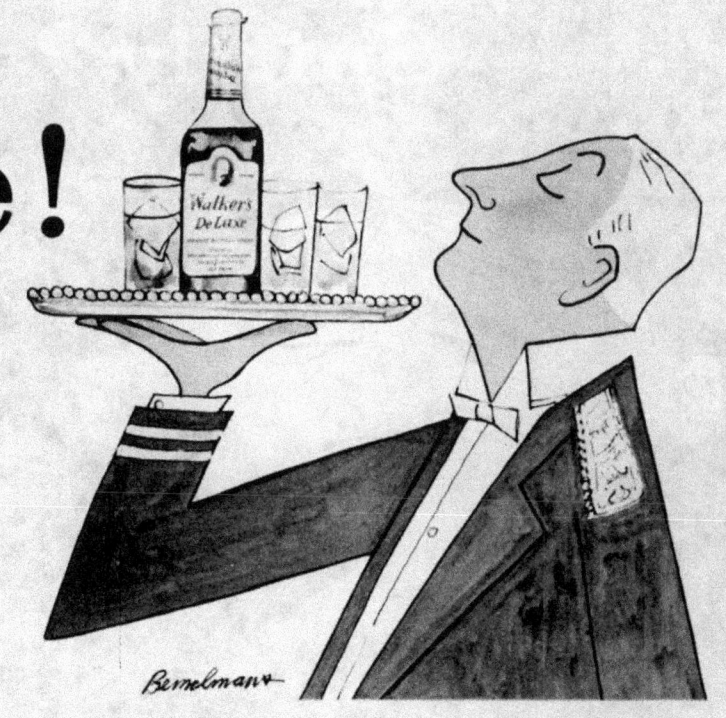

Deluxe!

Walker's
DeLuxe

7 YEARS SMOOTH...90.4 PROOF

Agency: Foote, Cone & Belding
Client: Hiram Walker & Sons, Inc.
Art Director: Orville Sheldon
Lettering Artist: Lettering Inc., Chicago

Tightly closed lines, which are staggered on both sides of the panel, present the lettering as a design pattern. Two colors were used to place the accent on "Bank of America." The freely drawn letters, done with a crayon technique, match the informality of the cartoon illustration.

 This poster contains a compatible combination of a lettered interpretation of Clarendon forms with tall, flat-sided Gothics. The bold and somewhat squat Clarendons serve as a counter-balance to the tall, concise trade name "Coldene." Again, minimum copy has left ample room for a potent display of the lettering and the cartoon illustration.

Sniffly ? Snuffly ?

coldene
catches your cold

Agency: J. Walter Thompson Company
Client: Coldene—Pharma-Craft Corporation
Art Director: Al Palmer
Lettering Artist: Bill Ficho—Ficho & Corley, Inc.

Agency: Johnson & Lewis Advertising, Inc.
Client: Bank of America
Art Director: George Kossman
Lettering Artist: Bill Hyde

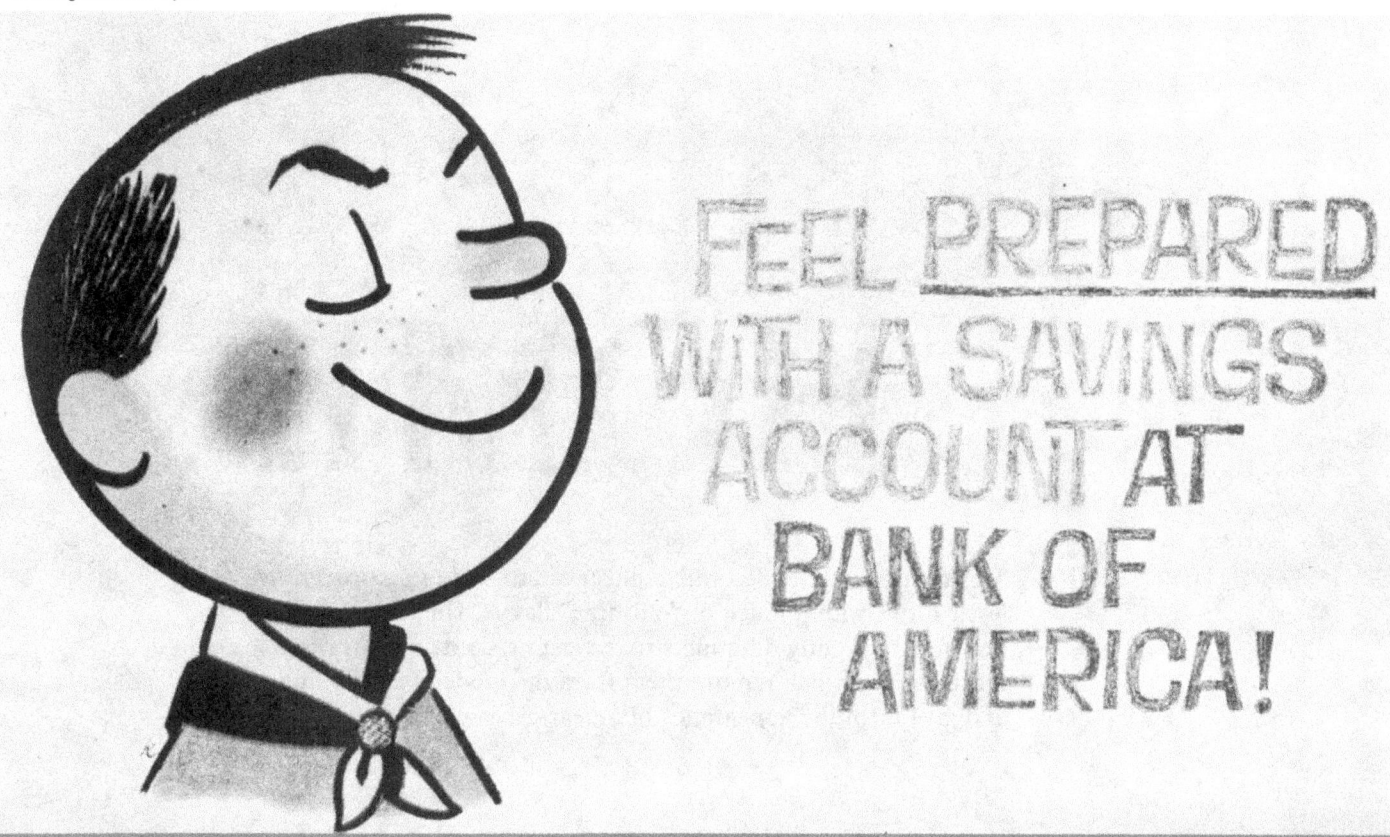

FEEL PREPARED WITH A SAVINGS ACCOUNT AT BANK OF AMERICA!

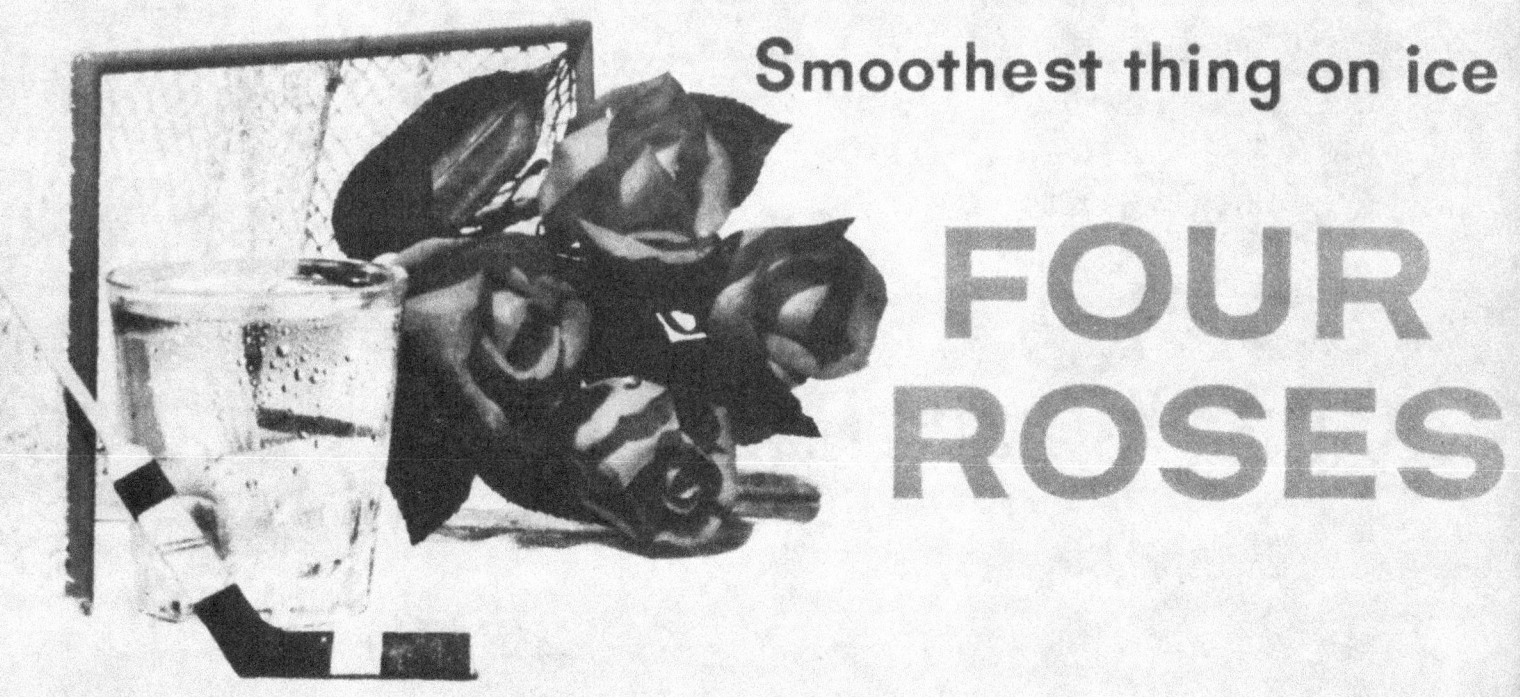

Smoothest thing on ice

FOUR ROSES

Agency: Young & Rubicam, Inc.
Client: Four Roses Distillers Company
Art Director: Arthur Cady
Lettering Artist: Not known

 Here again, an attractive, colorful illustration calls for no additional decoration by the letter styling. The lines balance well with the illustration and the trade name, "Four Roses," carries the color completely across the poster. The Extended Venus used for the trade name is a crisp style, well chosen for display letters.

BRINGS
HOME

 This poster, with its decorative illustration, called for conservative letter forms with a touch of "old-time" flavor. The letters, drawn with slightly differing stroke weights, contain sharply flicked serifs, which remove them from the modern classification and give them the appearance of a near-classic form.

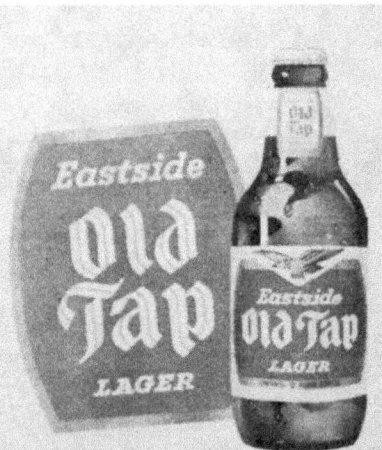 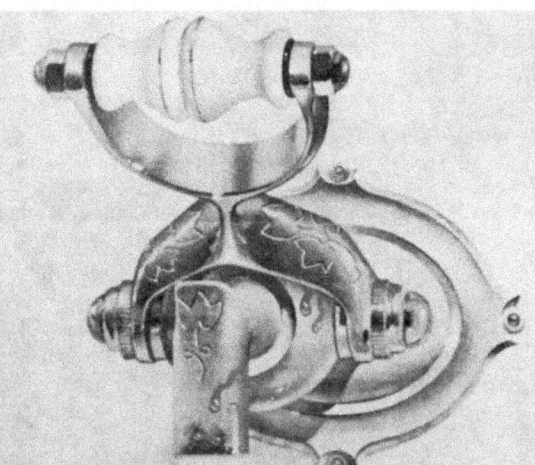

BRINGS HOME THAT TAP BEER PLEASURE

Agency: Young & Rubicam, Inc.
Client: Eastside Beer—Pabst Brewing Co.
Art Director: Robert Wheeler
Lettering Artist: Mortimer Leach

Client: Pabco Paint
Designer: Saul Bass
Lettering Artist: Maury Nemoy

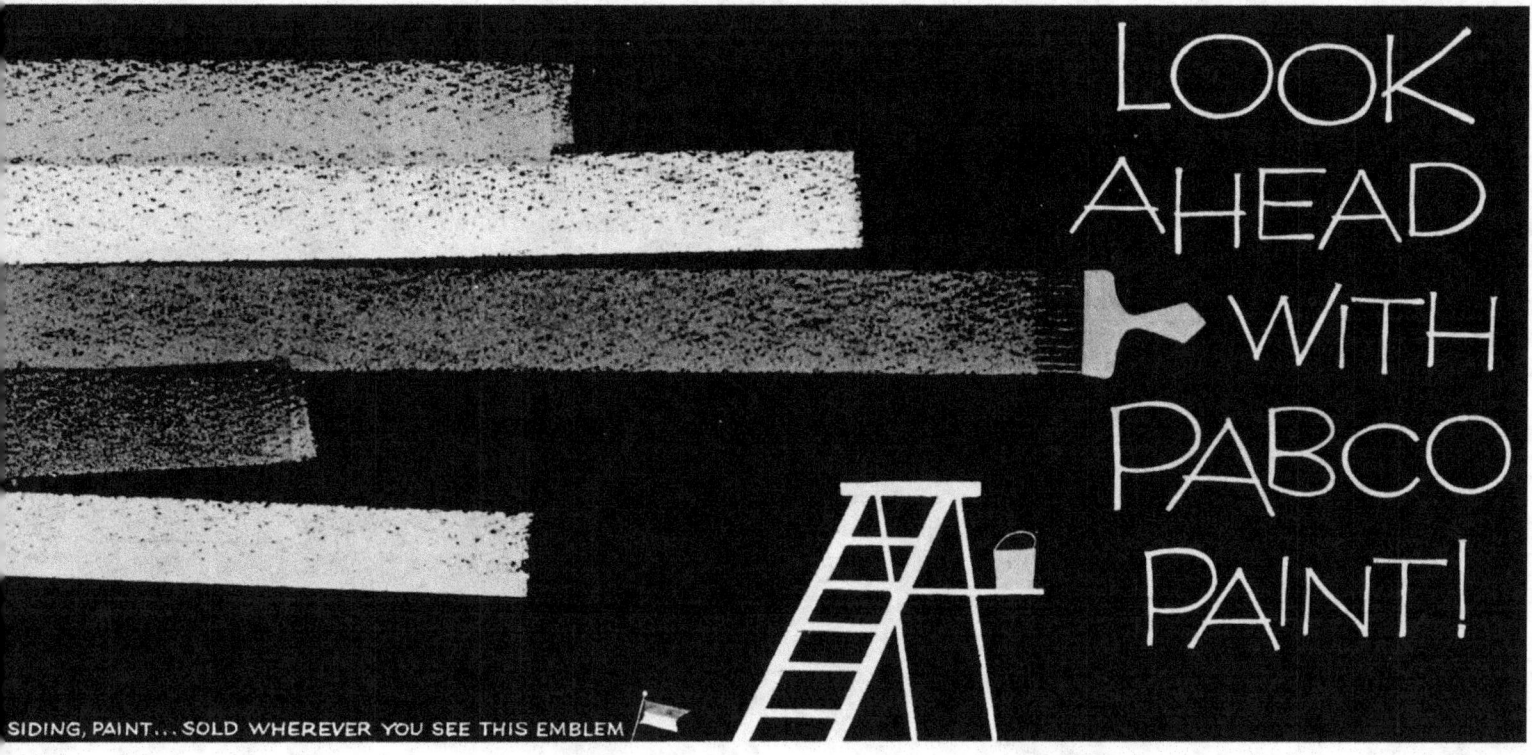

 The brushstrokes, drawn across this poster in differing colors, lead the eye directly to the message. Freely rendered and bounced letters, done in a single weight, provide additional action for the design of this display.

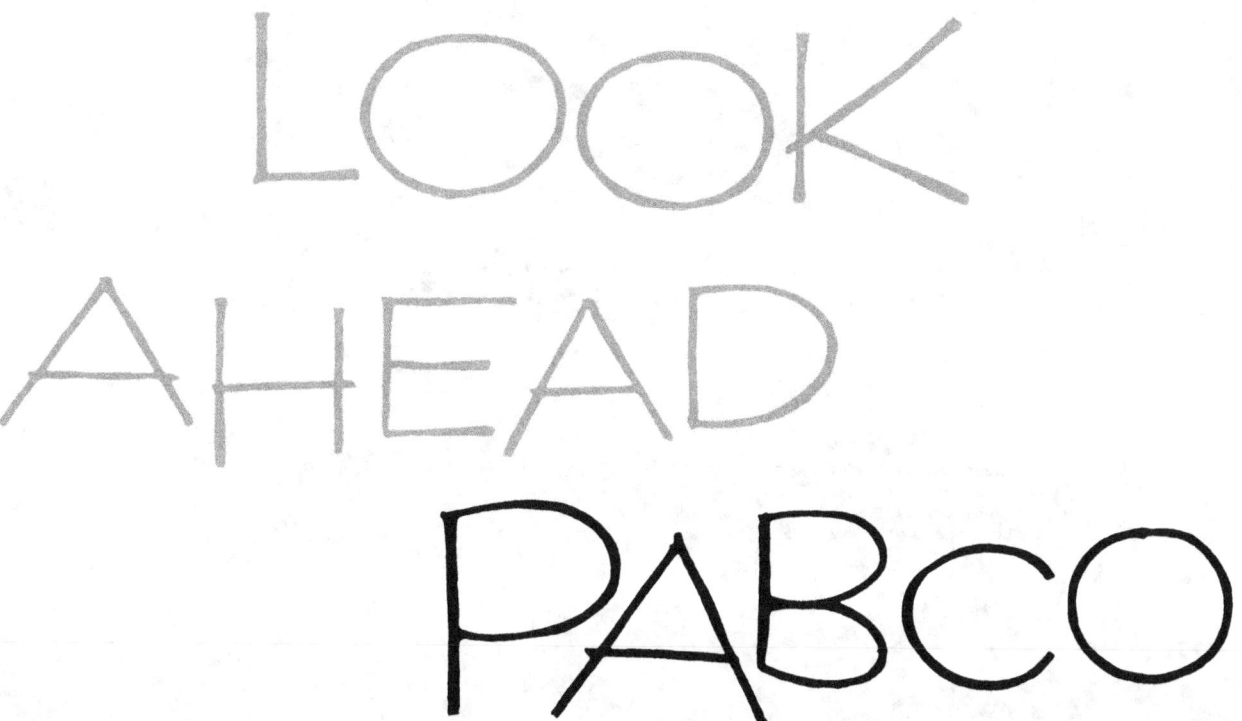

118

 This unusual arrangement, which places words done with widely differing letter styles within different colored panels, has considerable attention value. It would ordinarily be difficult to project a fast sales message with a design such as this, but when a well-known and widely advertised slogan like Morton's is used, one encounters no difficulty in reading it.

 The swinging line of Gothics on this poster has been employed as an element in the complete design. Following the action of the girl's body, the line produces the effect of an air-flow pattern. While the swing has been modified to avoid possible letter distortions, its action contributes to the rhythmic flow of the poster design.

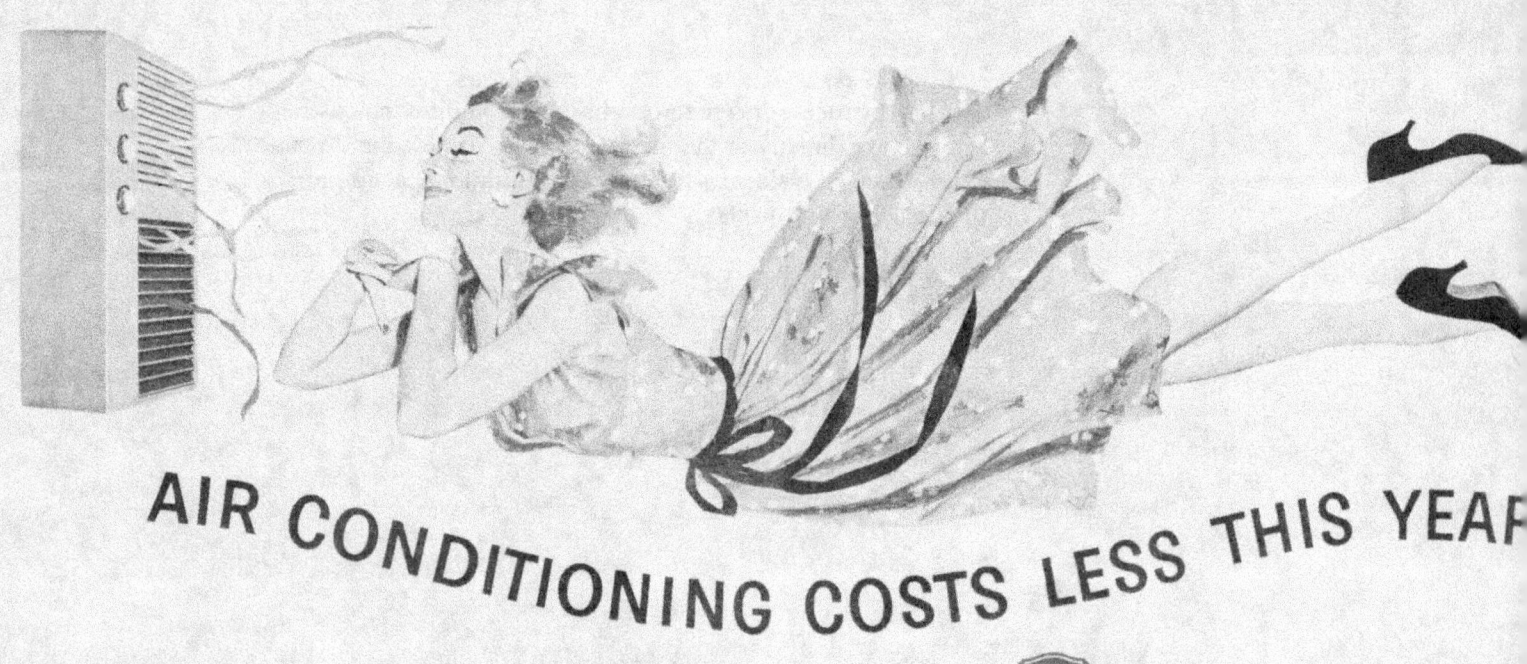

AIR CONDITIONING COSTS LESS THIS YEAR

SOUTHERN CALIFORNIA Edison COMPANY helps you LIVE BETTER—ELECTRICALLY

Agency: Young & Rubicam, Inc.
Client: Southern California Edison Co.
Art Director: Ray Pederson
Lettering Artist: Mortimer Leach

Agency: Needham, Louis & Brorby, Inc.
Client: Morton Salt Company
Art Director: Thomas R. Gorey
Lettering Artist: Carl Corley—Whitaker Guernsey Studio, Inc.

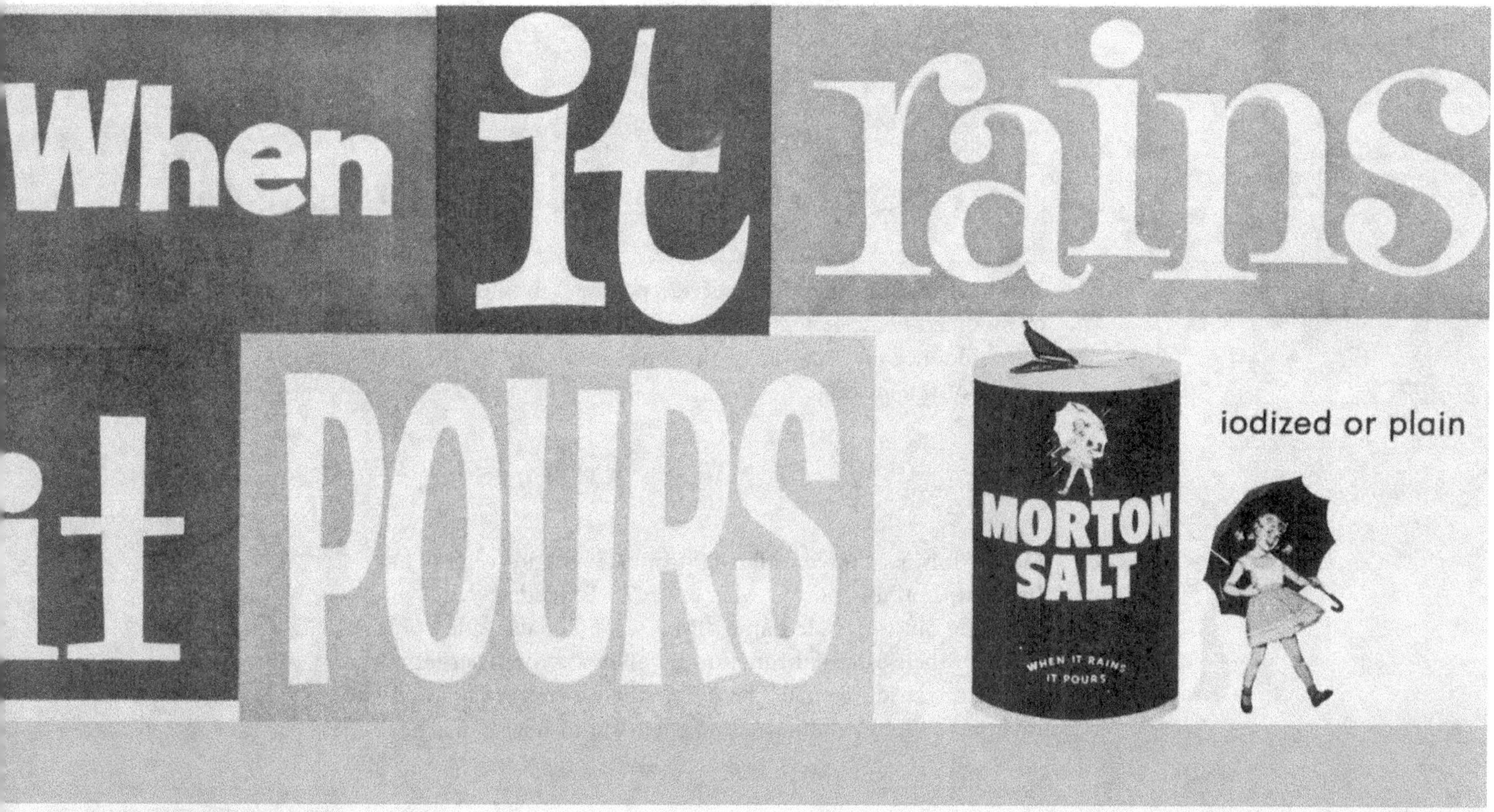

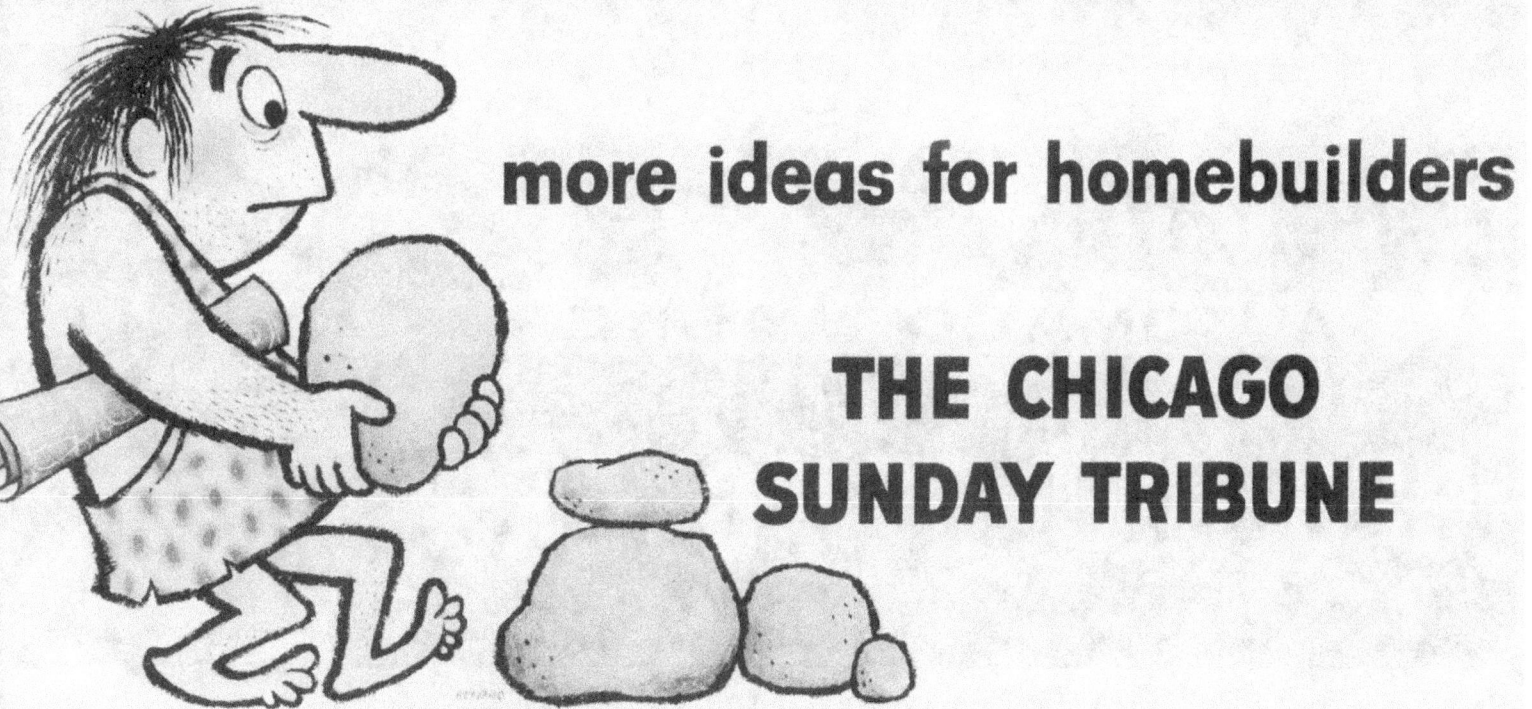

Agency: Foote, Cone & Belding
Client: *The Chicago Tribune*
Art Director: Jules Beskin
Lettering Artist: Bill Ficho—Ficho & Corley, Inc.

This humorous illustration, showing a cave man building his home with the aid of a blueprint, is a potent eye-catcher and calls for no further attraction by the lettered message. The concise, simply lettered statement is easily absorbed, in the same manner as one would read the title of a cartoon. The well-known name of *The Chicago Sunday Tribune* can be read at a glance.

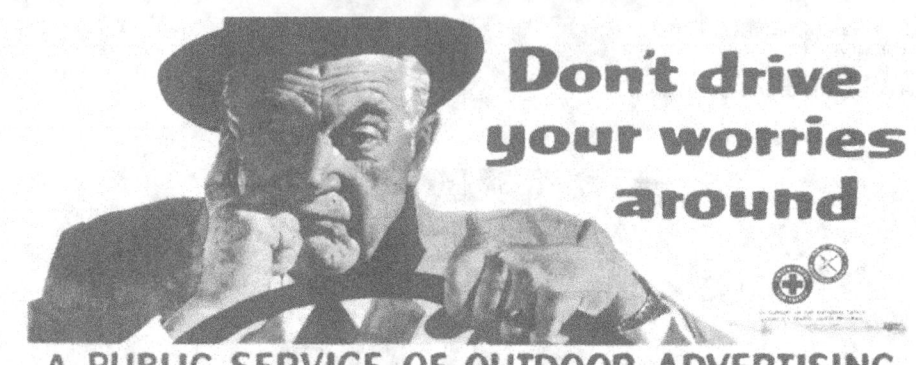

Client: Outdoor Advertising Association of America, Inc.
Art Director, Artist: Howard Scott
Lettering Artist: Sid Sevell

 The lettering on this public-service poster combines the qualities of modified brush letters and freely rendered Gothics. The subtle bounce and tumble of the letters adds to the informal aspect of the message.

 Gothic forms in three differing proportions and weights have been used on this poster, with the Bold Extended Venus booming out the trade name, "Maytag." The flat-sided Gothics perform their essential function by allowing for taller letters within a restricted area. These flat-sided forms are read quickly by a public long conditioned to their use in newspaper headlines.

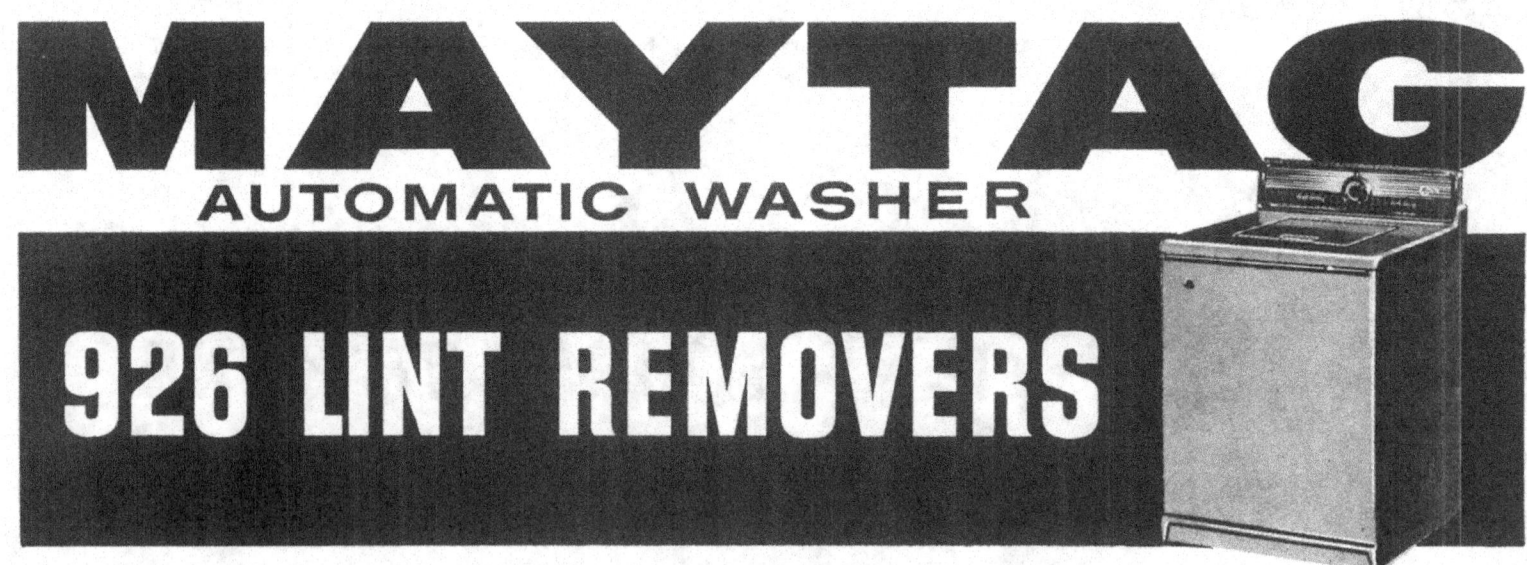

Agency: Leo Burnett Company, Inc.
Client: The Maytag Company
Art Director: Robert Weber
Lettering Artist: Kling Studios

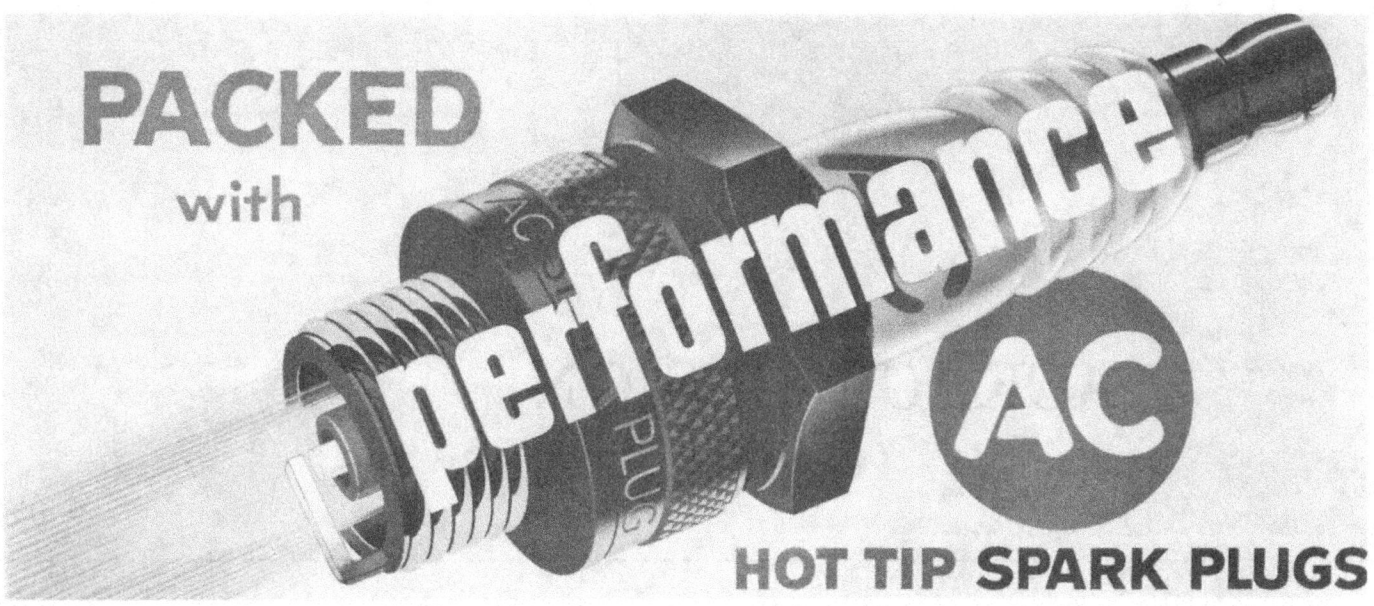

Agency: D. P. Brother & Company
Client: AC Spark Plugs Division, General Motors Corporation
Art Director: Paul R. Meyers
Lettering Artist: James A. Kelley

 Square Gothics, used for the word "performance" in the AC poster, once again allow for tall letters within a restricted width. These simple forms are clearly seen against the multi-toned values of the drawing of the spark plug.

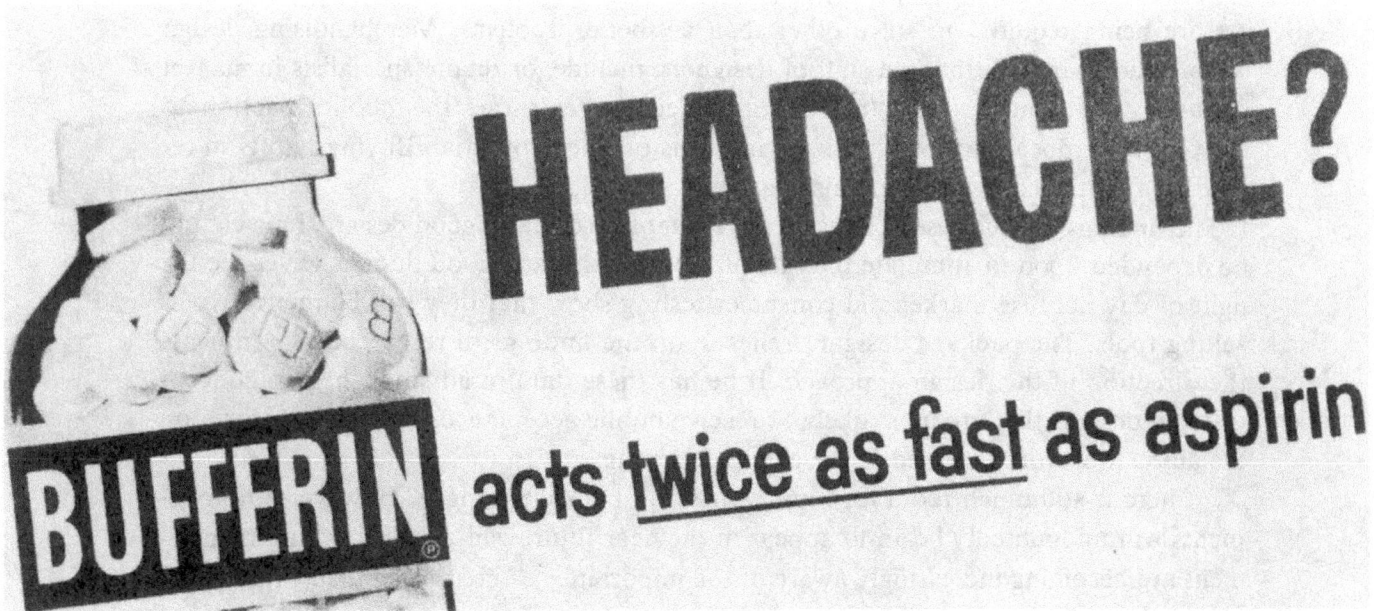

Agency: Young & Rubicam, Inc.
Client: Bufferin—Bristol-Myers Company
Art Director: George Infante
Lettering Artist: Sam Marsh Studios

 This Bufferin poster is a good example of a display ad that has been held to complete simplicity. The brief copy and the "posterized" drawing of the bottle combine to deliver a fast, effective message. Use of the trade name on the bottle as part of the copy line is advantageous here, allowing as it does for a larger lettering display. The small question mark provides additional space in which to play up the word "headache."

4 PACKAGE DESIGN

In comparatively recent years, package designing has become a major business in the industrial design field. New products, each requiring individual approaches to the design of their labels, containers, and cartons, are constantly being readied for the market. And long-established products are increasingly being presented to the public in redesigned packages, as marketers strive to meet new competition.

This tremendous growth of the package design industry has greatly increased the need for specialists in merchandising design. However, what was once a purely artistic approach to the design of a package, is now influenced by other factors. Design specialists are being required to solve other than aesthetic problems. Merchandising design organizations, in addition to a staff of designers, include, or retain, specialists in market research who conduct tests that are intended to determine the public reaction to the physical appearance of a package in terms of sales potential. Buying-habits in regard to a particular product are also carefully studied.

The findings of such research teams have established that a good design alone cannot be depended upon to stimulate the sale of a product. Many good designs never see the light of day because market and consumer testing show that they will be ineffective as selling tools. The package designer relies upon the findings of researchers to indicate the direction of the design approach. If he has these data in advance, he can concentrate on designs that are most likely to receive public acceptance, thus cutting down on the amount of work involved in the actual designing.

There is still much room for improvement in package designs. However, improvements will undoubtedly begin to appear in the near future, since industry and management are becoming increasingly aware of the importance of presenting their products in an appealing way.

In package design, a thorough knowledge of lettering and type styles is of utmost importance. Letters are an integral part of the design pattern. If they are poorly chosen or improperly drawn, the design, as a unit, is seriously damaged.

Because of the necessary integration of the letters with the complete design, the opportunities for unusual expressions are greater than those offered in space advertising.

Many letter designs that would be impractical for advertising captions can be used to advantage on a package, providing, of course, that they remain readable. Only someone with a sound background in the study of type and lettering development can be depended upon to successfully design unusual forms and radical departures from basic styles.

The shape of a container may exercise considerable control over letter proportions, as well as the choice of styles. When large letters are needed within a narrow space, condensed letters must be skillfully drawn and spaced to retain legibility. On a round bottle or can, the words must be held within an area that will allow for the complete reading of the product name when the container is faced directly.

Another factor that can affect the choice of letter styles is the surface texture on which the design is to be reproduced, whether it is paper, paper board, plastic, glass, etc. If changes in letter weights are likely to occur in the reproduction process, due to color bleeding on some textures, this must be anticipated when the letter styles are being selected.

The designer must also keep in mind the problems of sales promotion. The package design and the trademark should be planned so that they will hold a clear tonal quality when shown in black-and-white television commercials or when printed in halftone in black-and-white newspaper advertisements.

The type of product may narrow the selection of lettering to a particular category: such as dignified, traditional forms; bold, sturdy letters; gay, informal styles; letters which are chosen to appeal to men, women or children, etc. However, the tremendous variety of products on the market allows for the use of numerous forms of letter styling.

Once the style or combination of styles has been decided upon, I believe that only a highly competent lettering artist should be entrusted to prepare the finished lettering, if lettering is to be used. One still sees packages in which the original concept of the style was obviously sound, but the final design has suffered in reproduction because of insensitive or mediocre finished lettering.

When designs are being planned for the packaging of a new line of products or for the complete redesign of an established line, the trademark styling is usually planned for additional uses. It should be adaptable to space advertising, stationery, truck signs, building signs, shipping cartons, and other applications, without need for design changes, in order to maintain the identity of the manufacturer. The terms "corporate image" and "corporate identity" are now familiar ones to management, advertising agencies and industrial designers. Advertising agencies present this image in magazine and newspaper advertisements. Package designers symbolize the image through an interpretive design for the trade name.

The package designs shown on the following pages are accompanied by descriptive information provided by the designers. These packages, produced by some of the country's best-known men in this field, have successfully performed their function: to stimulate the sales of the product for which they were designed.

124

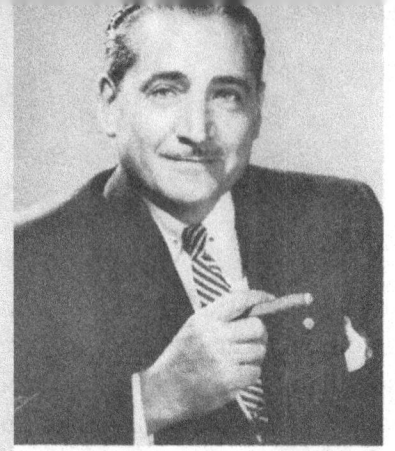

FRANK GIANNINOTO
Frank Gianninoto and Associates, Inc.

Frank Gianninoto is one of the founders of the industrial design profession and one of the first to specialize almost exclusively in package design and merchandising counsel. He has been responsible for developing new design concepts for some of the country's leading manufacturers of packaged goods. His intimate relationship with supermarket growth and new package design development has helped to make self-service marketing centers the success they are. His belief in design as an international language has taken him to the most important centers of Europe to lecture on our American design and marketing philosophy.

"Gianni" is the only package designer to maintain complete design facilities on both coasts—in New York and Los Angeles. Frank Gianninoto and Associates, Inc. was established in 1931. Prior to that time, "Gianni" was art director at Batten, Barton, Durstine & Osborn, Inc.

Last year over $3 billion worth of merchandise was sold in Gianninoto-designed packages. These ranged from sleek, high-styled containers for the cosmetic industry to fast-hitting, hard-sell designs for the self-service market.

Typical Gianninoto clients are Borden's, Chesebrough-Pond's, Crown-Zellerbach, Dole Pineapple, Dr. Pepper, Du Pont, General Foods, Johnson's Wax, Kaiser Aluminum, Lever Brothers, Nash's Coffee, Philip Morris, Seagram's, Foremost Dairies, M. J. B. Coffee, Richmond-Chase, Brown & Williamson Tobacco Corporation, and Thomas J. Lipton.

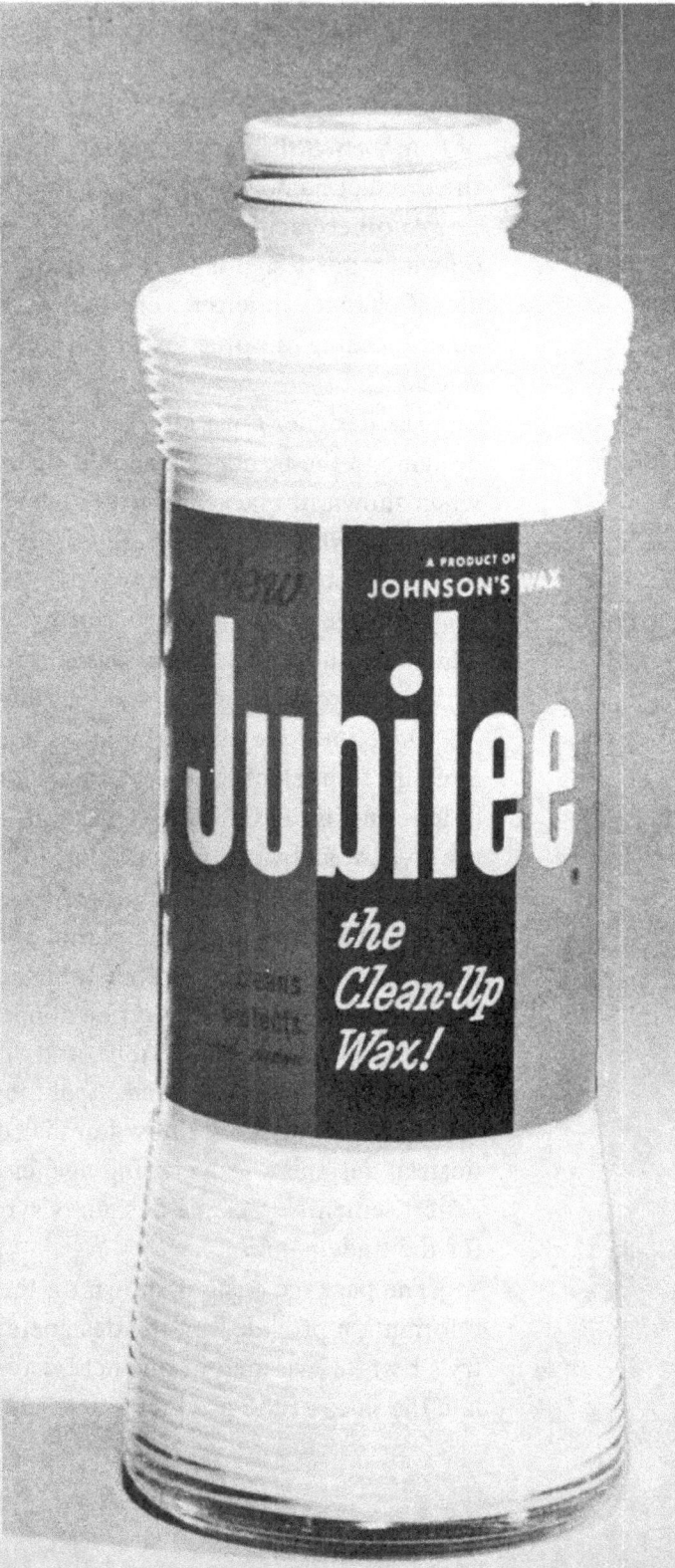

"Conforming more closely to what Mrs. Consumer really wants in a floor-wax container, the new Jubilee wax bottle is shaped for easy gripping. A ripple pattern in the jar overcomes an important anxiety—that the bottle will slip out of the user's hand.

"The new label design—vertical bands of bright red, black, and bright blue—together with the new logotype for 'Jubilee' in sunny yellow, suggests gaiety with honesty and ease of work through its simplicity. The package is festive, and the simple design gives a strong impression of cleanliness and function without the need of toil."

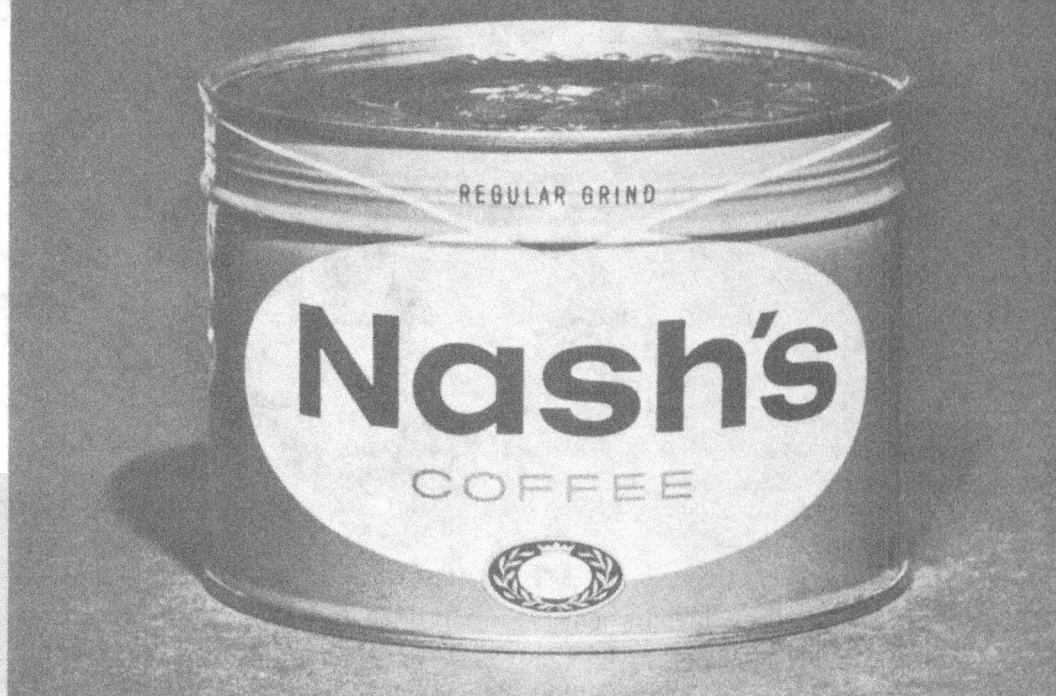

"The new design exemplifies our belief that coffee packaging, to achieve maximum sales, should be suggestive of good taste and pleasure and should serve as a reminder of the enjoyment and companionship that come from lingering over a second cup of coffee. The design is also calculated to convey the spirit of Nash's advertising slogan, which declares that the product is 'an honest blend.'

"Chief color of the new package is a strong red, a reminder of the richness and the full-bodied flavor of the product. A new modernized logotype in coffee-brown appears against an oval background of white and is readily legible on a crowded supermarket shelf. In a much smaller version of the oval at the base of the design is the initial 'N,' surrounded by a garland and topped by a crown. This decorative treatment given to the letter 'N' trademark adds a regal look to the over-all design. Additional descriptive copy (type of blend), also printed in brown, is positioned in a distinctive, simulated-gold color, triangular shape at the top of each can.

"The same basic design is used for the institutional line. The triangular device in the basic design is repeated as an over-all background pattern on the measured service bags. All packages combine a classic, rich feeling with modern simplicity. All are readily identifiable and boldly distinctive."

▶

"A new symbol has been created for Pond's creams that better reflects the product's high quality. This 'manikin' shape is also used in outline on the caps. The styling of the name 'Pond's' is classical in design and, although smaller than on the old label, it is just as legible, if not more so. These are three-color labels (differing for each cream) using a dark and light tint with a gold crown and manikin outline. The caps are printed in the gold hue."

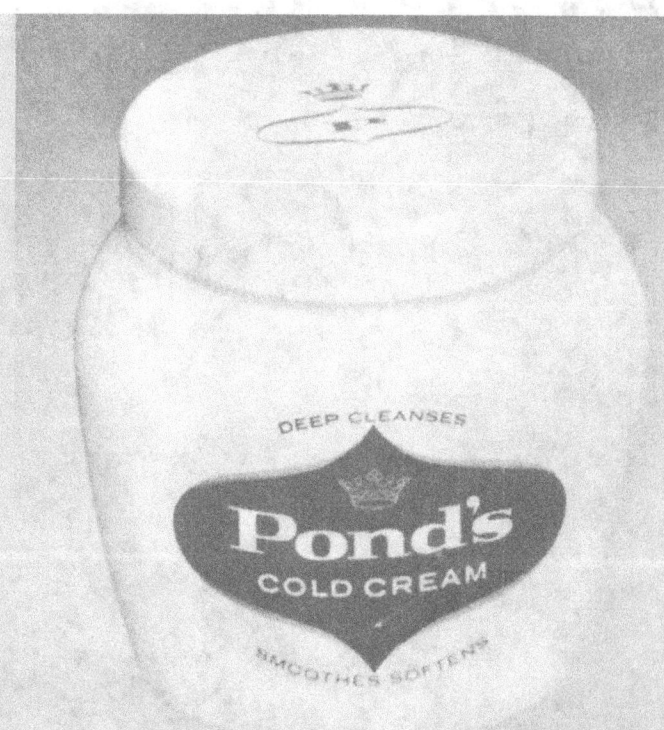

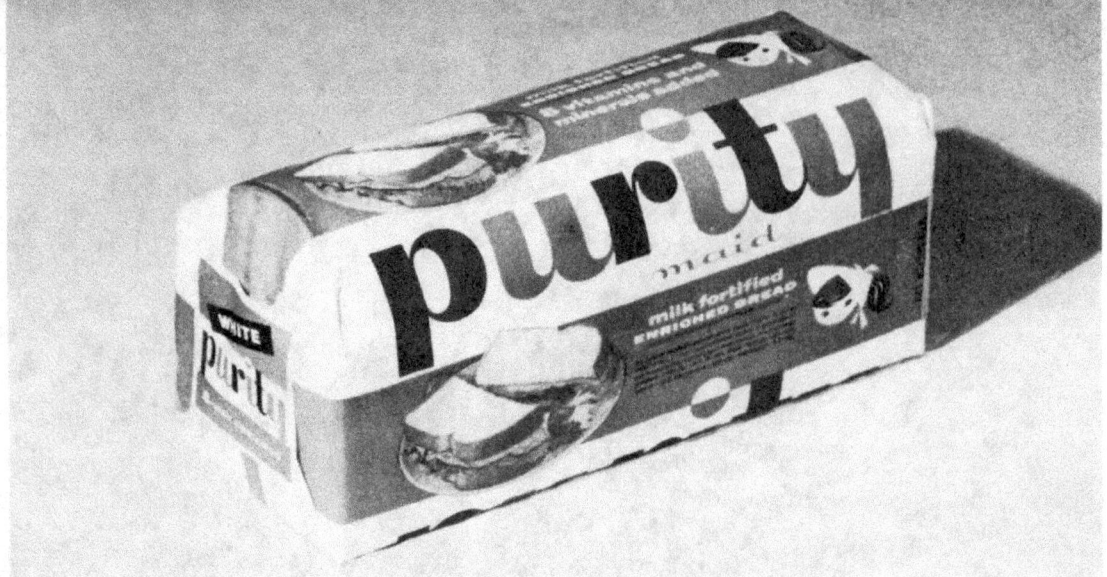

"These bread wrappers are part of an over-all redesign program—a start-from-scratch operation—undertaken by Purity Baking Company. This company, operating only in West Virginia, felt it was important to gain corporate identity throughout its entire line.

"A new, appealing, sun-bonneted 'Purity Maid' symbol was evolved from the company name and appears on the wrappers and cartons of every item in the Purity line. It is a line illustration of a little girl in a Shaker bonnet (suggesting the freshness and old-fashioned goodness consumers want in bakery products), and said symbol appears on all packages along with the large, informal lettering of the brand-name logotype and bright panels of color and food illustrations. The style of lettering used in the Purity logotype was selected because it suggests maximum friendliness and youthfulness, and is product and brand related.

"The new wrap's basic design is alternating red and white bands. Running the full length of the white bands is the name 'Purity' in giant, lower-case letters, alternately red and brown. Beneath is the word 'Maid' in small red script. On the red band is the Purity Maid trademark and promotional copy. This same design appears on the wraps for other types of bread, cakes and cookies in Purity's line, with identification simplified by replacing the red band with other colors that best complement each product variety.

"Purity bread end-labels are similar to the wrap design, for easy point-of-sale identity.

"Purity Maid wrapped up this package redesign program by incorporating its new trademark and king-size brand name and design on everything, including trucks, shipping cases, stationery, building signs, checks, and other items."

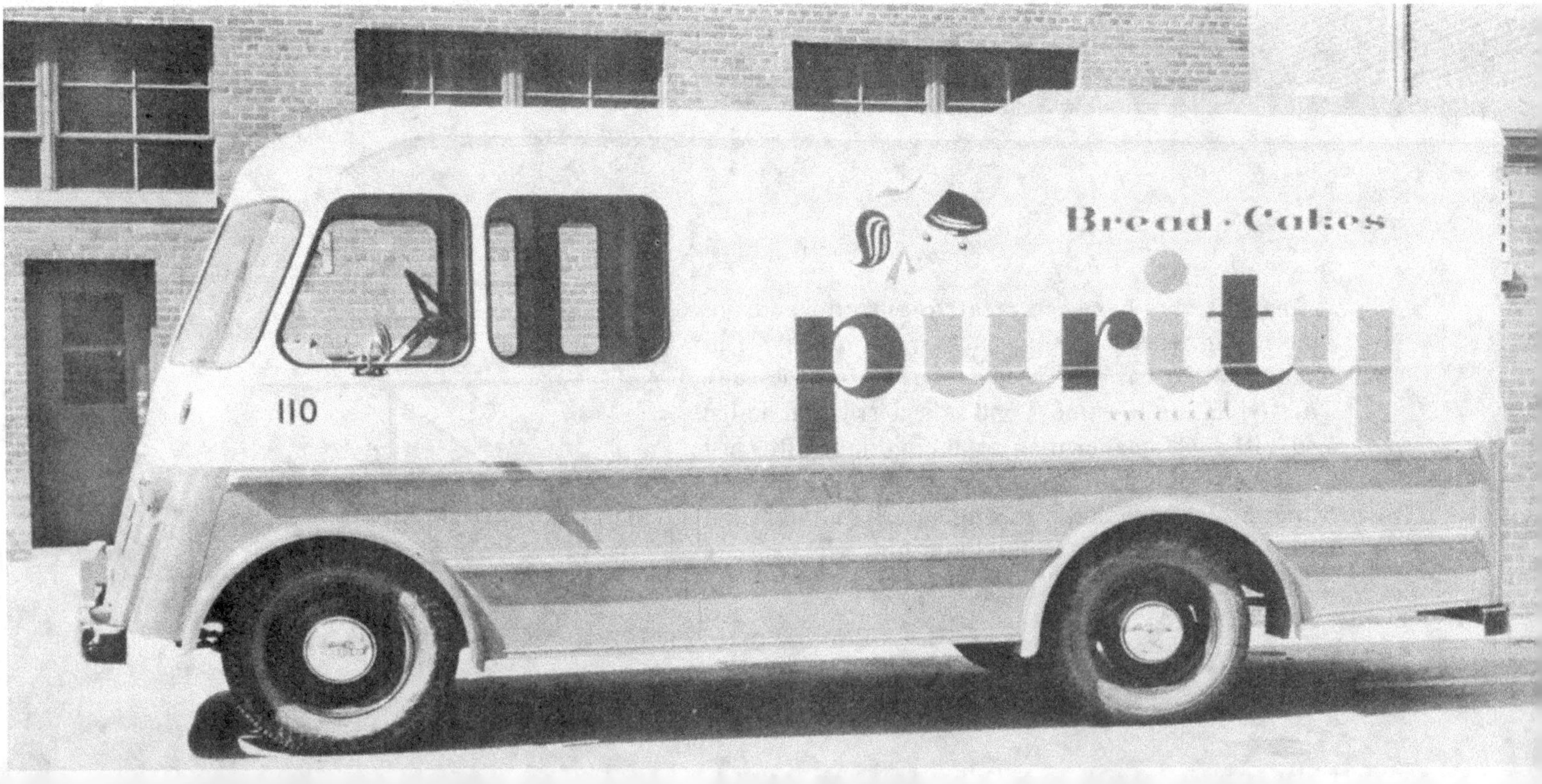

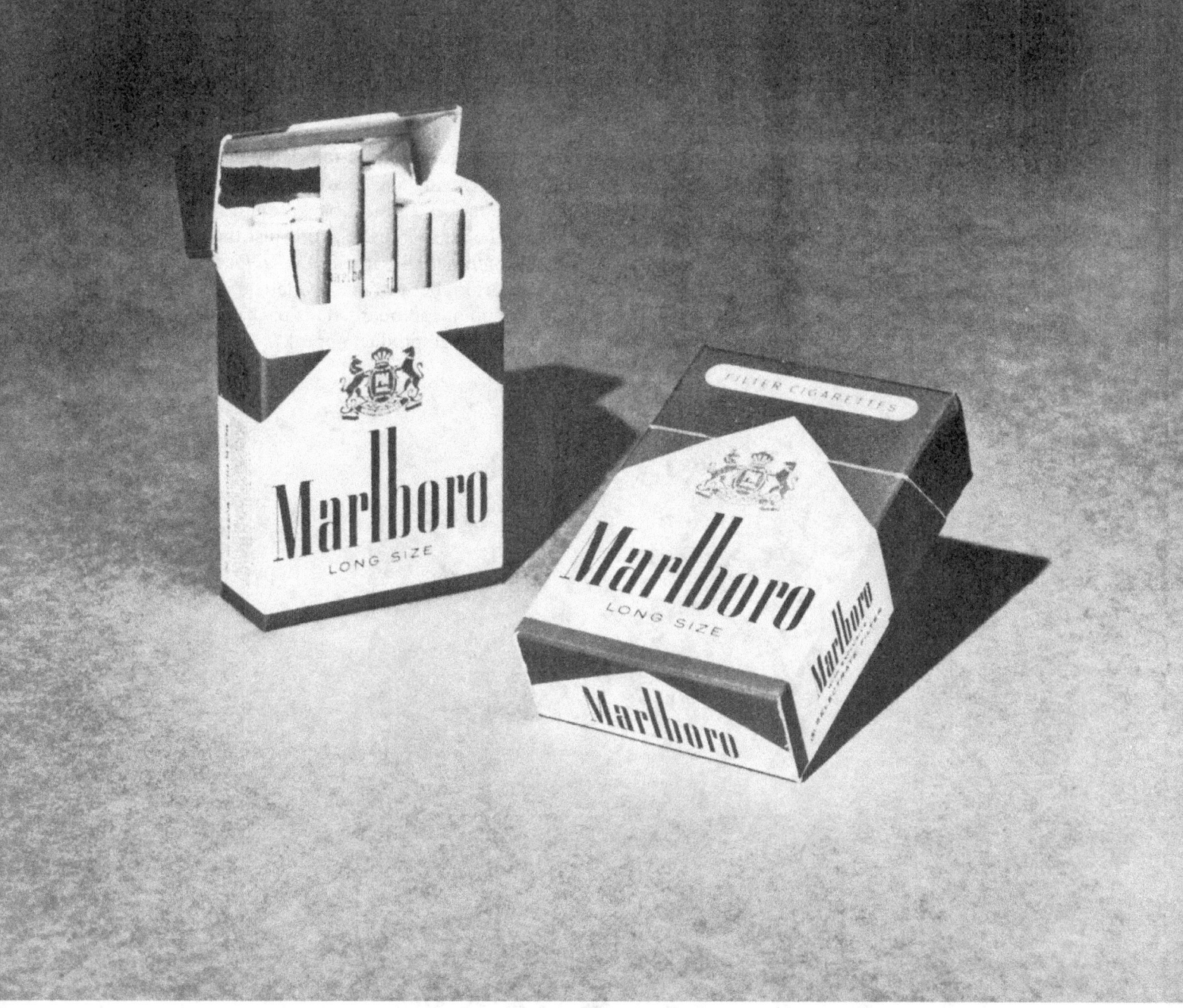

"Chief design features red, white, and black color scheme; white pyramid shape or house design; and condensed, modified, classical lettering for brand name.

"Philip Morris crest, originally in a screen of blue-black, has recently been revised and now appears in gold with red center. This further enhances the appearance of the package and gives a high-quality connotation.

"In addition, the design has been adapted to a new king-size soft pack—or cup label package—which is now on the market as well as the flip-top box. The new design represents a high point of success in sales for any package in recent times."

Designs and comments on these pages by FRANK GIANNINOTO AND ASSOCIATES, INC.

"The high quality of Seagram's V O is reflected in this luxurious, gold-foil package. Introduced for Christmas gift purchasing, it is planned as an all-year-round gift carton. The colors are maroon, metallic blue, and white. The blue oval shape makes an ideal background for the gold V O name. The stenciled lettering, in reverse on the maroon panel, adds just the right touch for 'imported' and was designed to suggest maximum quality in gift giving. Deep and varying degrees of embossing have been used on this carton, both in the V O letters and the trademark shield, which is first printed in white on 20-point foil board. This package leans heavily on lettering for styling: the result—good taste and high product appeal."

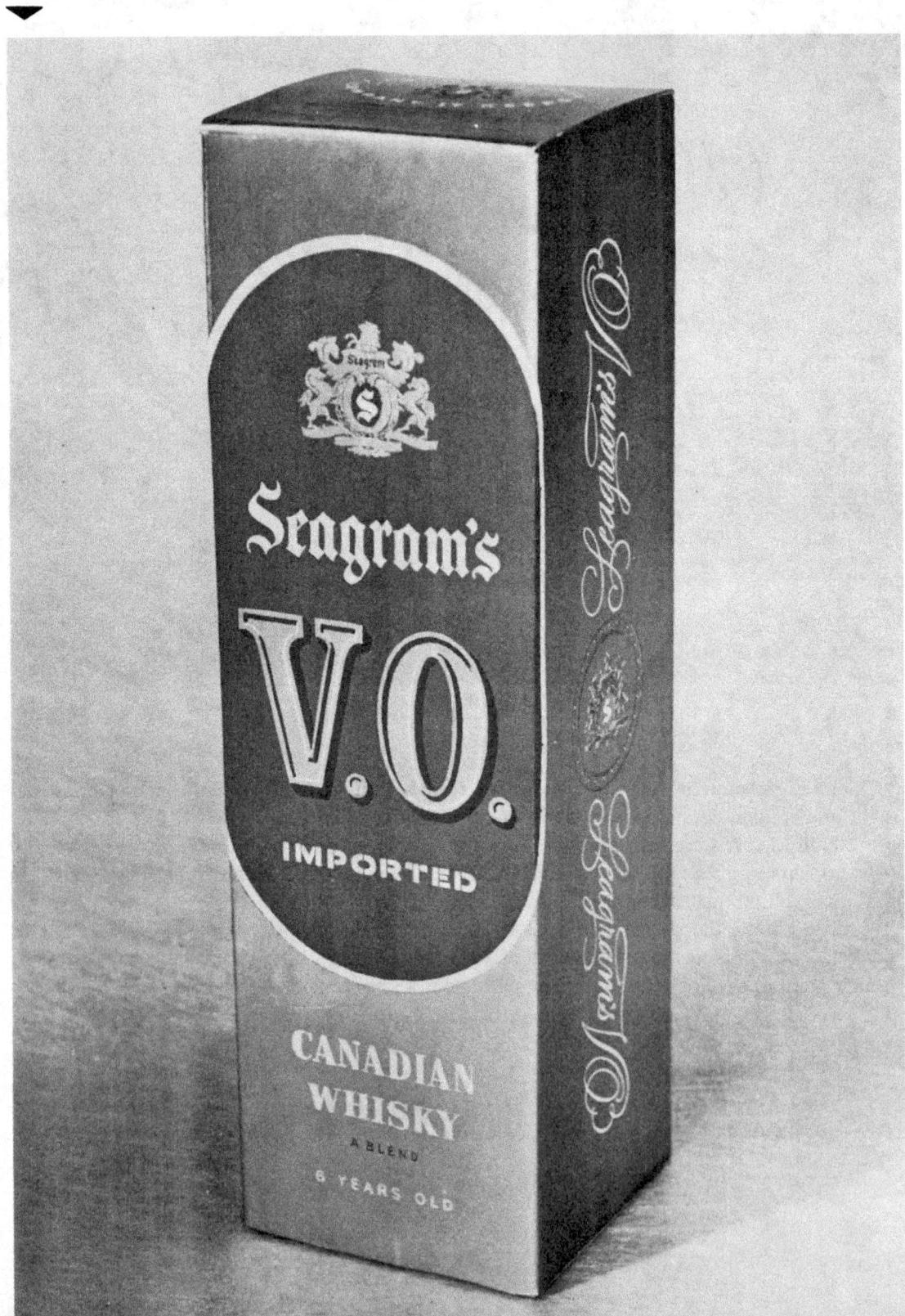

Designs and comments on these pages by FRANK GIANNINOTO AND ASSOCIATES, INC.

"Both product and package are fresh and modern, and both were developed after exhaustive research into consumer preferences.

"The Spud design is clean and lively and it connotes quality. The package is the famous flip-top, crush-proof box used for Philip Morris' Marlboro packages. The Spud box is clear white and bears a broad horizontal panel of intense blue-green, suggesting coolness (for Spud is a mentholated cigarette), accented by a distinctive border of bright red. A rich effect has been achieved by overlaying the red strip onto the blue-green panel, and this adds special drama to the package in photography or on television. The name 'Spud' appears in classic Roman Forum style lettering on the blue-green field."

▼

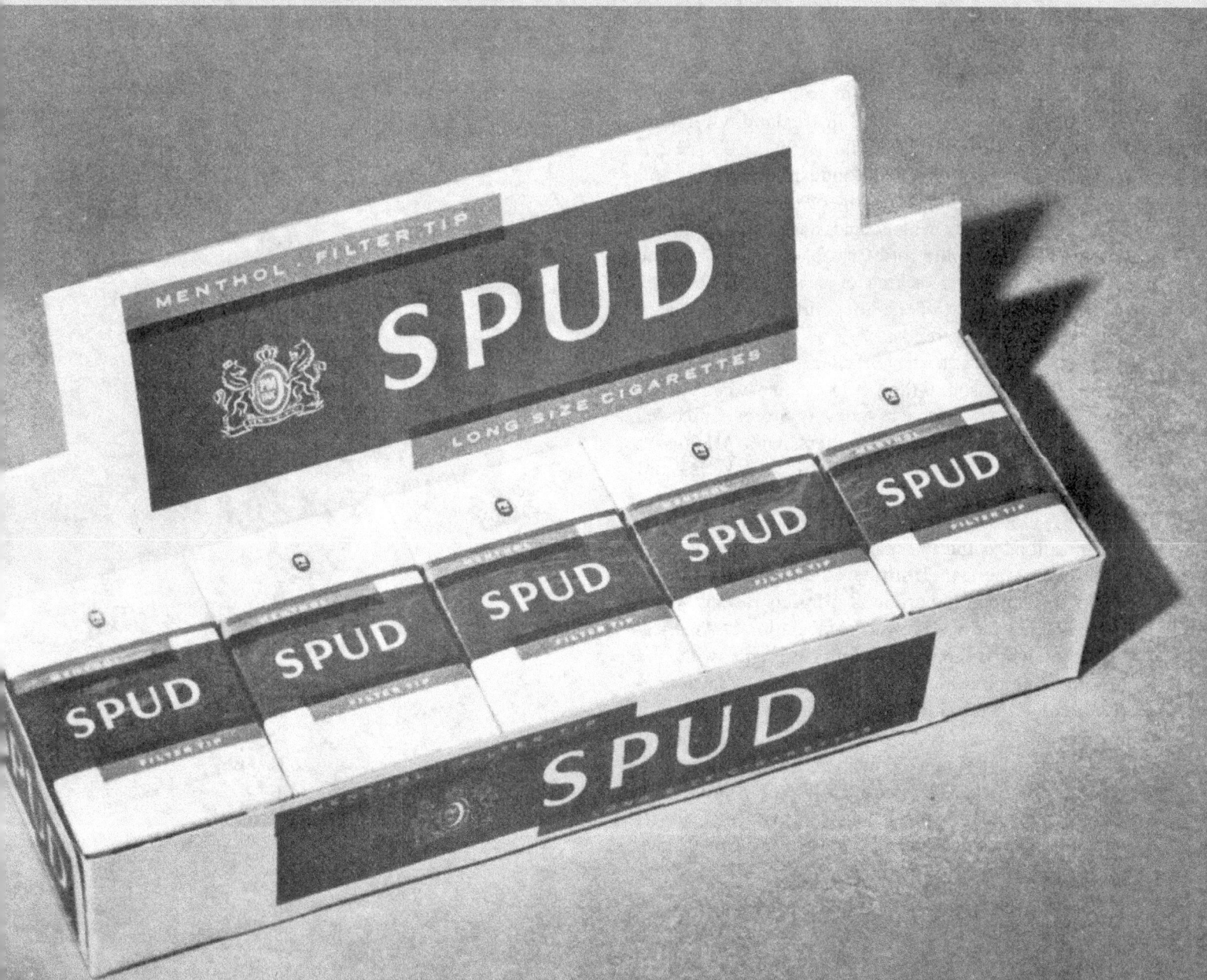

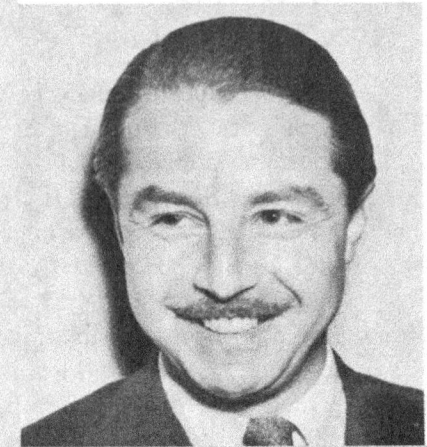

WALTER LANDOR
Walter Landor and Associates

Walter Landor, internationally known industrial designer, has been making news in various industries for years with his sales-producing product and package designs. His talents, with which he has won many awards and prizes, have been applied to a wide range of industrial design.

His work has varied from the design of nail packaging for U. S. Steel to food and beverage packaging, trademark design, World's Fair exhibits, visual identification for a huge, international, pipeline construction project, industrial architecture, and store designs.

Mr. Landor was educated in England, Germany, France, and Switzerland. In the early 1930's, he co-founded England's first firm of industrial designers and was elected the youngest fellow of the Royal Society of Arts. He travels widely and has made extensive trips to Europe, South and Central America, and the Caribbean islands in search of new design concepts and to keep abreast of the latest international design and merchandising trends.

Mr. Landor's roster of clients includes Lucky Lager, Paul Masson, Granny Goose, Sunsweet, Standard Oil, Crown-Zellerbach, Safeway Stores, Spreckles Sugar, U. S. Steel, Lever Brothers, Olin Mathieson Chemical Corp., Swift & Co., American Bakeries, and Stitzel-Weller Distillery.

The Landor group has won awards from such organizations as the Package Designers' Council, New York; the American Institute of Graphic Arts, New York; the Foreign Operations Administration, Washington D. C.; and the Brewers' Association of America, Chicago, which honored Landor designs with the Grand Championship Design Award for five consecutive years. Mr. Landor is a co-founder and director of the Package Designers' Council. He is also a member of the Food Packaging Council, an advisory organization limited to 100 key people in the food industries. In 1957, the California College of Arts and Crafts awarded him an honorary Doctor of Fine Arts degree.

"Decorative calligraphy forms the main design element of this wine bottle for a noncommercial vineyard, which limits its production and numbers its bottles. Colors are black and red on Strathmore double-deckle ivory stock. Design of the label and neck pamphlet by Walter Landor and Associates."

▼

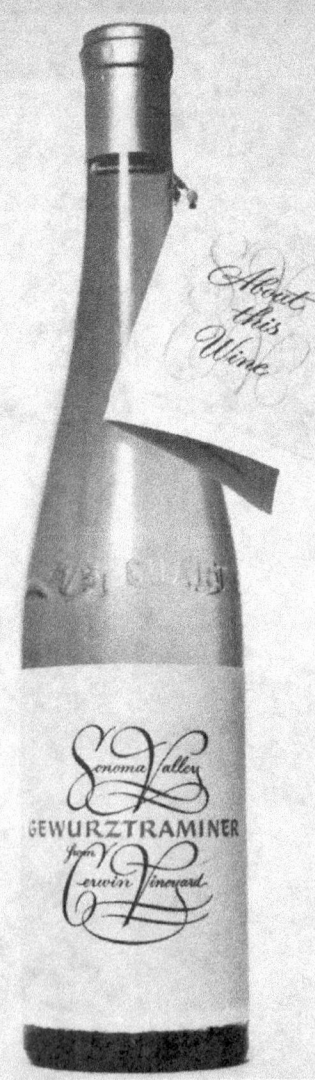

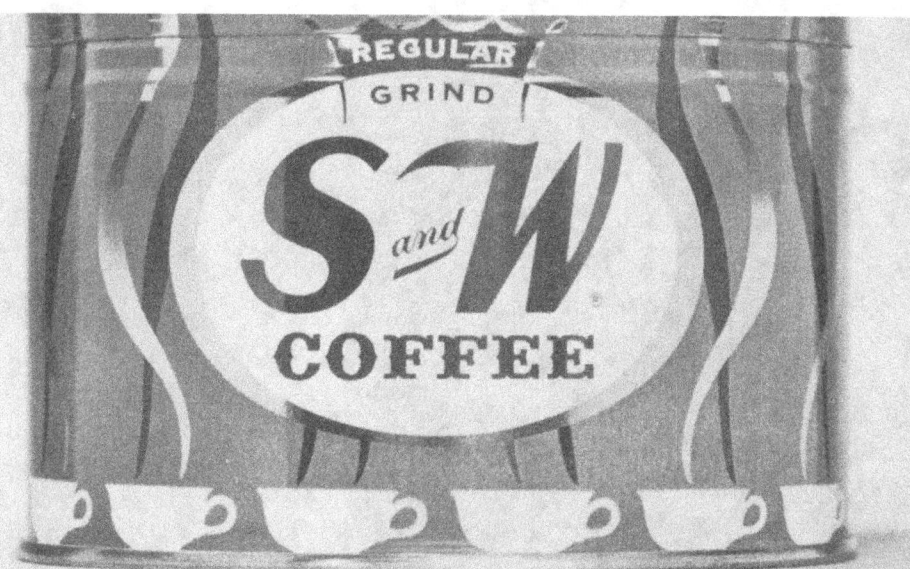

"The underlying aim of this vacuum-can design was to stimulate by graphic means the psychological associations of aroma, warmth, and home and hearth, which coffee has for most consumers. A basic commodity has been endowed with desirable individuality through meticulous design. The S & W design is based on a rich pattern of swirling gold and coffee-brown 'aroma lines' rising from a row of cups. Printed in transparent inks against the opaque red of the can, these lines of vapor inject a happy note by also suggesting party streamers. All copy, which has been kept to the indispensable minimum, is spotlighted in a white oval bordered by gold. The traditional S & W logotype, slightly modified to make it more contemporary, is printed in transparent green, assuring brand continuity with the many other products of this prolific manufacturer. The

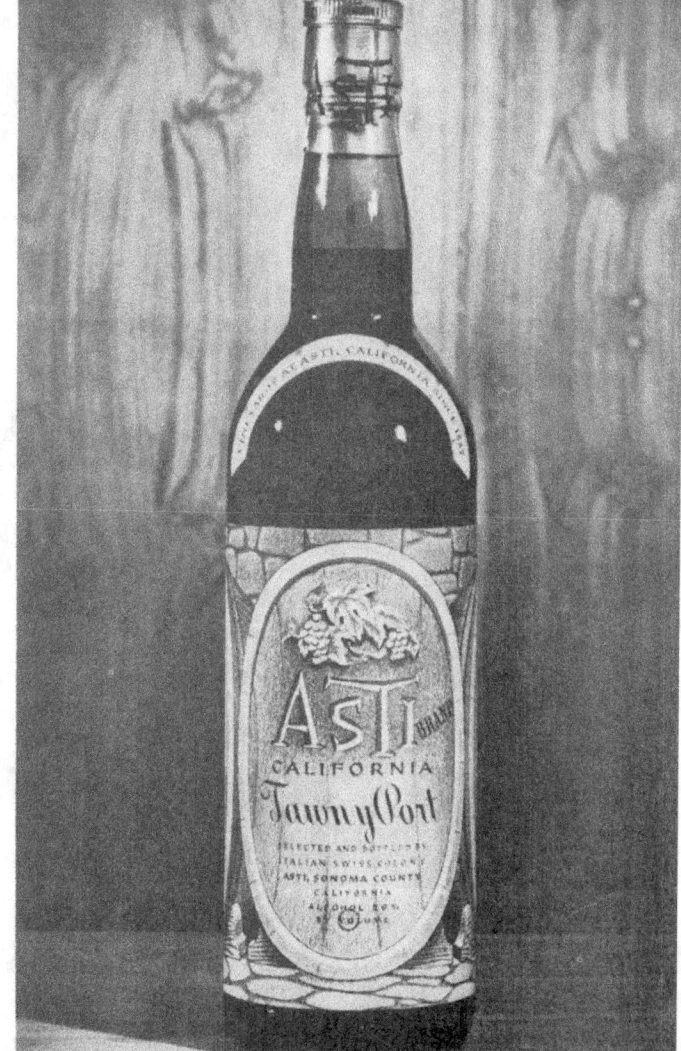

word 'coffee,' lettered in deliberately old-fashioned style and printed in a warm brown tone, contributes to the luxury look. Grind information is spelled out in straightforward fashion in a small crown resting on the top edge of the oval.

"The S & W coffee-can design was developed in conjunction with an extensive research study undertaken with the aid of the Institute of Motivational Research. A large number of designs were exposed to consumer testing before the final choice was made."

"Oaken casks in which Asti Wines are aged supplied Walter Landor with a unique and powerful central theme in the packages he created for this new premium offering by Italian Swiss Colony. Just as important is the manner in which he made an unmistakable trademark out of the brand name. Emphasis on the 't' instantly tells how it is pronounced. Nationwide dealer acceptance greeted the new line—a victory credited by Italian Swiss to the unusual appeal of its packages as well as to the prize-winning quality of the product."

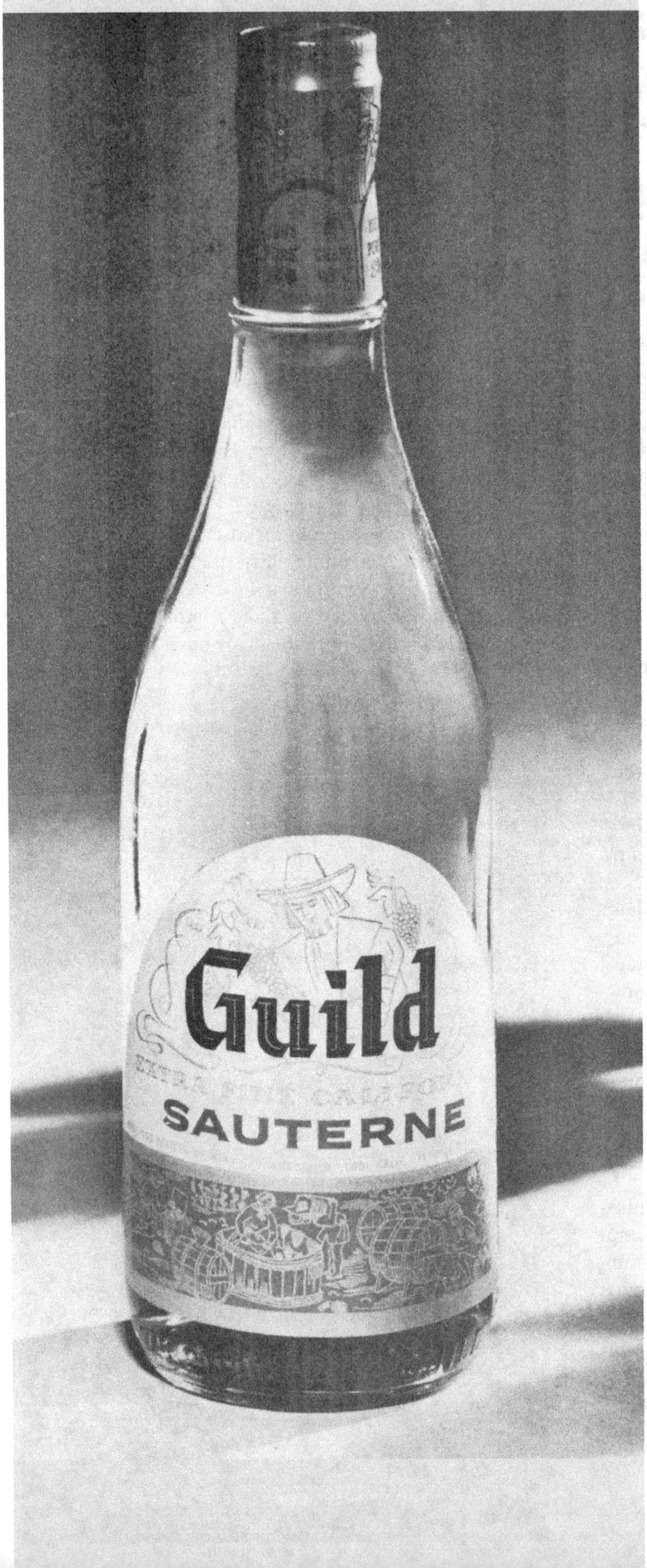

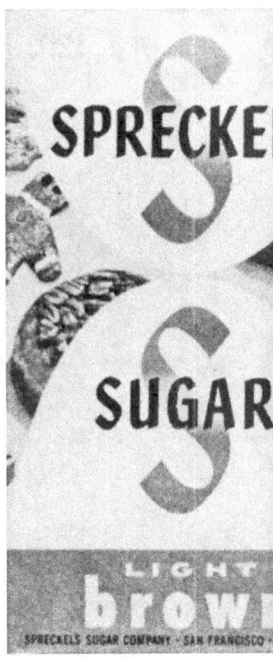

"The label tells a story of wine making and wine tradition in addition to simply identifying a product. When Walter Landor and Associates undertook this design project for the Wine Growers Guild, one of the main requirements was that the new label be equally suited to both dessert and dry wines. Guild markets both types.

"Studies indicated that the Guild labels then in use did not possess the dynamic qualities which tie in closely with the consumers' emotional attitudes toward wine and wine making.

"Howard Williams, general manager of the Wine Growers Guild, states that 'our findings convinced us that Guild's exclusive wine-making story must be visually conveyed by the label. We asked Walter Landor to translate the findings of our consumer research into design results and to undertake a thorough restyling program for the Guild.'

"On the new label, the Guild name is shown in black, in stylized Beton lettering, hand lettered with a gold in-line. The variety name, as well as the background color of the illustration panel across the bottom, runs in a light maroon—actually a special color made by the ink maker to match the designer's sample. All other label elements—the illustration behind the brand name, the two small text lines, the bottom panel border, and the contained line illustration—are printed in gold for an exceptionally effective 'quality' effect. Shelf appearance, likewise, is excellent, and brand name and varietal name are easy to see. A well-styled, cellulose neck band completes the ensemble."

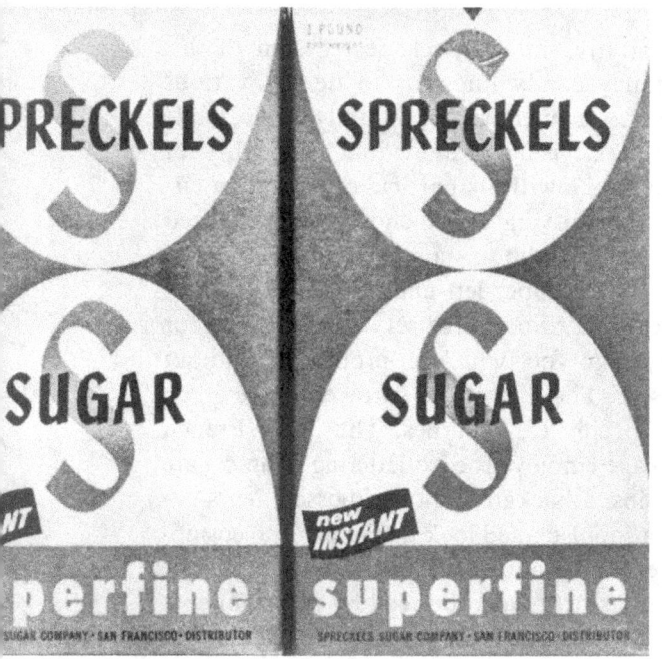

"This design program embraced the company's line of sugars (superfine, granulated, confectioner's and brown). Appropriate color combinations and vignettes serve to differentiate the various sugar types. However, one over-all design scheme relates all the items in the line. The design is based on an hourglass motif, combined with hand lettering based on Lydian type. The latter was selected with an eye to good reproduction in black-and-white advertising media, especially television. The large 'S' in each of the two hourglass panels is used as a branding device to equate Spreckels and sugar in the consumer mind. The entire design scheme attempts to realize the ideal trademark: the total package."

Designs and comments on these pages by WALTER LANDOR AND ASSOCIATES

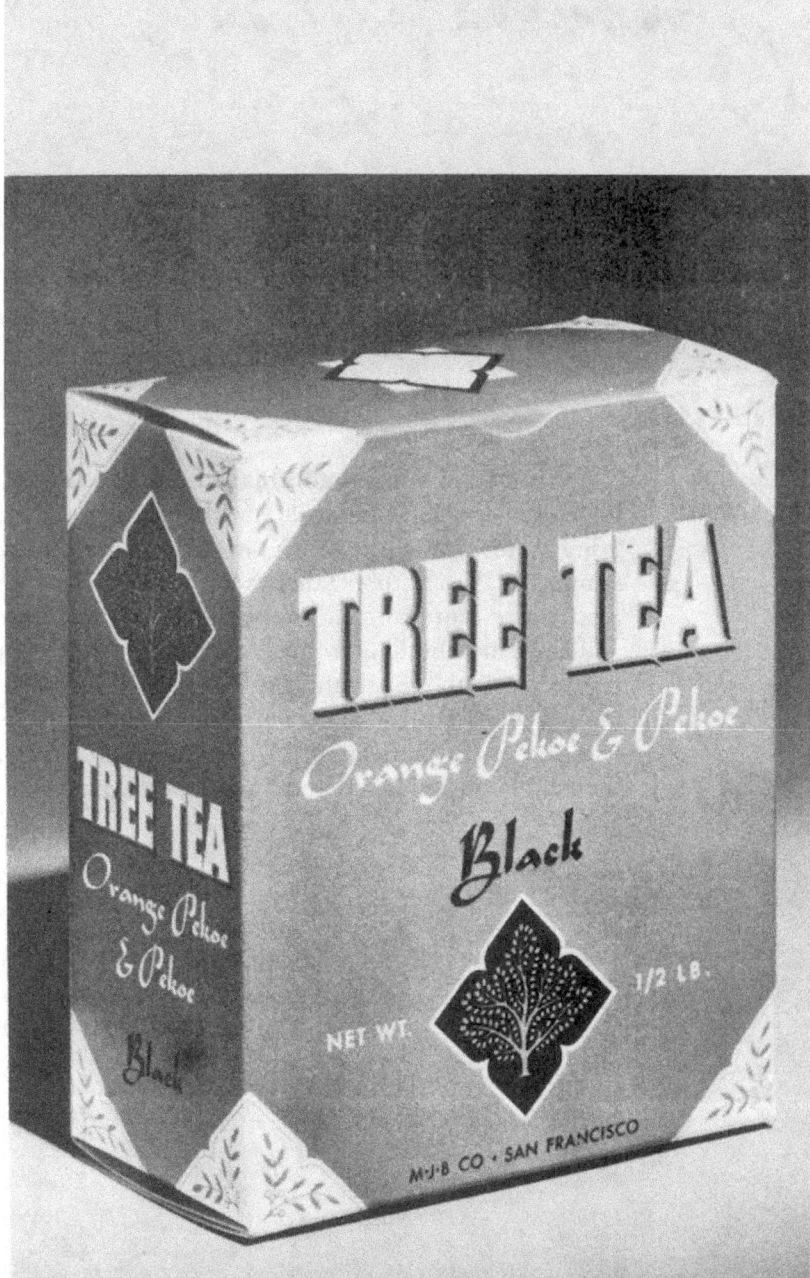

"Surface design of this package aims at projecting the Far Eastern origin of tea. The hand lettered 'Tree Tea' is in the style of Condensed Copperplate Gothic, while the words denoting the tea type are in Legend script, which has a distinct Oriental flavor. Other design elements aid and abet this over-all scheme—including the colors, which are Chinese red, black and white."

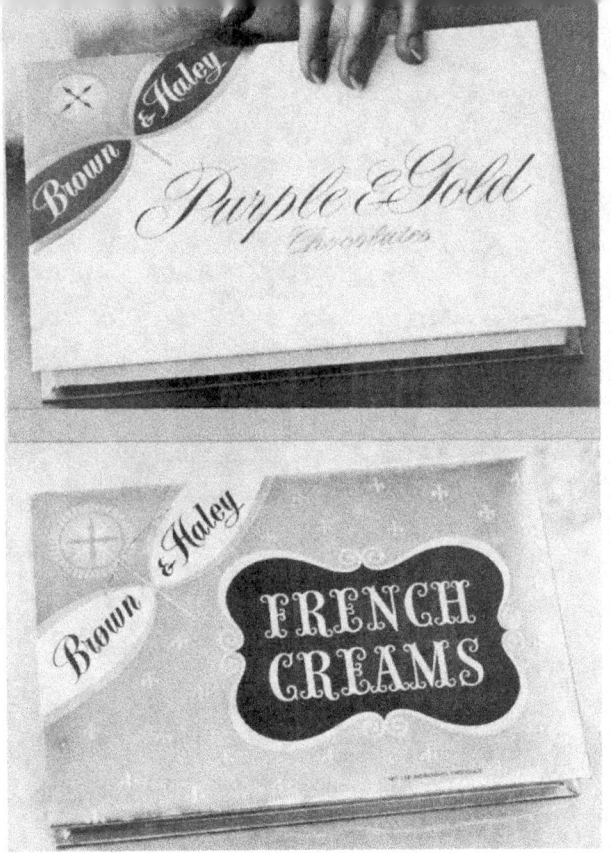

"The dual objective in the package redesign of this company's fancy candy line was to tie the various products together as members of a family group, while at the same time devising an individual personality for each, in accordance with its particular marketing circumstances. The unifying device chosen was a stylized lollipop with twisted ribbon—a symbol appropriate to the product—in the upper-left-hand corner of the various packages. The ribbon area serves as a setting for the company logotype, which is prominent without being obtrusive. The rest of the surface area is given over to the specific candy types. Thus, the 'French Creams' package employs rococo lettering in an ornate frame set against a background of embossed fleurs-de-lis to convey a sophisticated look that appeals to cosmopolitans. The 'Purple and Gold' package, which is the highest priced assortment produced by the company, uses deliberate restraint in limiting itself to a design scheme of formal Spencerian script in royal purple against a white background, blind-embossed with white crowns."

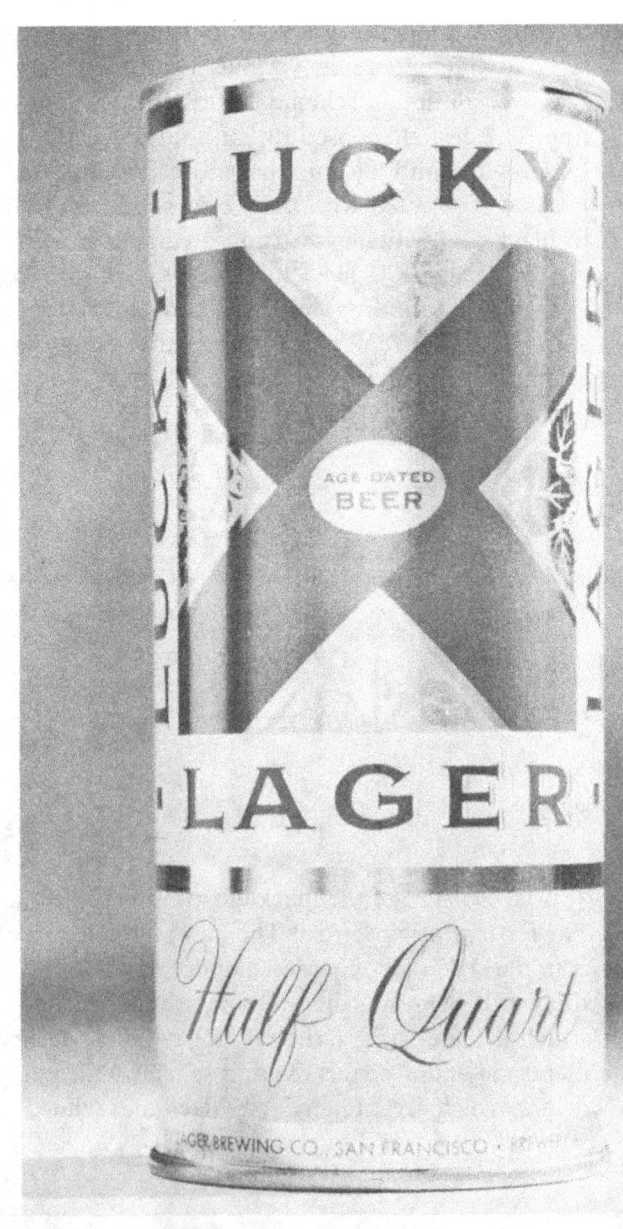

"Sophistication and glamour have been added to the Lucky Lager label without sacrificing the major identifying factor of the 'big red X,' which has become so familiar to Western beer fanciers in the years since Repeal. Since more women are buying beer these days, and since distribution through supermarkets is becoming increasingly important, the designer had to make the new label especially attractive to women shoppers, without loss of male interest. Five colors are used on the aluminum-foil labels and on the metal cans."

Designs and comments on these pages by WALTER LANDOR AND ASSOCIATES

"This Hawaiian Golden Punch can is the result of close collaboration between the Walter Landor design group, Pacific Hawaiian and its advertising agency, Atherton Mogge Privett, Inc., Los Angeles.

"The design is based on a horizontal leaf treatment, conceived to minimize the breaks in American Can Company's wide-beaded can, which is used by Pacific Hawaiian Products because of its resistance to buckling. Sharing the front panel with the leaves, and superimposed upon them, is an actual-size illustration of the drink in a tall, stemmed glass and a blossom from the passionflower vine. This combination of bold shapes makes a strong image for the brand in all advertising media, even where color is unavailable, such as in black-and-white TV and newspapers.

"Brand and product identification appears on the uppermost of the three broad leaves. The word 'Hawaiian' is highlighted in traditional lettering in white with gold in-line. In their treatment of 'Golden Punch' which is printed directly below in gold, lower-case italics, the designers have taken advantage of the can's beaded structure. Taking into account the fact that large fruit-juice cans are usually displayed on bottom shelves at supermarkets, they located these words along the wall of the top break. This causes the identification copy to look tilted and much increases visibility when seen from above by the consumer.

"The color scheme of the new design juxtaposes metallic and regular lines to achieve an extraordinarily rich effect. The veined leaves alternate forest green and magenta to accent the tropical theme. These colors are cooled by the use of golden lime green for the over-all background, suggesting the clear, fruity flavor of the drink and imparting a chilled look to the can when the consumer sees it on the store shelf."

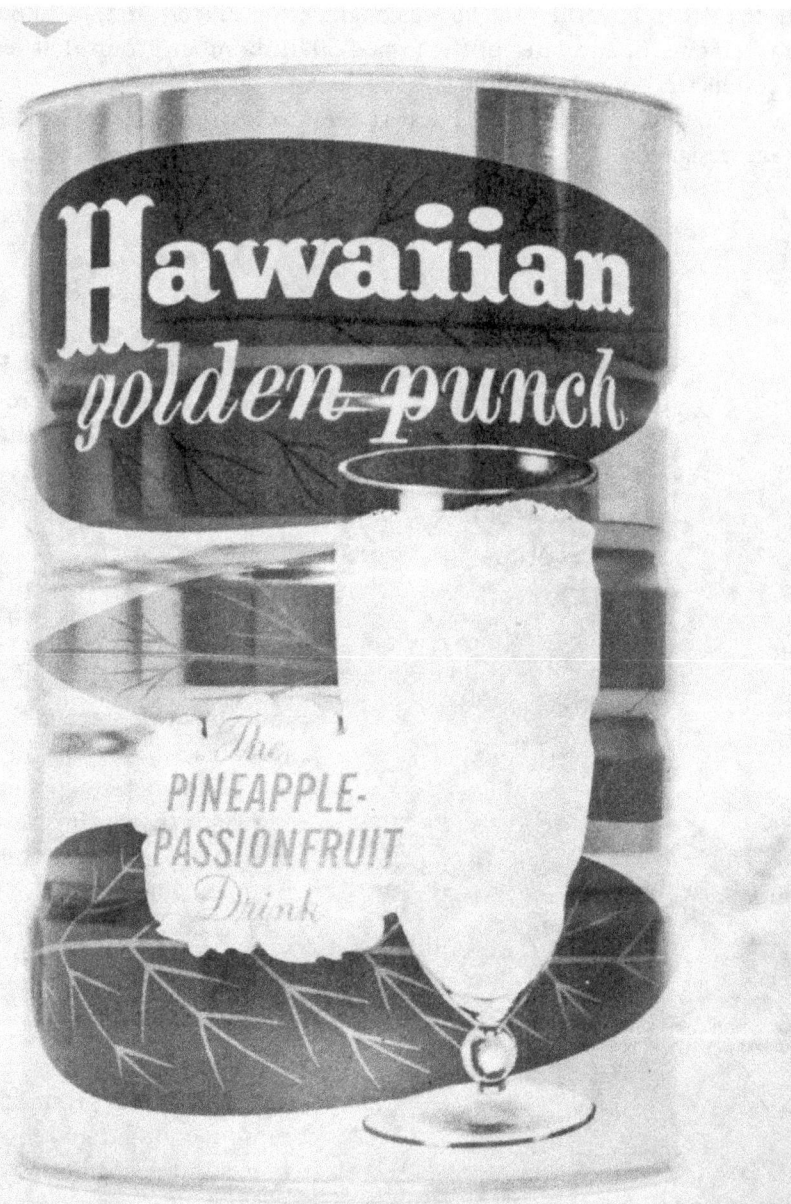

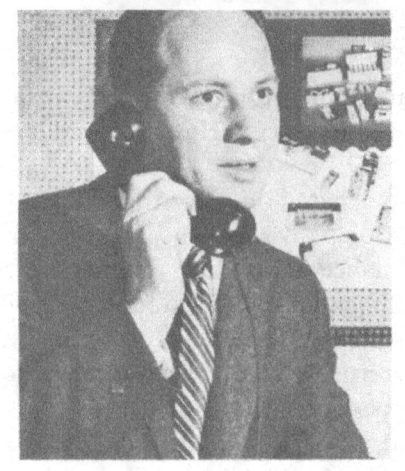

GERALD STAHL
Gerald Stahl Associates

Head of the New York industrial design firm, Gerald Stahl Associates, Gerald Stahl is one of the younger men among America's foremost industrial designers. Many of the product design and development programs, packaging projects, and corporate-identification plans for which he and his firm have been responsible have been heralded as establishing new standards in design and marketing.

Among his clients are many of the country's best-known corporations, including: Waring Products, Stanley Works, Jones & Laughlin Steel, American Chain and Cable, General Foods Corporation, United States Plywood, American Hardware, U. S. Industries, Inc., and Nichols Wire & Aluminum.

Mr. Stahl received his degree in industrial design from the Rhode Island School of Design, and opened offices as Gerald Stahl Associates thirteen years ago.

During the Second World War, he was engineering officer, first, of Experimental Flight Test and Development, and later of the famed 509th bomber group that tested the atomic bomb and conducted bomb operations against Japan.

He is a fellow and director of the Package Designers' Council, the professional society of U. S. package designers.

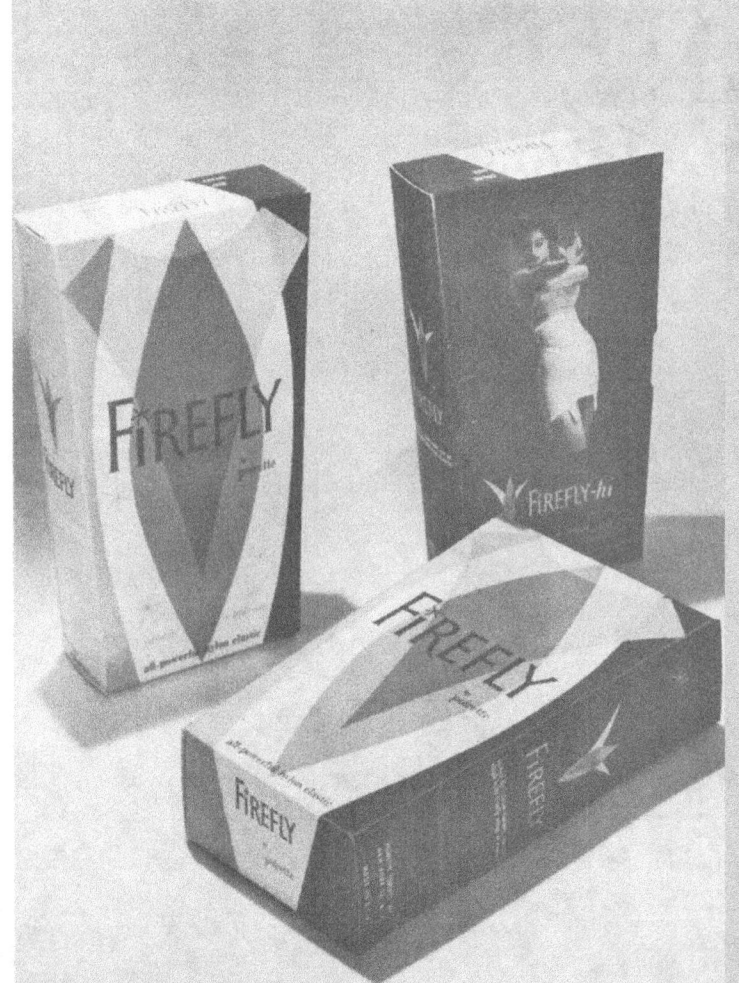

◀

"Lettering design for the Poirette Corsets, Inc., 'Firefly' girdle package is finely detailed but free in form to achieve a product image of femininity and freedom in wearing. The use of the star to dot the 'i' provides an additional accent of allure for the woman shopper."

▶

"Among the first industrial corporations to adopt the consumer-goods marketing plan of 'corporate imagery' design, the Jones & Laughlin Steel Corporation has won awards as well as new industry-wide recognition with its outstanding trademark.

"Shown here applied to a variety of packaging and advertising layouts, the powerful 'JL' symbol, designed by Gerald Stahl Associates, introduces a unique use of letter design and format.

"The new mark utilizes powerful letter-line imagery to portray industrial authority. Simplicity and clarity of the design permit consistency of its use in all media.

"The 'JL' mark is used most often in yellow against a green ground; but its black-and-white reproduction attains equal force, with strong and immediate recognition."

"Recently, U. S. Industries, Inc.—which developed in one decade from a one-product to a multiproduct company with 14 national and international divisions —began promoting its new 'corporate image' and trademark.

"This is the first time in the company's history that all divisions will be linked visually with one mark and one look.

"Formerly, USI had one parent-company mark— the letters 'USI' against a field of 'wings.' As it acquired various companies—including those that engineer and produce water tanks, electrical fittings, oil-well pumping equipment, heavy-duty engine lathes, milling machines, stainless-steel cookware, control systems for guided missiles, etc.—USI acquired, simultaneously, a separate trademark and identity for each division.

"Last year, as part of an over-all marketing scheme, USI chiefs felt that this lack of unity and direction, via a series of unrelated division identities, had to go.

"The new USI mark will be used in two ways: as a trademark by itself, and as a part of the advertising signature in promotional material, with the name of each USI division alongside it. It will, in addition, be used in a geometric-design pattern in all printed matter, motion pictures, outdoor signs, shipping stencils, ads, products, shipping crates, containers, wrappings, factory signage, billboards, etc."

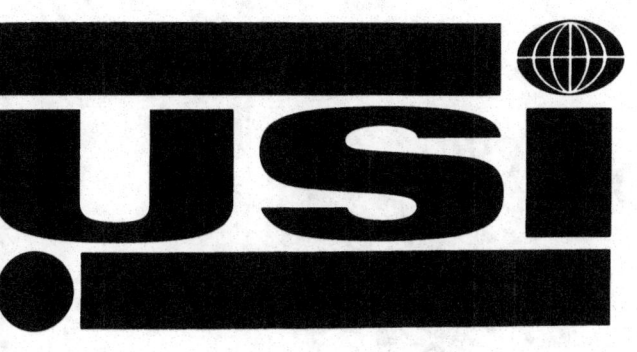

"New corporate-identity format for all 14 national and international divisions of U. S. Industries, Inc. will include this newly designed trademark, developed by New York industrial designers, Gerald Stahl Associates.

"Letter form is prominent design element. Image idea is to promote authoritative, dominant, and modern company with activities of international scope (note globe which dots 'i')."

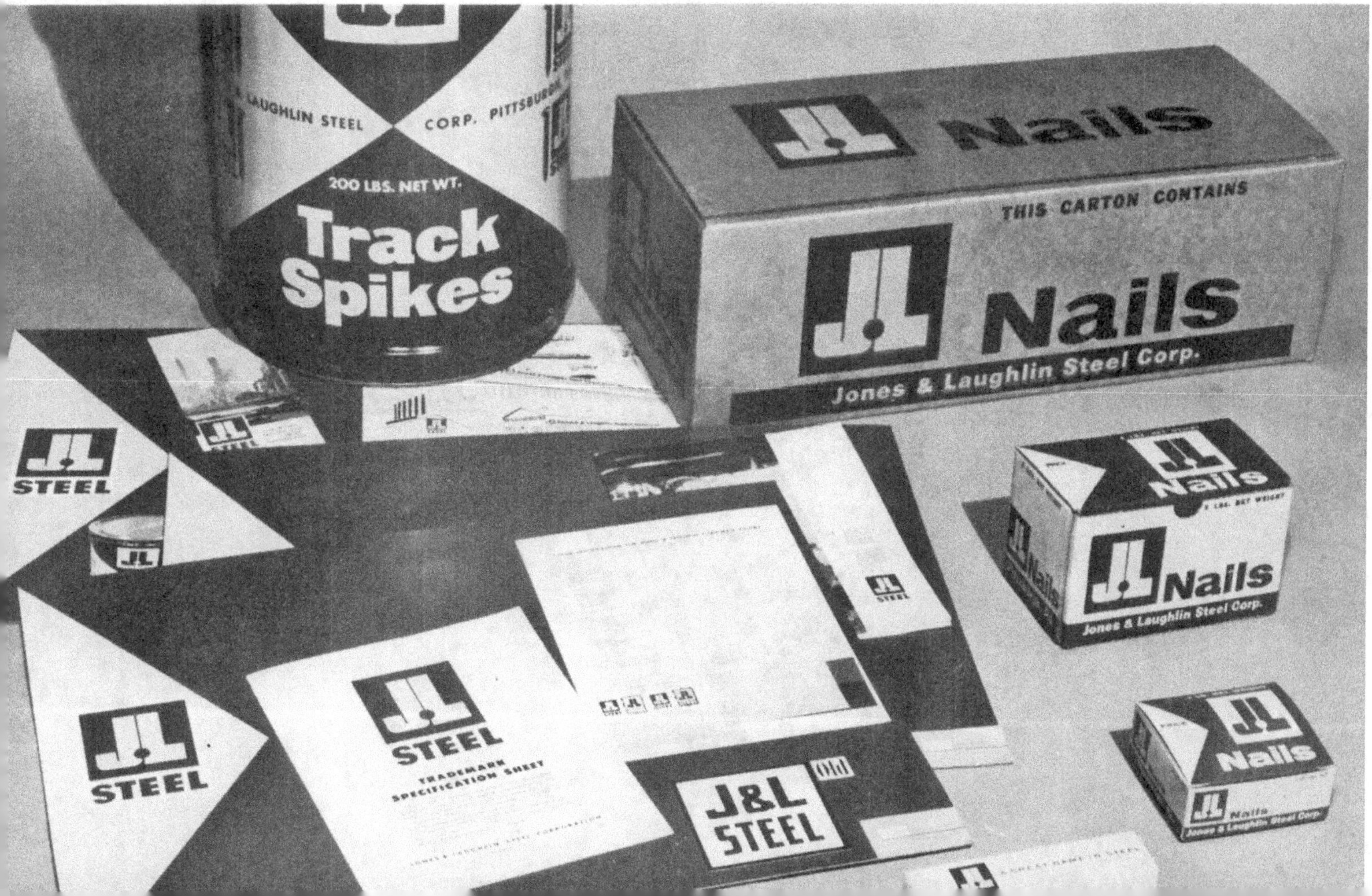

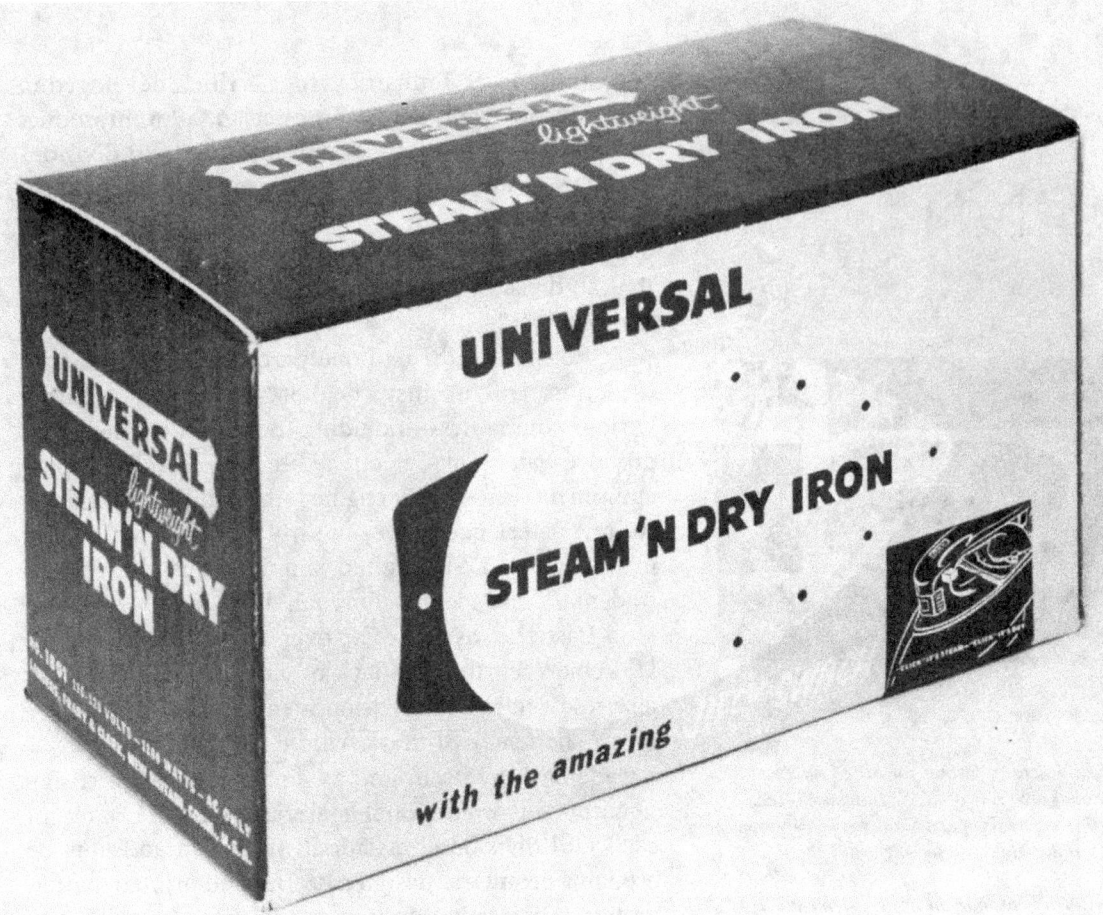

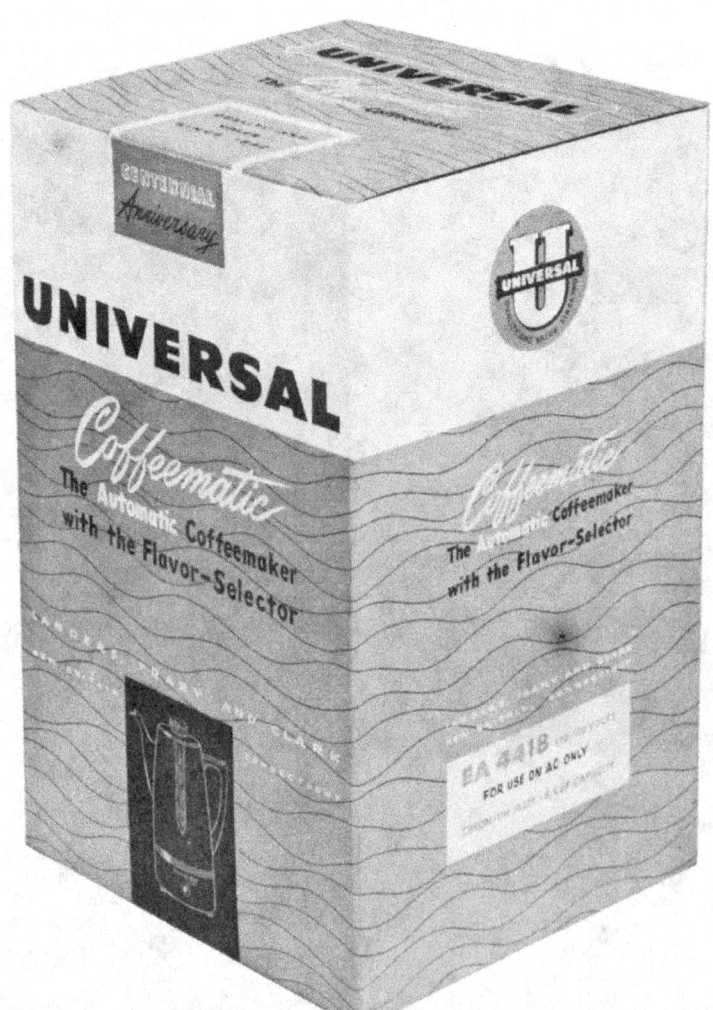

Designs and comments on these pages by GERALD STAHL ASSOCIATES

"Lettering design for these Universal-brand products promotes a quality look as well as strong product identity. Integration of script lettering adds a homey, warm, feminine touch to take the product out of 'industrial' frame. 'Universal' and 'Steam 'N Dry Iron' are lettered in black against a deep pink field. Base of the iron is shown in white. The 'Coffeematic' and 'Beam-O-Lite Iron' have coffee-brown package colors to promote visual brand unity."

"Of special importance in the packaging redesign project for the American Chain & Cable Company, is the versatile use of design elements throughout its various lines. Shown here, for example, are 'WEED' chains, ACCO's automobile tire chains and accessories. To associate this line with the ACCO company and simultaneously maintain strong identity of the 'WEED' brand name, the yellow-and-blue, link-design pattern, used with clean ACCO trade-name lettering, works well."

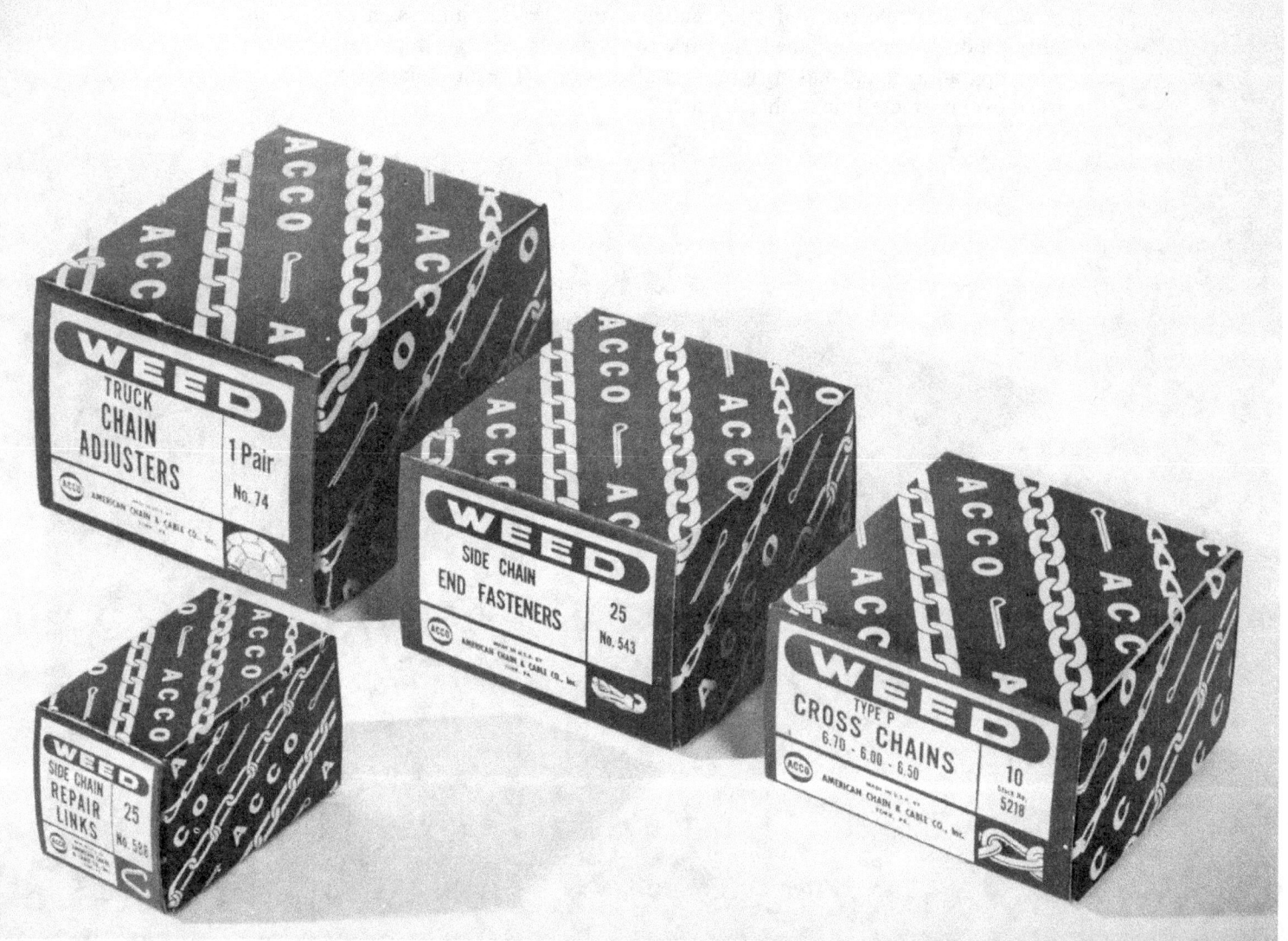

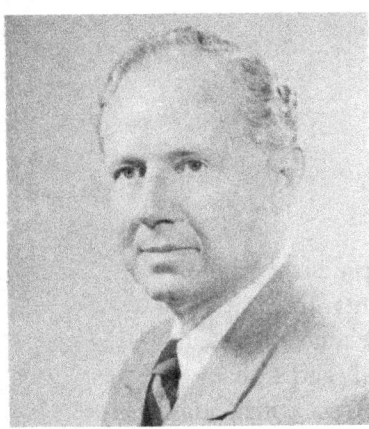

Mr. Francis E. Blod, president and creative director, founded Francis Blod Design Associates, Inc., New York, over fourteen years ago. This nationally known industrial design firm includes among its clients such companies as Farrington Manufacturing, Lily-Tulip, Mennen, Squibb, Tung Sol Electric, Lehn & Fink, Wallace Laboratories, and Warner Lambert.

Mr. Blod is a board member and president emeritus of the Package Designers' Council, an organization of leading package designers in this country. He is a graduate and trustee of Pratt Institute's School of Industrial Design and the recipient of many national design awards.

In addition to his more than twenty years' experience in the practice of product and package design and development, Mr. Blod has broad experience in retail merchandising.

"The design of this logotype was based on a modified Lydian. The objectives were to improve the legibility at point of sale, under supermarket self-service conditions, and to enhance the quality appeal of a long-established product to encourage new purchasers. The gold vignette was conceived to develop a thirst appeal inherent in a well-frosted can of beer. The particular hue and value of gold was selected to further enhance the over-all impression of a quality product. We maintained the basic red Krueger oval but improved the color, upgrading it and making it more contemporary. The ale maintained the green oval characteristic of this product."

Francis E. Blod, art director
Ray Spillenger, designer

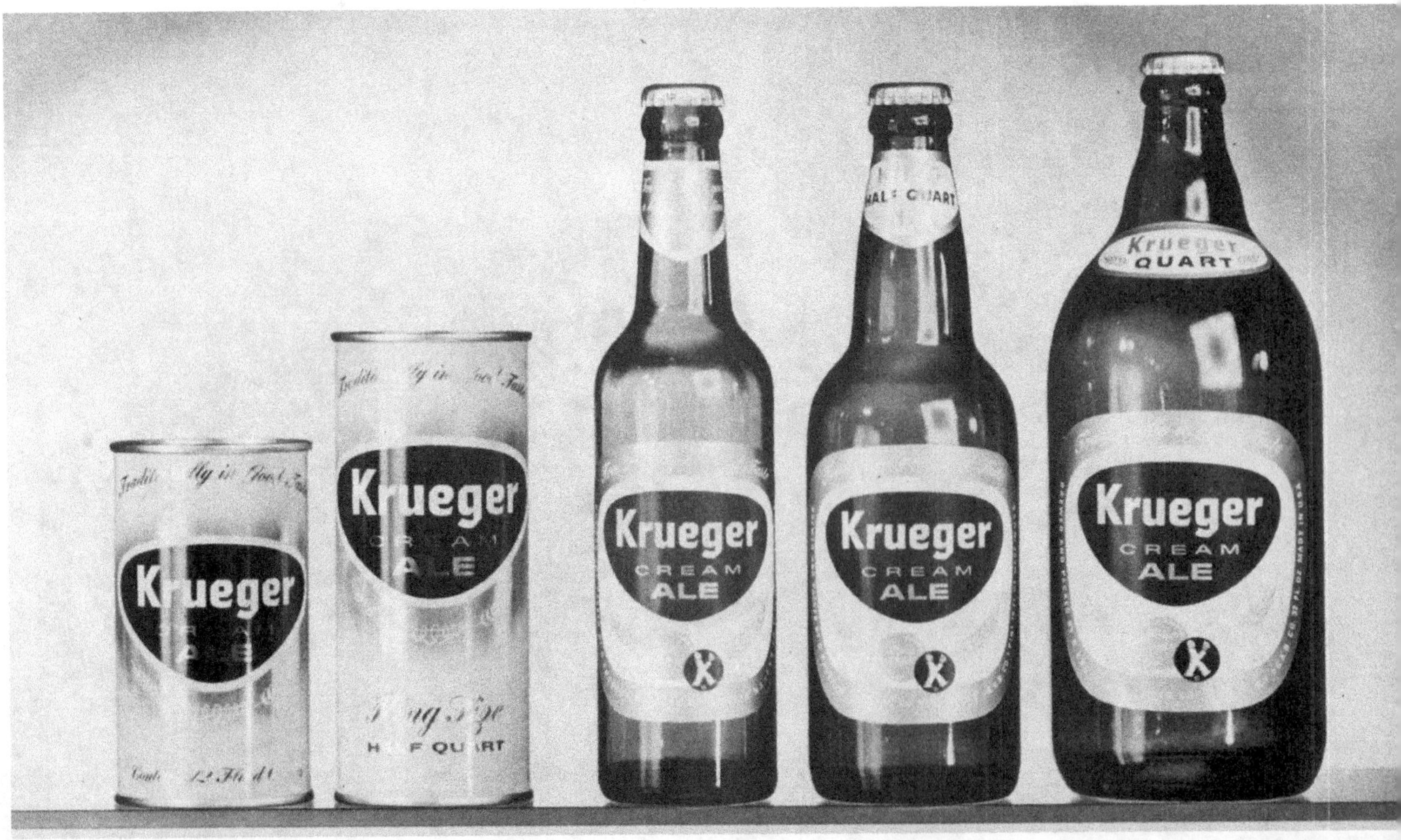

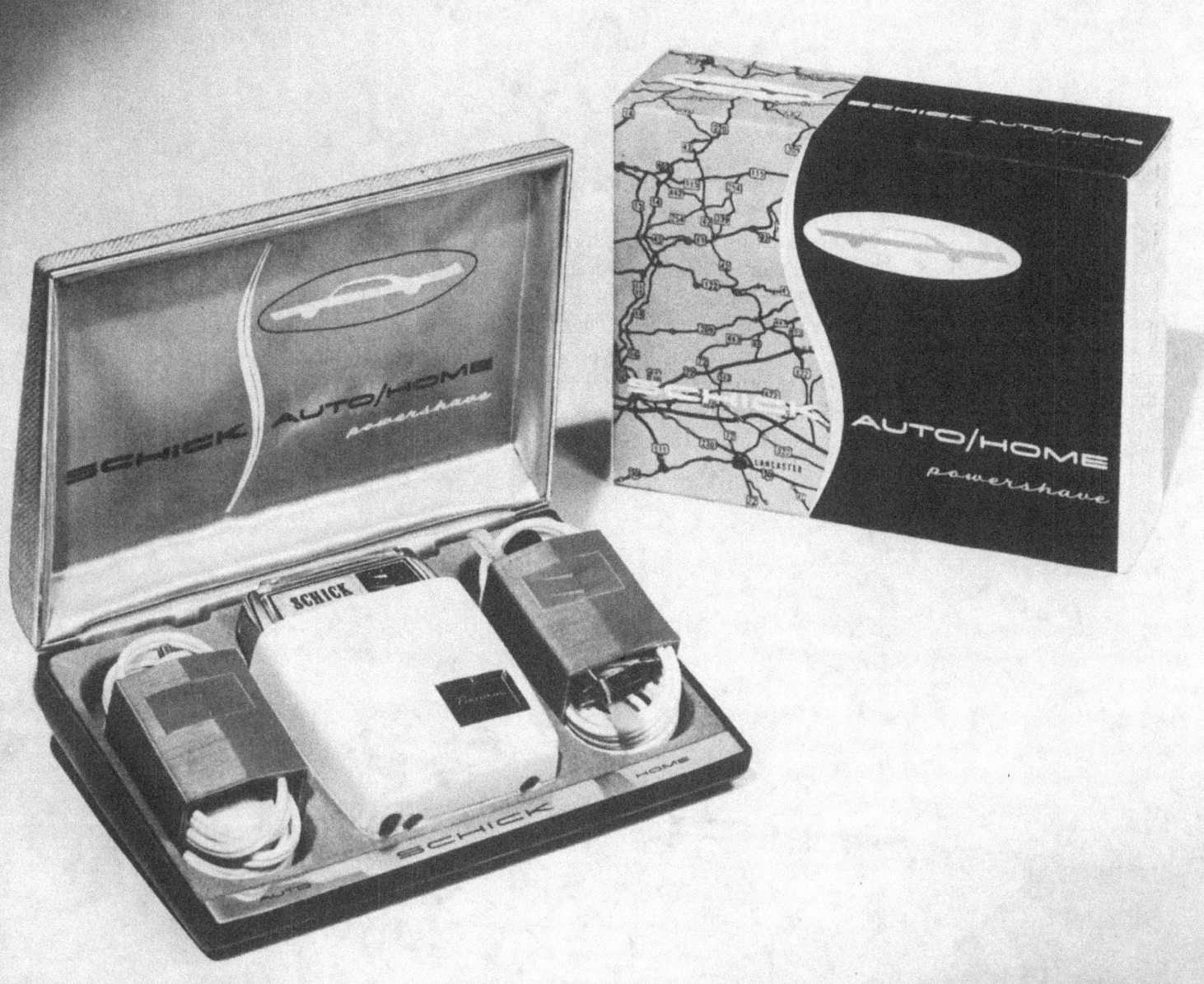

Francis Blod Design Associates, Inc.
Marian Franco, designer

"A stylized car and a highway 'S' were combined with a road map to dramatize the usefulness of a new auto/home electric shaver that Schick recently introduced. The carton was developed to give Schick a distinctive package, using easily identifiable travel symbols. These graphic symbols were developed for display strength on the carton and in the luxurious case interior, as well as for effectiveness in advertising and sales promotion."

"Graphic symbols of multiple speakers combined with a pronounced electronic-impulse pattern were designed to appeal to the discerning hi-fi devotee in selling a 'matched pair' of beam power amplifiers. In this comparatively new field, Tung Sol believed that the typical, amateur hi-fi customer is usually unaware of the availability of products of this type. So, to encourage display of the product, a package dramatizing end-result benefits was designed. The package maintained family identity with other Tung Sol products."

Marian Franco, designer

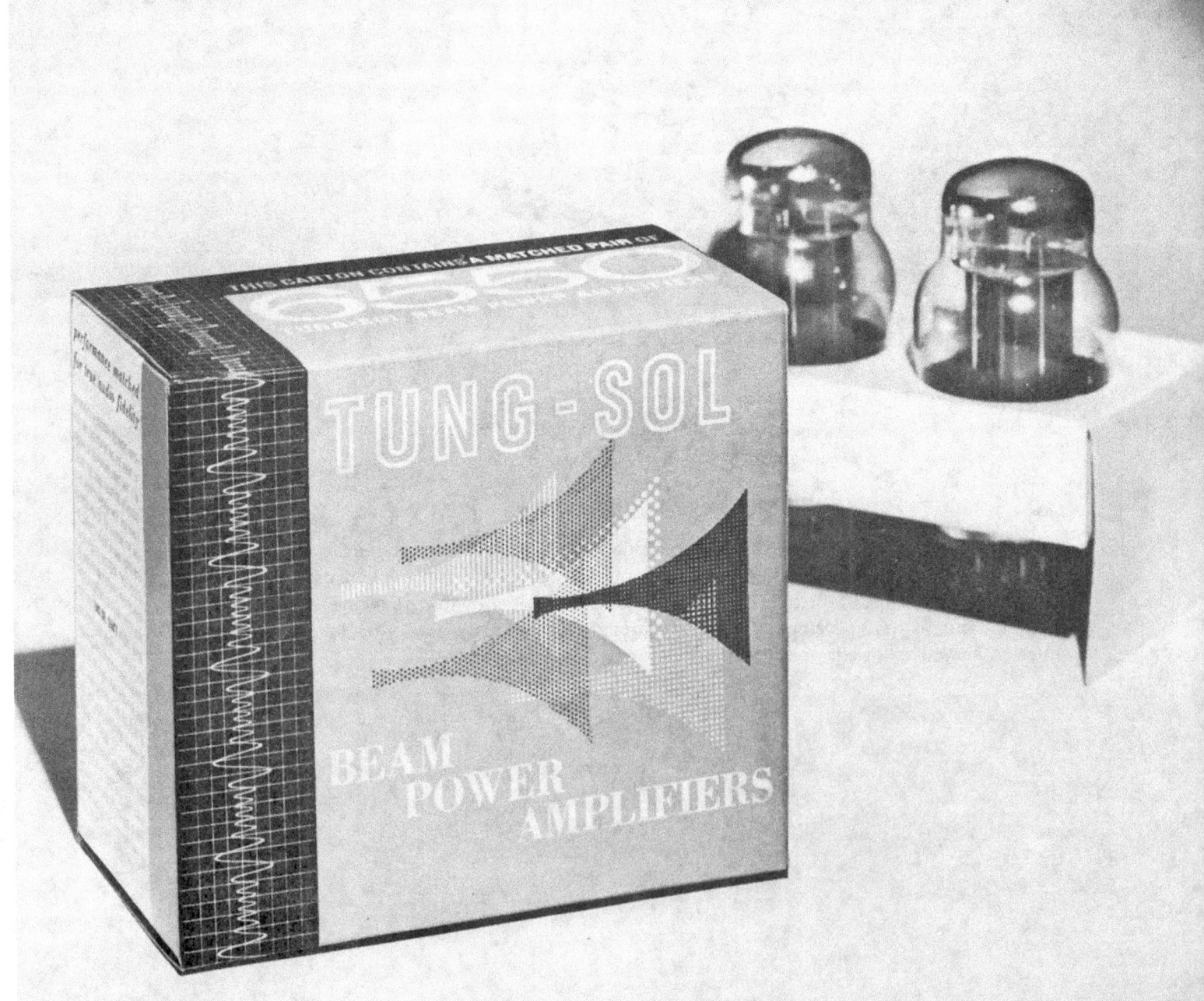

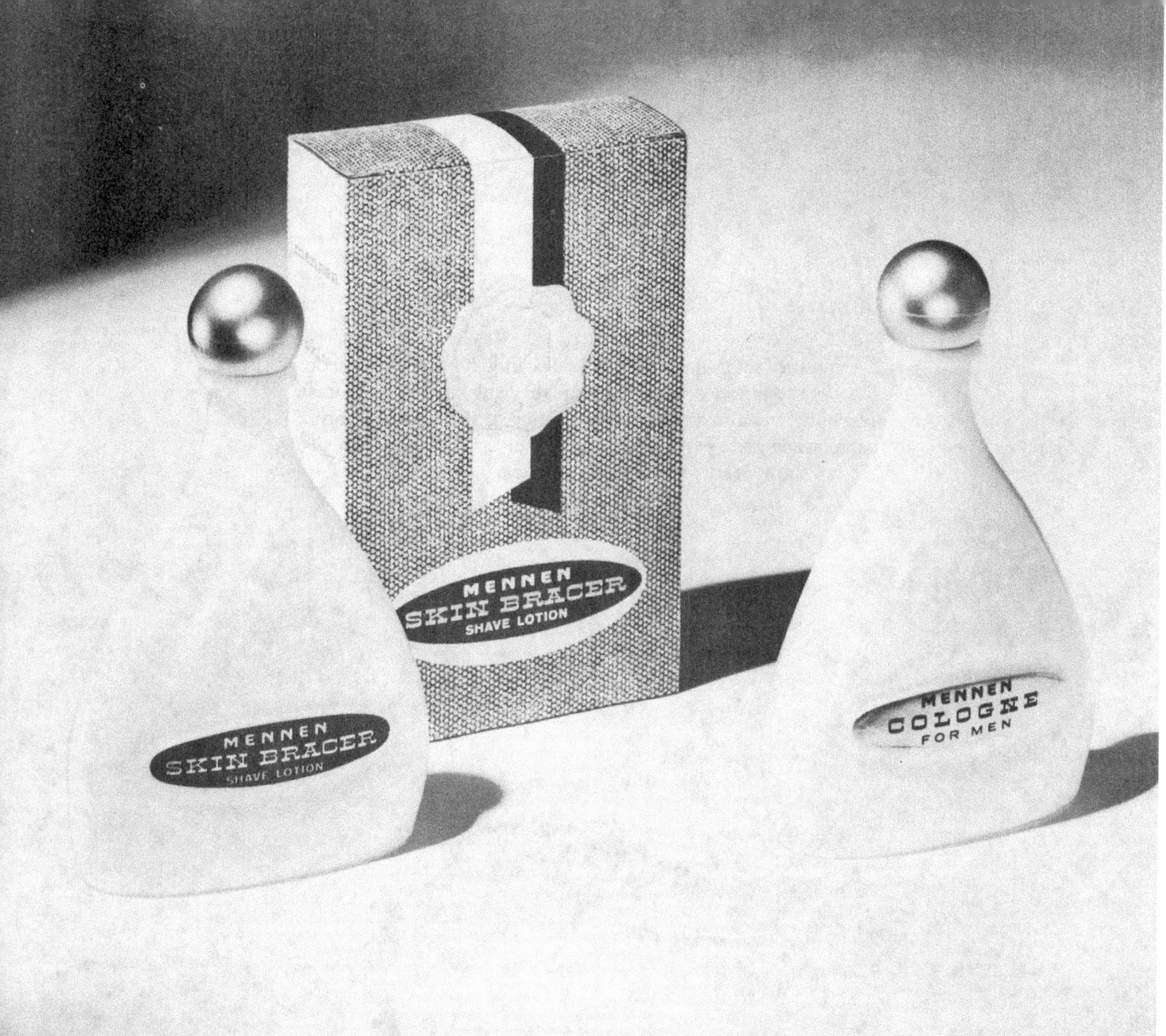

Bernard Bresky, designer

"This new packaging for men's toiletries will give the Mennen Company representation in higher priced products designed to appeal to the gift-buying consumer. This type of luxury line will appeal, not only to men, but to the woman gift buyer, who represents an important factor in this market.

"The Mennen Company did not want ultra-sophisticated, cosmetic-looking packaging but, rather, a deluxe, masculine effect, reflecting good taste. A look of luxury is enhanced by the gold crest displayed against a black-and-white ribbon on the outer box. Quick brand identification is achieved by the Mennen name on the labels of both decanter and box and by a raised 'M' on the bottle. The tweed-like background on the package identifies the product as masculine, yet has eye-catching appeal for the woman shopper."

Designs and comments on these pages by FRANCIS BLOD DESIGN ASSOCIATES, INC.

"A modified semi-uncial form was designed for the Ambassador logotype to reflect the European quality and that of aged brew. Legibility was also a major consideration in this name. A grayed ochre, wood-grain pattern was selected for the background to give the can the appearance of an oak beer keg."

▼

Francis E. Blod, art director
Fred Feucht, designer

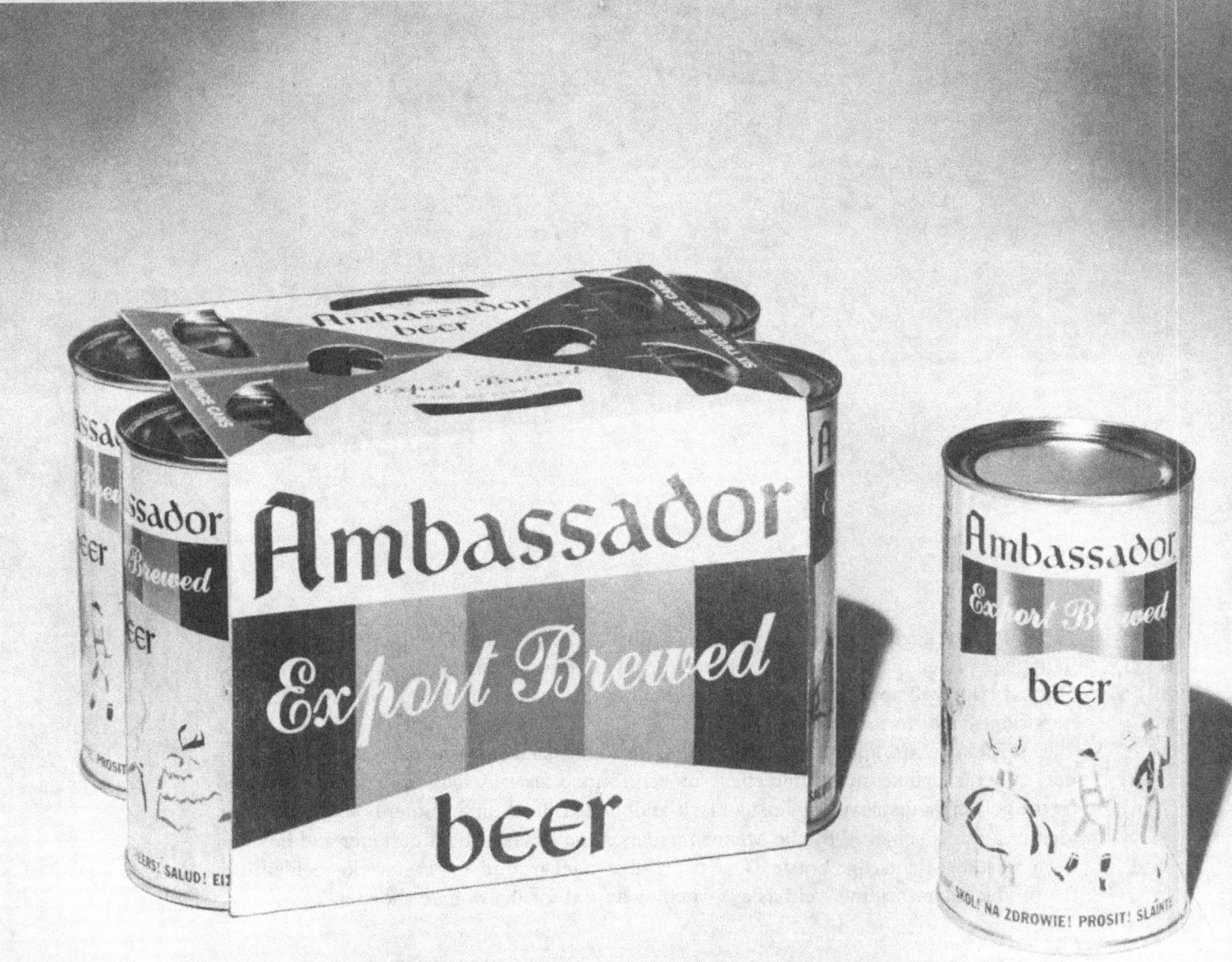

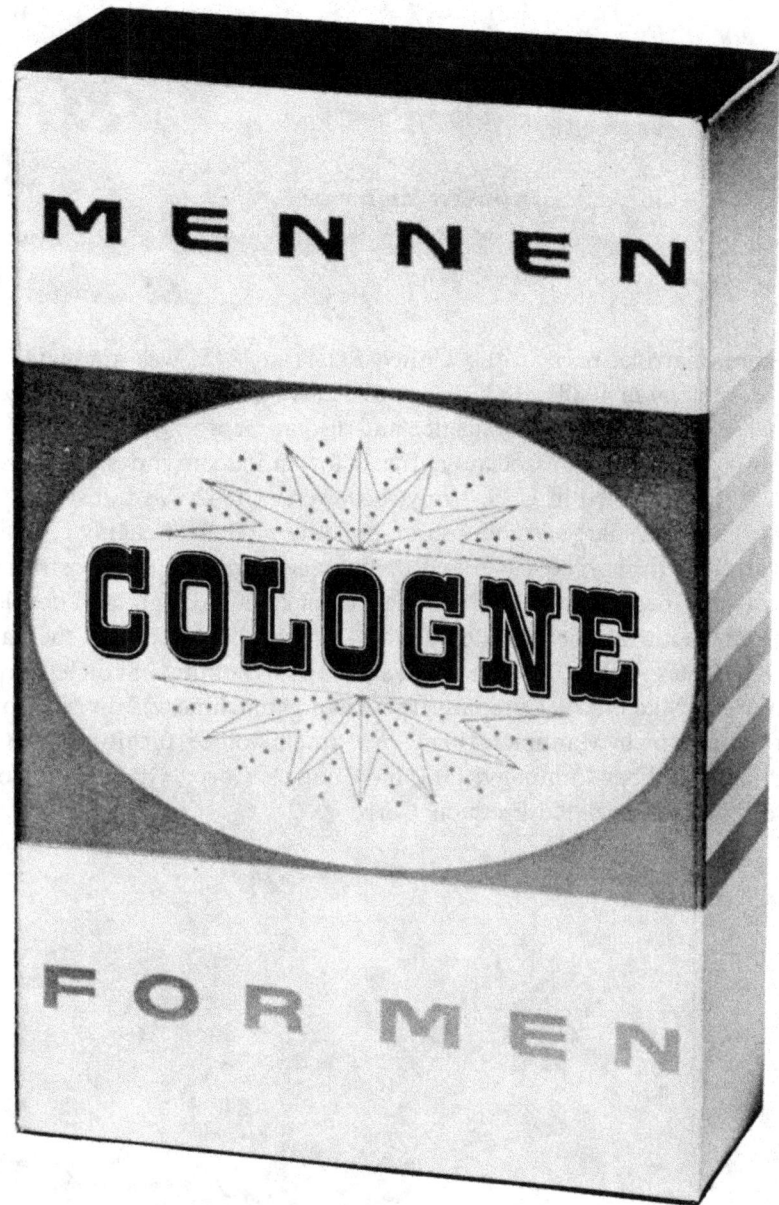

Bernard Bresky, designer

"A redesigned Old Towne form for the word 'Cologne' was selected for its masculine quality and also because it reflects the corporate personality of the Mennen Company. An ornate letter style was designed because of the romantic quality of the product. Great care was taken to maintain the legibility of the name for maximum impact on the retail shelf. The Mennen logotype was relettered in an extended form to give it added quality and a more contemporary style. Gold was used, in addition to the traditional Mennen green, to give the product an upgraded appearance."

Designs and comments on these pages by FRANCIS BLOD DESIGN ASSOCIATES, INC.

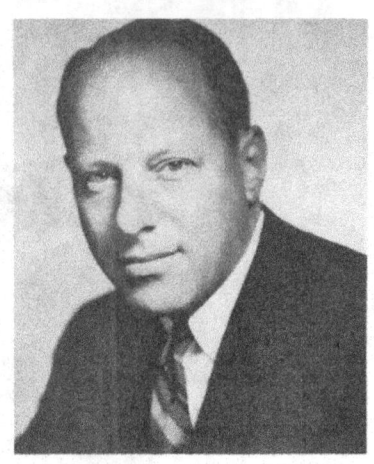

ROBERT ZEIDMAN
Robert Zeidman Associates

Robert Zeidman, married, born in the United States in 1915, was graduated from Carnegie Institute of Technology in 1938 with a degree in industrial design. Did postgraduate engineering study at Case School of Applied Science and also at George Washington University. From 1939 to 1941 was employed as associate designer for an industrial design engineering concern in Cleveland. In 1941 enlisted in U. S. Army; however, in 1942 was transferred to Navy where he set up and ran world's largest model shop, building models of enemy coastal areas for amphibious invasions. Discharged 1946, and commenced practice of industrial design in New York. His firm now specializes in product design, packaging design, and development of new products for manufacturing clients, who include 43 industrial concerns in the Eastern and Midwestern United States. Some of these are as follows: Hamilton Skotch Corp.; Chap Stick Company; Wright Machinery Company (packaging machinery), division of Sperry-Rand Corp.; Corry Jamestown Manufacturing Corp. (metal office furniture); Eisendrath Glove Company; Pioneer Rubber Company; Graphic Controls Corp.; Otto Bernz Company; Aetna Industrial Corp.; and Associated Products Corp.

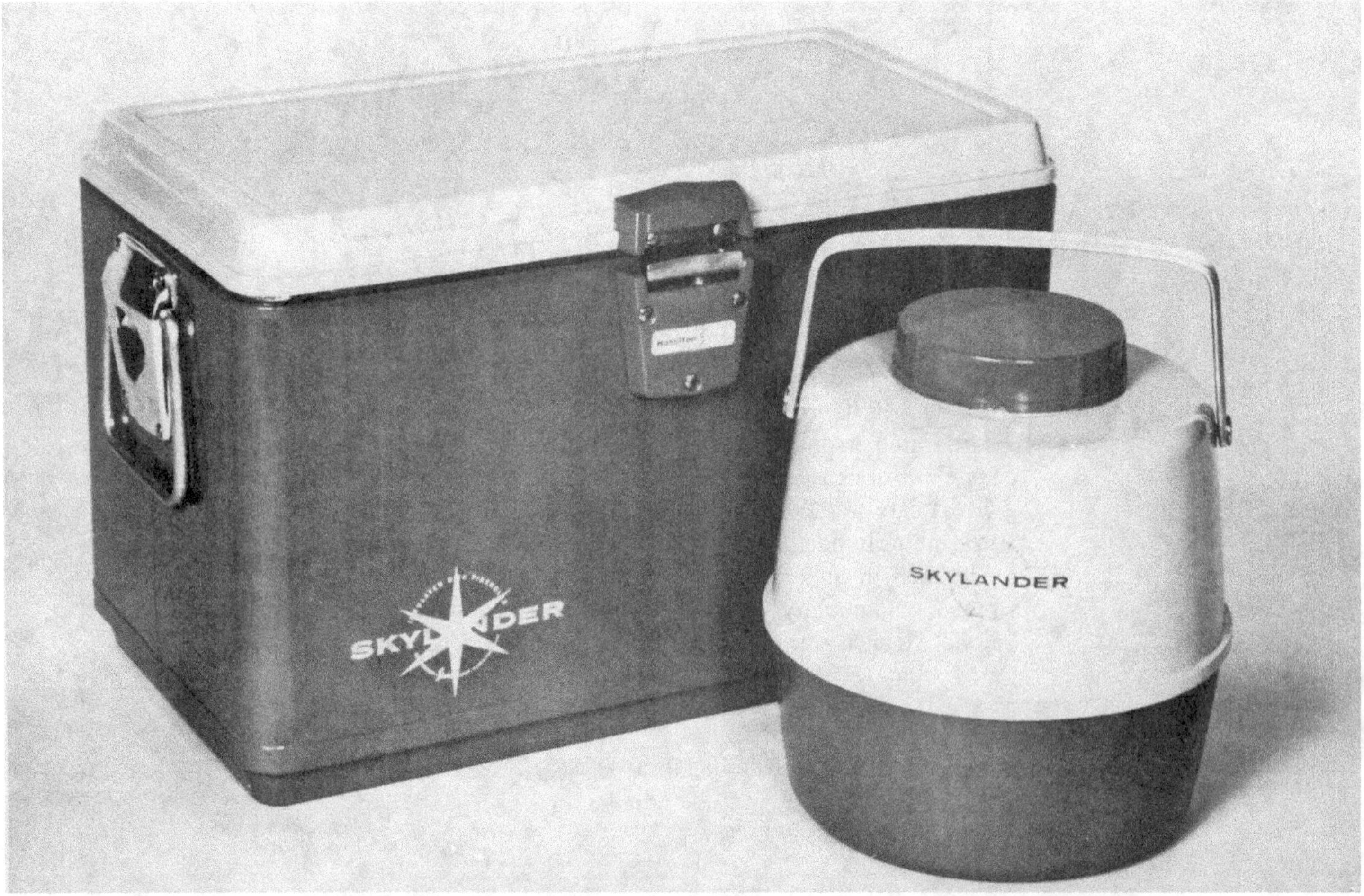

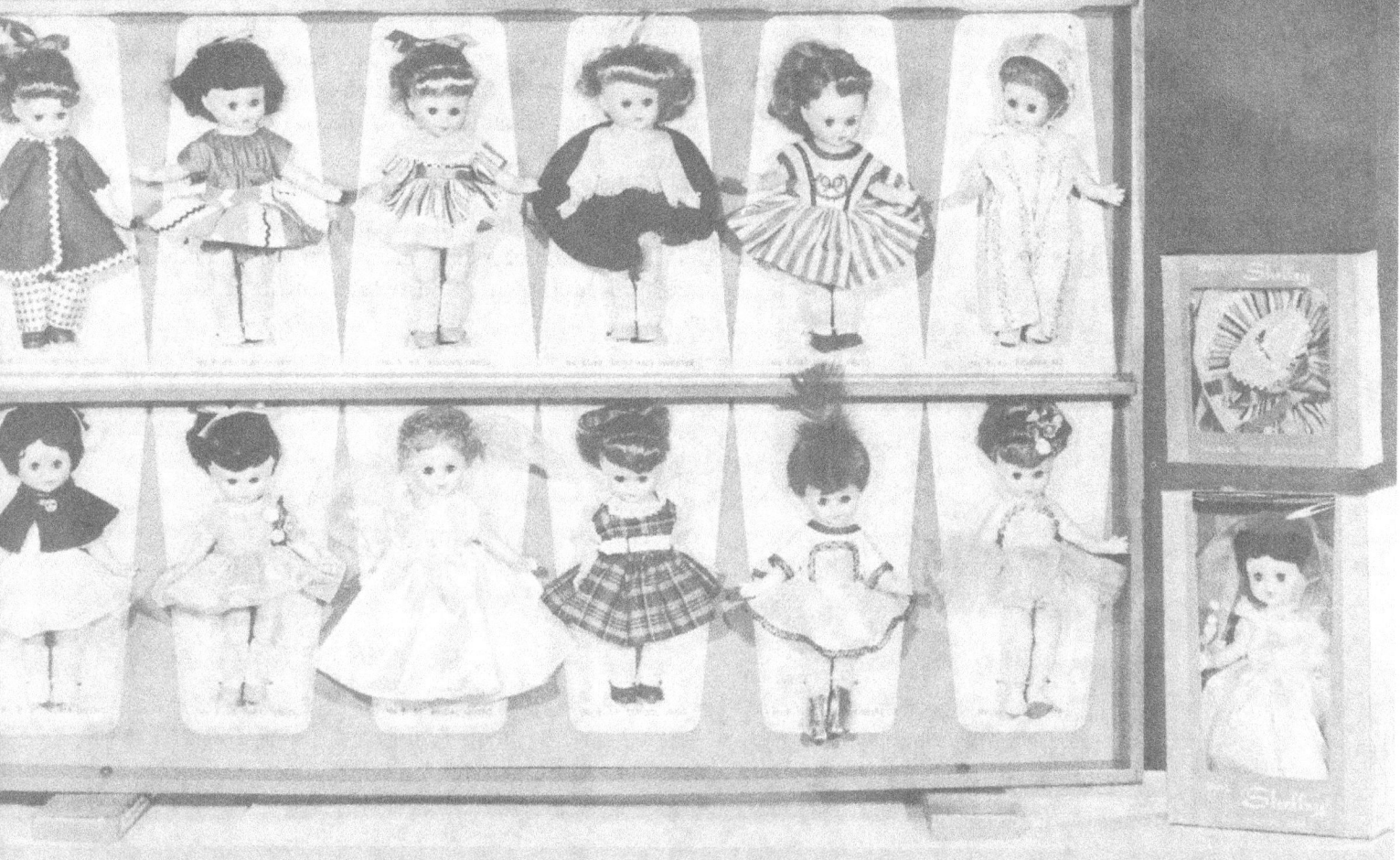

▲

"This pink-and-gold color scheme typifies the gaiety and playfulness necessary in children's doll packages. The logotype was designed for its distinctiveness and remembrance values."

◀ "Red, white, and blue decals stand out on reverse shades of blue on jug and cooler. The relatively sophisticated lettering was chosen to convey the concept of the modern outdoor family on the move."

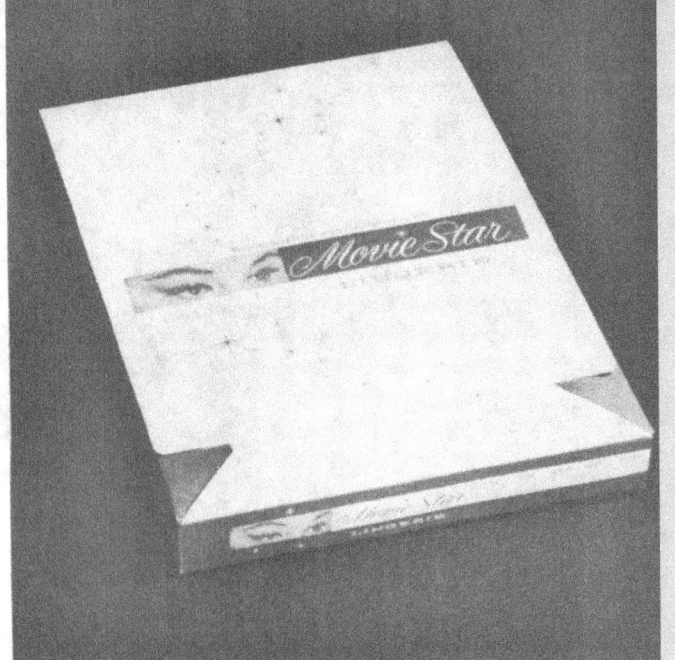

"This was a one-color package—either in black, midnight blue, or a 'purplish' cerise. The lettering and colors were chosen for their high-fashion quality in order to further glamorize a low-priced item."

"Here, a dramatic effect, plus an office-like appearance, was required to successfully promote this line of office-secretarial equipment. Red, white, and blue are the colors."

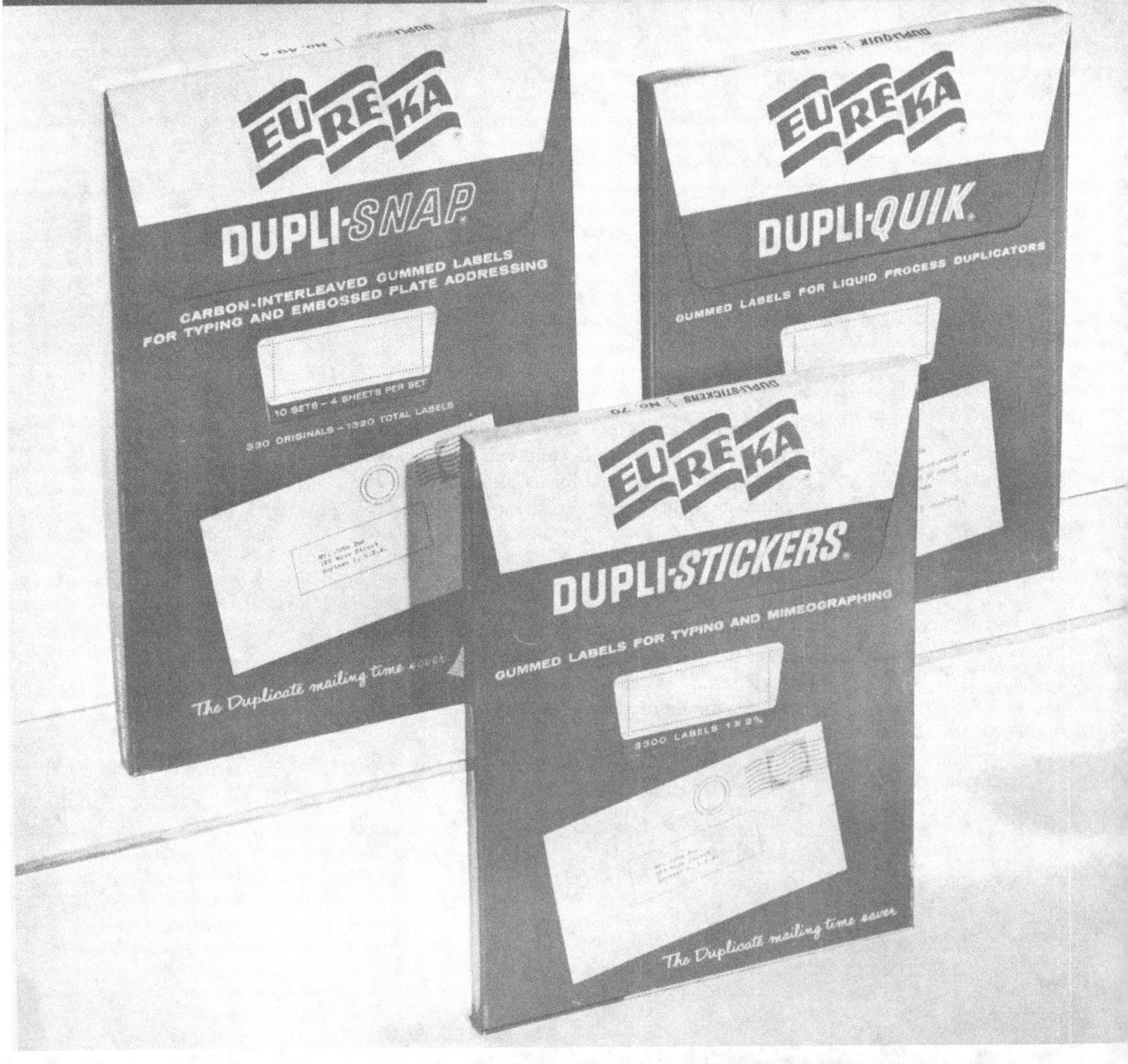

Designs and comments on these pages by ROBERT ZEIDMAN ASSOCIATES

"Colors: Aquamarine and ochre, in combination, offer a clean, antiseptic appearance. 'Sea Breeze' is in designed letters so that maximum legibility is attained along with a 'friendly personal look'."

▼

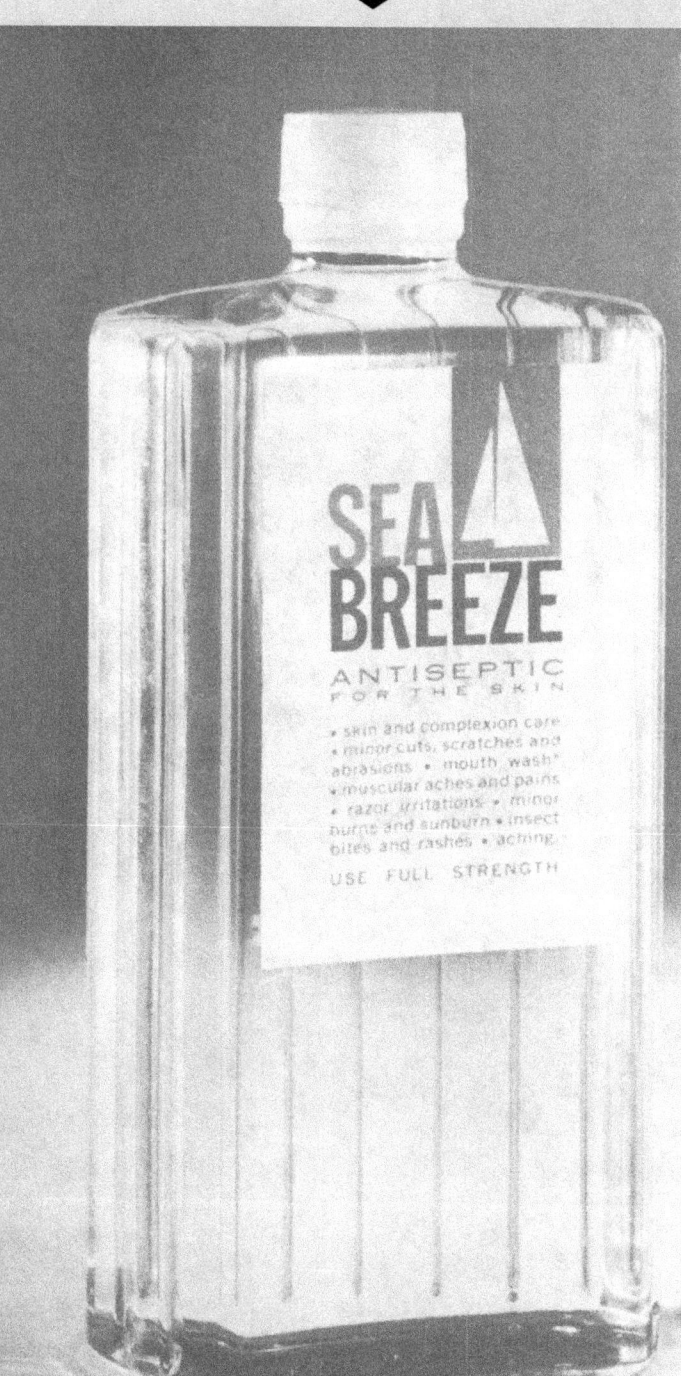

Designs and comments on these pages by ROBERT ZEIDMAN ASSOCIATES

"These new decanters and apothecary jars for Cresca candies doubled the price of the product but kept the sales at the same level. This highly successful example of what better packaging can do illustrates both the early 'Americana' traditional, plus the modern, home-decor decanter. Black, gold, and a range of high-fashion pastel shades are employed here."

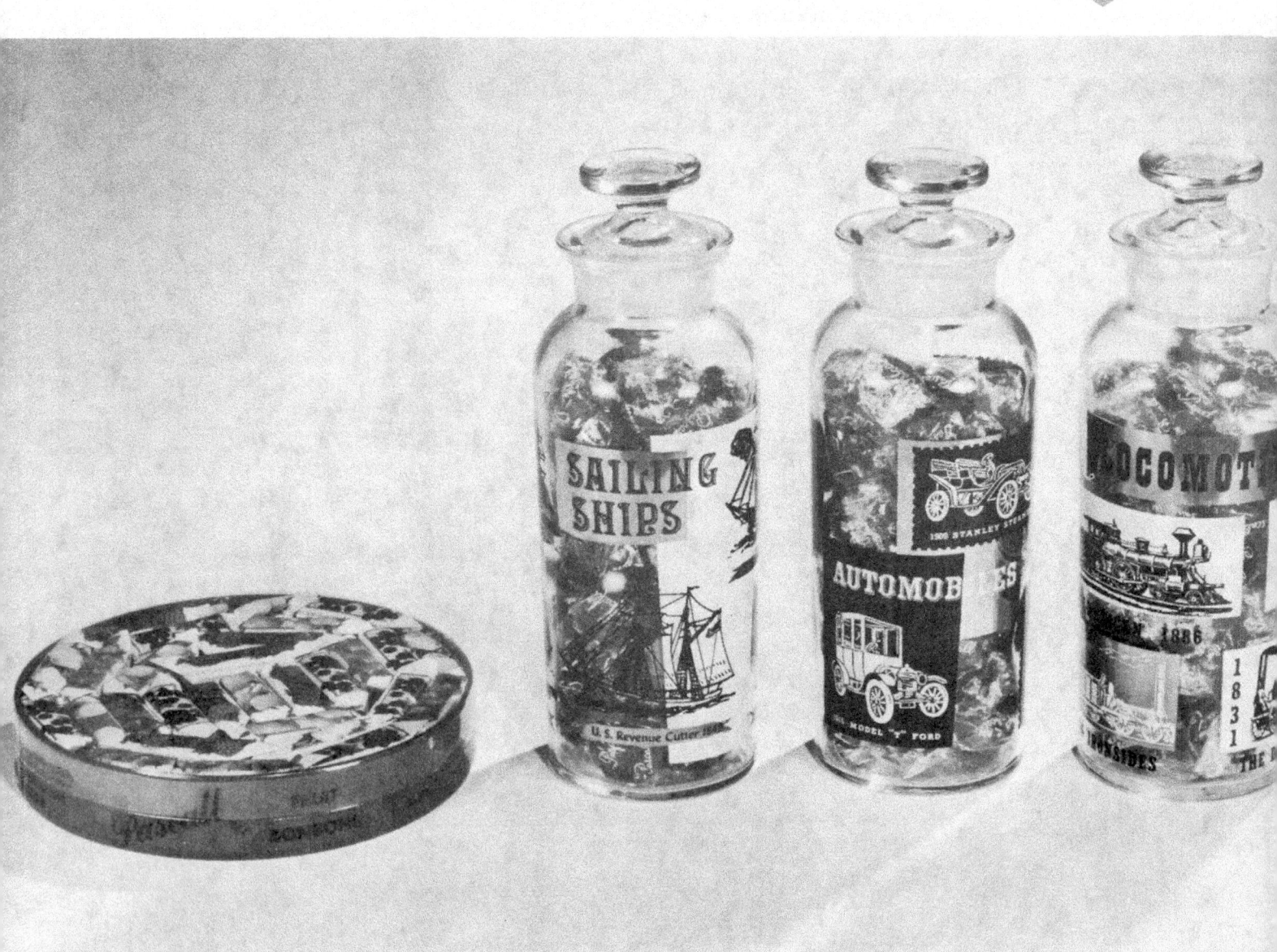

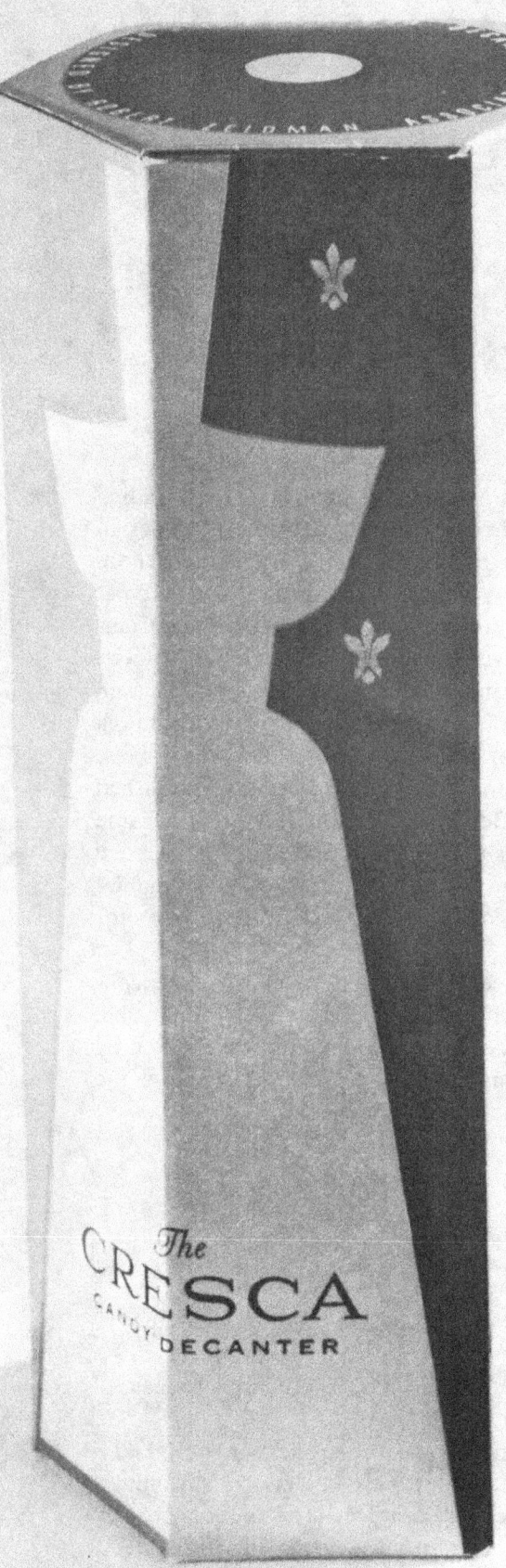
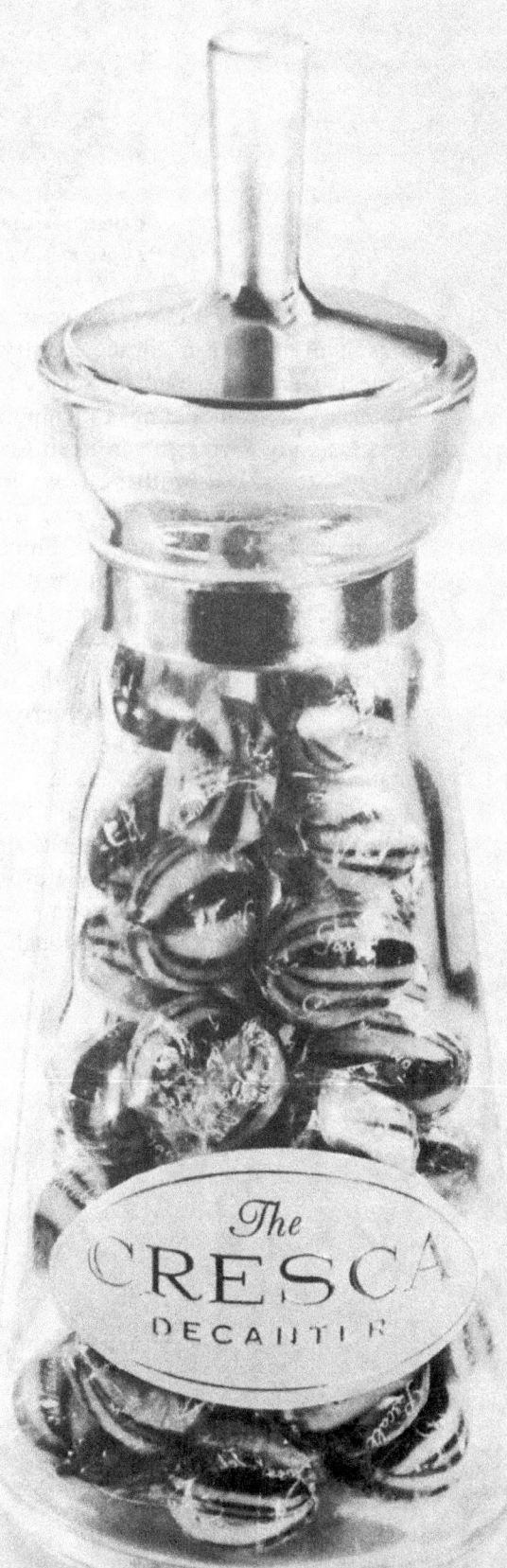

152

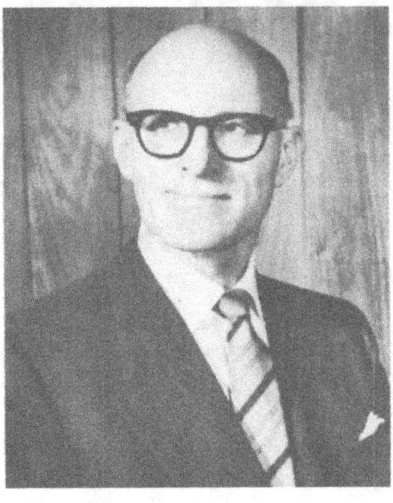
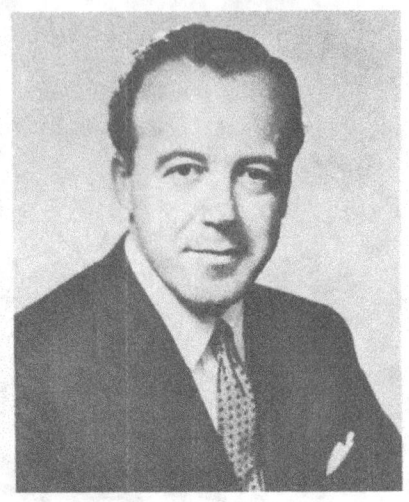

GORDON LIPPINCOTT   **WALTER MARGULIES**
Lippincott & Margulies, Inc.

Started in 1946, and incorporated in 1947, Lippincott & Margulies is now among the leading consultant design firms in the country. In the first decade of its operations, some 1,000 design projects were completed for such clients as Campbell's Soups, General Electric, the Hilton Hotels, American Seating, Cincinnati Milling, General Precision Laboratories, Royal Typewriter, Fanny Farmer, Penn Fruit Co., Glenn Martin Aircraft, W. T. Grant, American Community Stores, Piel Brothers, Lever Brothers, Parke-Davis, Emerson Drug, and many others.

The two managing partners, Gordon Lippincott and Walter Margulies are both well known in the design world. Mr. Lippincott, a graduate of Swarthmore College and Columbia University, formerly taught at Pratt Institute and was for many years associated with the late Donald Dohner, pioneer industrial designer. He is author of "Design for Business," published in 1947. Mr. Margulies is a graduate of the Ecole de Beaux Arts in Paris. He first became known through his designs for the International Exposition in Paris, and later for the New York World's Fair. He was formerly associated with the Statler hotel chain as a leading designer, during which time he pioneered in creating the combined living-sleeping hotel rooms first employed in the Hotel Statler, Washington.

From its inception, Lippincott & Margulies has pioneered the introduction of broader concepts to the field of industrial design. This "composite approach" has been responsible in large measure for the steady growth of the firm. At L & M, no design job is undertaken by one man. Instead, a team—composed of L & M designers and representatives from the client's management—works through the problem from beginning to end.

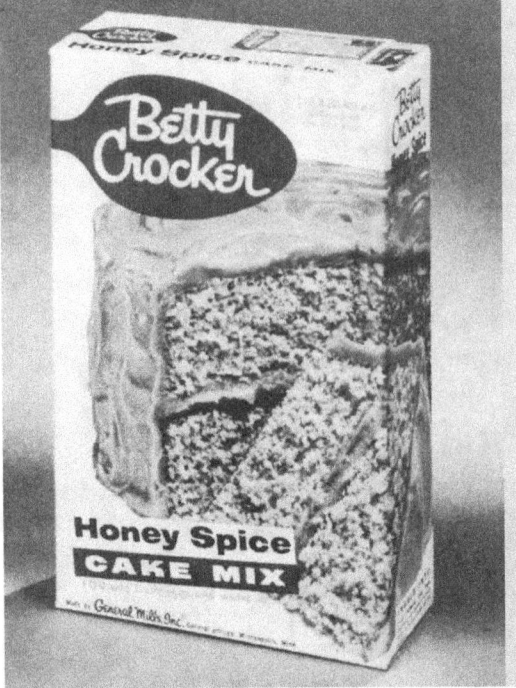

"One of the hottest competitive lines in the supermarket today is the cake mix. Manufacturers are constantly making changes in their cake-mix packages to meet the competition.

"The Betty Crocker cake-mix package, designed by Lippincott & Margulies, pushed General Mills into first place saleswise in cake mixes. The spoon symbol makes an effective 'flag' in mass display and provides a unique brand image. The picture of the cake is more mouth watering than ever."

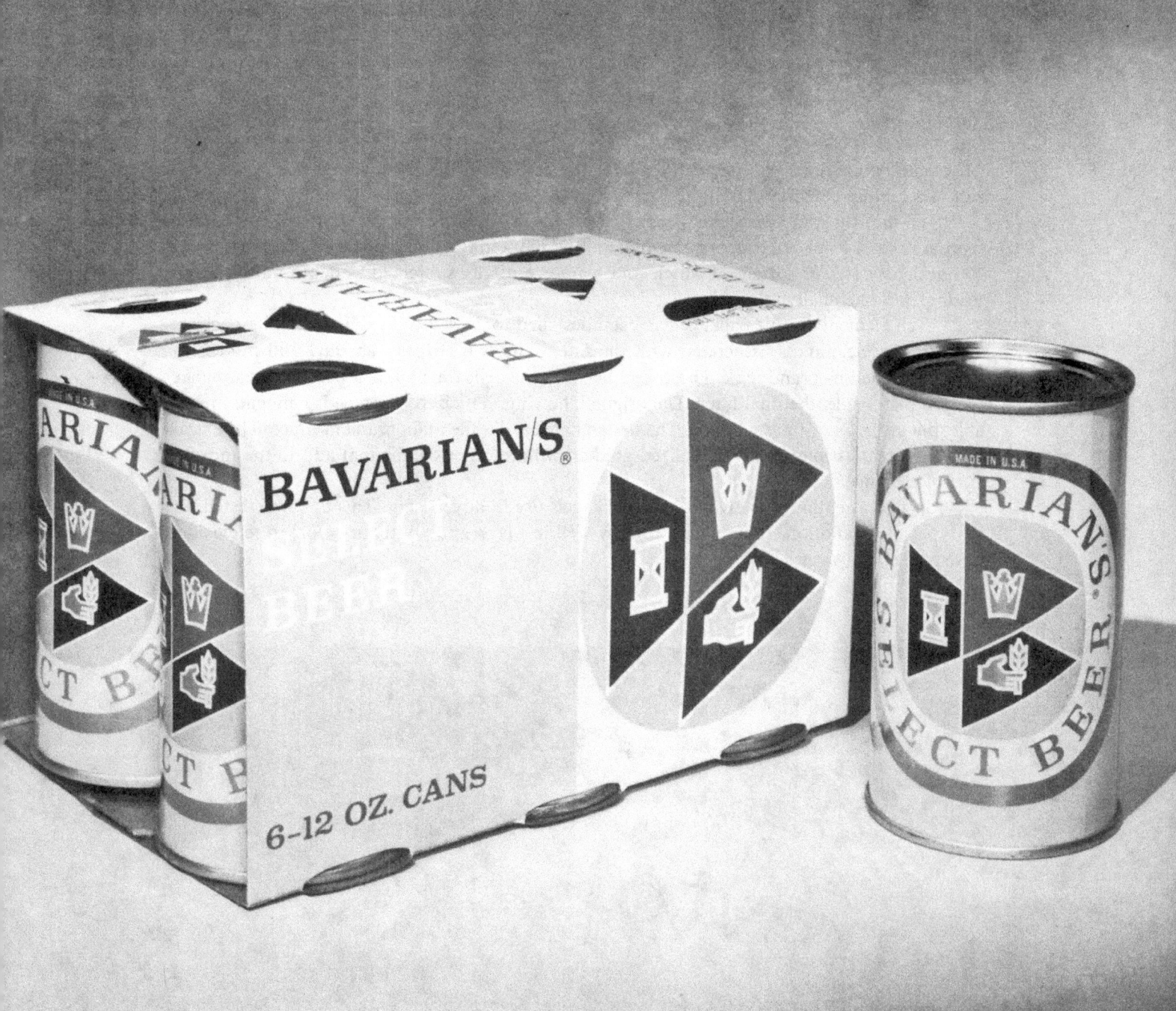

"Lippincott & Margulies not only redesigned the package for Bavarian Brewery, but the company's graphics were given a going-over to establish a new corporate identity, centered around the L & M-created trademark.

"Research disclosed that Bavarian's old label and trademark gave the impression of an old-fashioned beer. The new design is fresh in appearance, using symbols to make the point that Bavarian is brewed in a modern way by skilled German brewmasters. The colorful 'three flags' brandmark in red (top), blue (left), and green (below) catches the eye with its sharp juxtaposition of powerful triangular forms. Stylized symbols within the triangles get across the message of 'tradition' (crown), 'time' (hourglass) and 'skill' (hand holding stalk of barley). Letter forms in gold plus gold oval encircling the new brandmark convey strong images of quality. The light background serves to focus attention on the symbols. A versatile brandmark, it is equally adaptable to the company's cans, bottle labels, carry-packs, shipping cartons, or trucks."

"The bold twin-striped package that contains the new Dual Filter Tareyton cigarette is the result of a unique design-research program.

"Ten months' time was taken, four of which were spent in nondesign work, to produce this package. A team of designers, researchers, and marketing experts pooled their efforts. Over 100 designs were submitted, of which four were eventually subjected to depth motivational testing, and one finally selected.

"Each element on this package has been designed to do a specific job. The white package suggests the cleanliness associated with the filter. The two stripes—abstract and modern—make a compelling brandmark. These together with the delicate, double tobacco leaf announce the product inside, the dual filter. The original, flowing, italicized logotype is eminently readable, but at the same time subdued. The design here carries the main brand message. The extra-thin, gold tear-strip and the formalized gold crown are other details that add to the impression of elegance.

"Special attention was given to the package's use in advertising. This one was tested for all types of promotion. It shows up equally well in black and white, or color; in television, newspapers, magazines, and on posters."

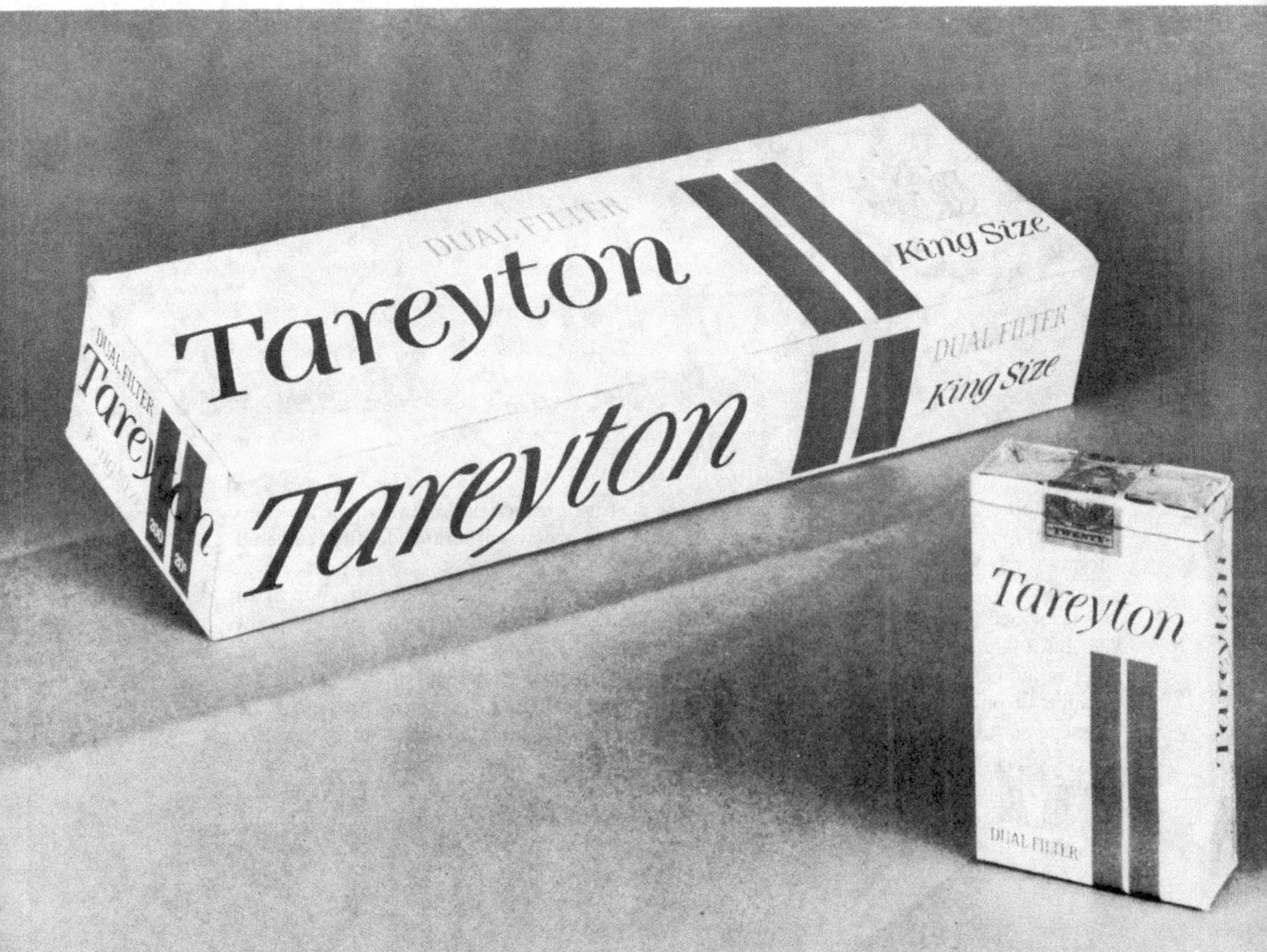

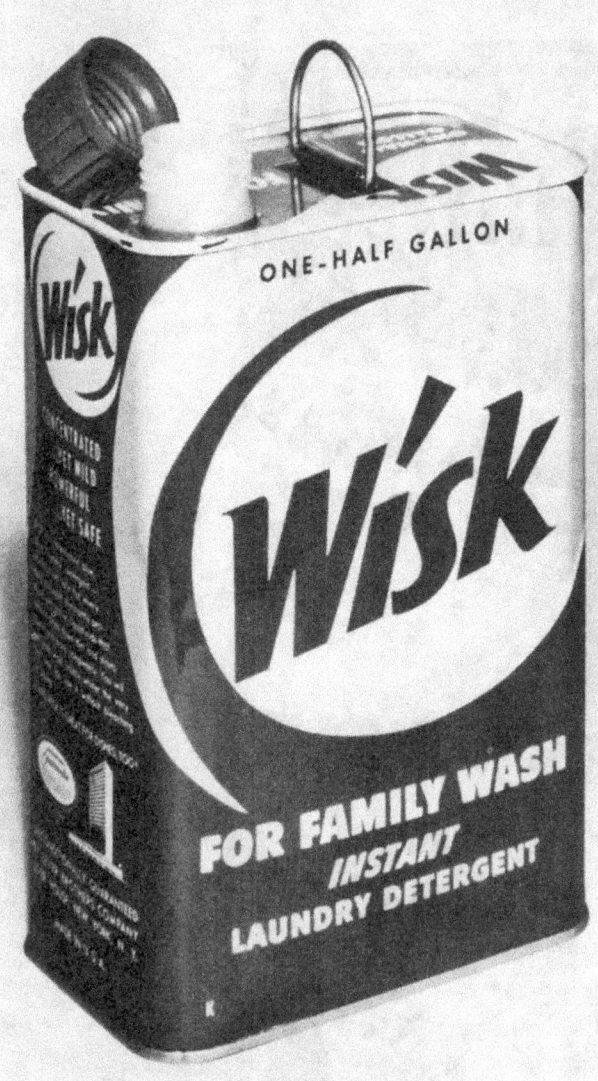
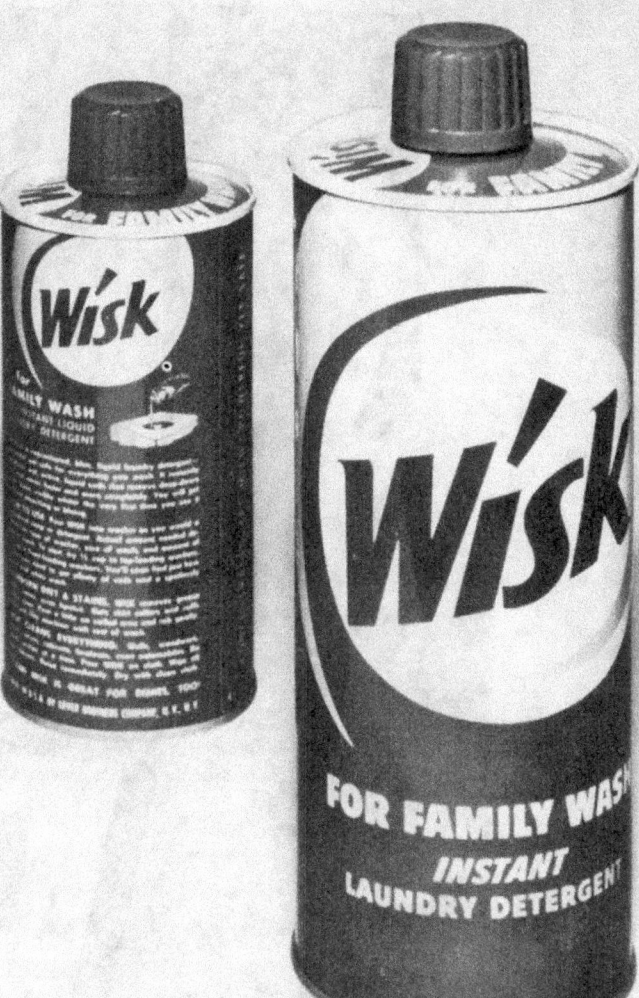

"Research which preceded the 'Wisk' design showed that, while women prefer detergents for heavy-duty housework, they seek, at the same time, some of the familiar 'safe' and 'soft' feeling of mild soap. The new package would have to reflect this feeling. Still another task would have to be performed by the package—it would have to establish a clear-cut differential for the new product, for research indicated strongly that homemakers consider all detergents 'pretty much the same.'

"Designers Lippincott and Margulies worked also on the selection of a name for the product—one that would compete successfully with those on the market, and, simultaneously, one whose letter configurations would make it suitable for unique letter forms, appropriate for both the product and container. The decision was not to depart from the tradition of terse names in the detergent market. Thus, 'Wisk' was tested, along with a dozen others, and won as a concise name suggesting fast action and fulfilling the other requirements.

"After development of a suitable container with an efficient pour spout, graphic design was the next step. The result: gay and bold colors—a bright red background and cap to attract attention in busy supermarkets, and a yellow and white swirl pattern to suggest washing-machine spin action. Against this, a sturdy-looking, highly readable, and distinctly lettered 'Wisk' logotype appears in deep blue. All sell copy was kept off the front panel to achieve a clean and uncluttered package face."

Designs and comments on these pages by LIPPINCOTT & MARGULIES, INC.

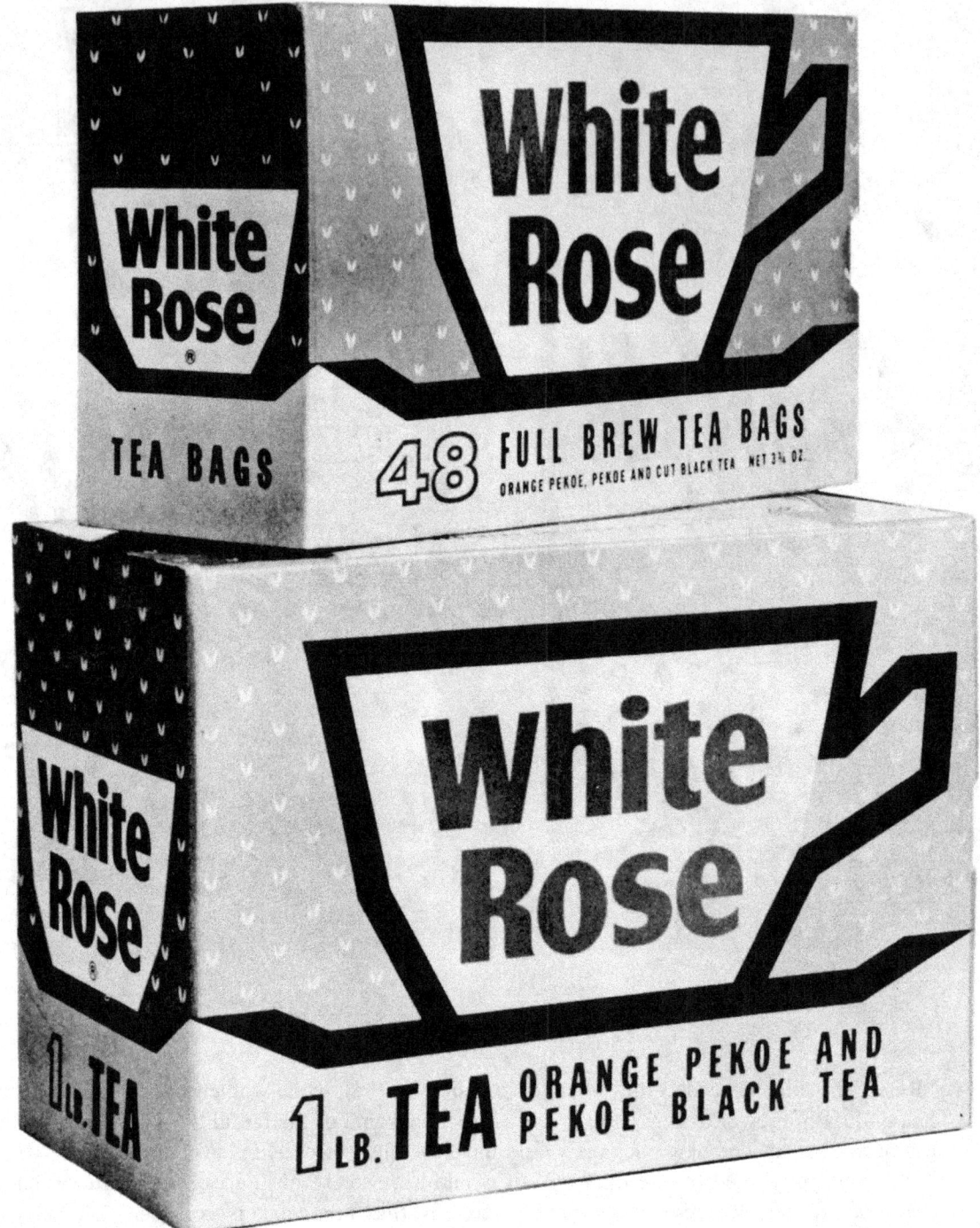

"The L & M design for White Rose features the brandmark concept. The bold, tea-cup motif is designed to 'move' off the package and on to printed ads or television screens. It has the masculine characteristics which research indicates are necessary for the merchandising of tea. However, taken as a whole, the new design, which also features a delicate, tea-leaf background pattern, has a strong appeal to women, as its colors are smart and fashionable and its design clean and pleasing.

"Market testing has proven that the White Rose tea package is quickly identified on the shelves and gives White Rose a strong visual impact in today's self-service markets. Retention of the White Rose logo, though streamlined and simplified, maintains the valuable 25-year-old equity established by this famous brand name."

Designs and comments on these pages by LIPPINCOTT & MARGULIES, INC.

"The smart, simple design for the Mayfair cigarette package features two equal areas, white and a soft, tobacco brown, chosen to reflect a high degree of good tobacco taste. They are vertically divided up the center of the package. The word 'Mayfair' appears along the white half; the descriptive words 'filter tip' and 'king size' are printed inconspicuously in yellow ochre on the brown panel. Also on this panel is a stylized lantern design, suggestive of the Mayfair connotation. Thus, each element—color, design, and graphics—makes its individual contribution to the total, integrated brand statement that is the Mayfair package."

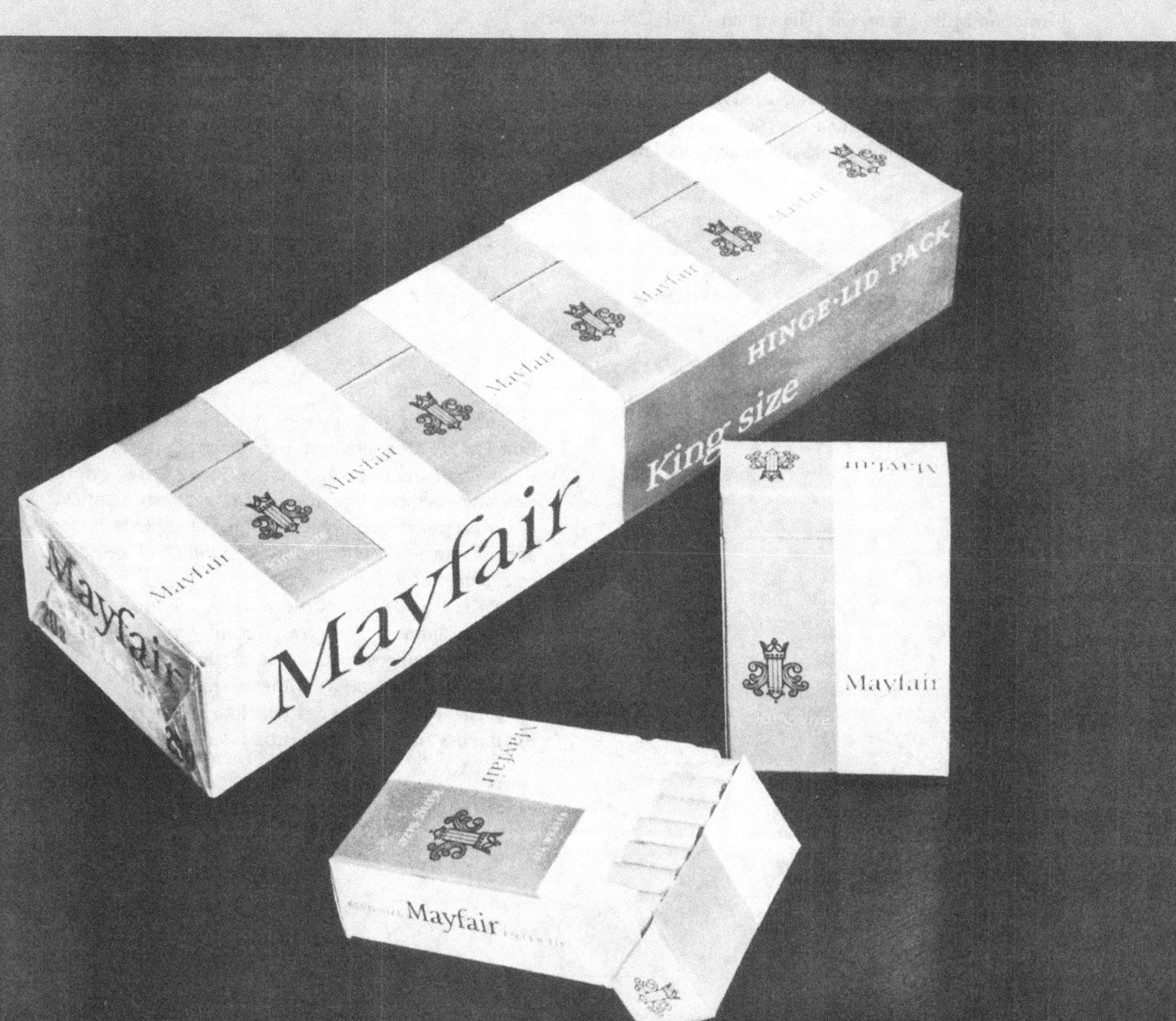

158

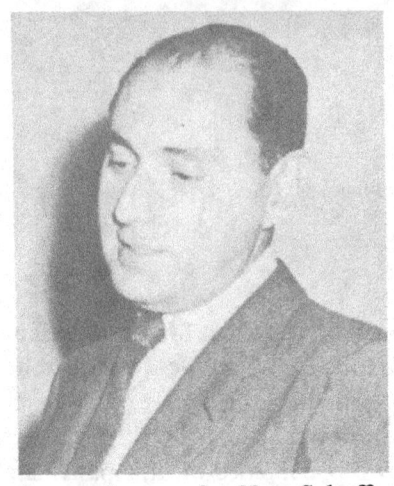

JEROME GOULD
Gould and Associates, Inc.

Born in Chicago. Studied art in Chicago and Los Angeles. Co-art director for Hart Schaffner & Marx, Chicago. Three years in Army Air Force (designer in training films and visual aids). Established a free-lance practice in Los Angeles in 1946. Work has received many awards. Part-time instructor in design at Chouinard Art Institute in Los Angeles four years.

Art director and design consultant for such national accounts as Budweiser, Coca-Cola, Max Factor, Ford Motor Company, Cole of California, Hart Schaffner & Marx, Sahara Hotel of Las Vegas, Huntington Hartford Enterprises, Capitol Records, Chrysler Corporation, Carnation Milk, Union Oil, The Gruen Watch Company, etc.

Currently in assignment with: Anheuser-Busch, Paul Masson Vineyards, Reddi-Wip, Standard Oil of Indiana, Bireley's, Pacific Finance, Great Lakes Carbon Corporation, Cole of California, Ambassador Hotel, Alfred A. Knopf, Doubleday & Co., Hunt Foods, Louis Milani Foods, Convair, Grumman Aircraft, Aerojet-General, Toni Products, Fluor Corporation, Security First National Bank, Manufacturers Trust Company, Citizens National Bank.

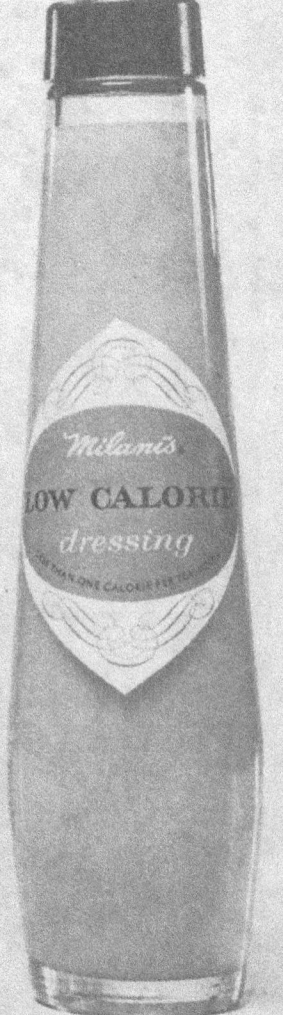

"Client desired a totally new design idea for Milani's Low Calorie Dressing bottle. In analyzing the problem, I arrived at the following conclusions: A low-calorie dressing need not be packaged in a 'pharmaceutical' container and label. It is possible to inject appetite appeal into what is basically a product of necessity rather than of desire.

"The tall, slender bottle was designed to impart a feeling of slimness through an elegantly conceived form. It has been suggested that the bottle be promoted to serve a secondary use as a flower vase.

"The label no longer looks like an ℞ prescription but implies and holds out a promise of appetite appeal."

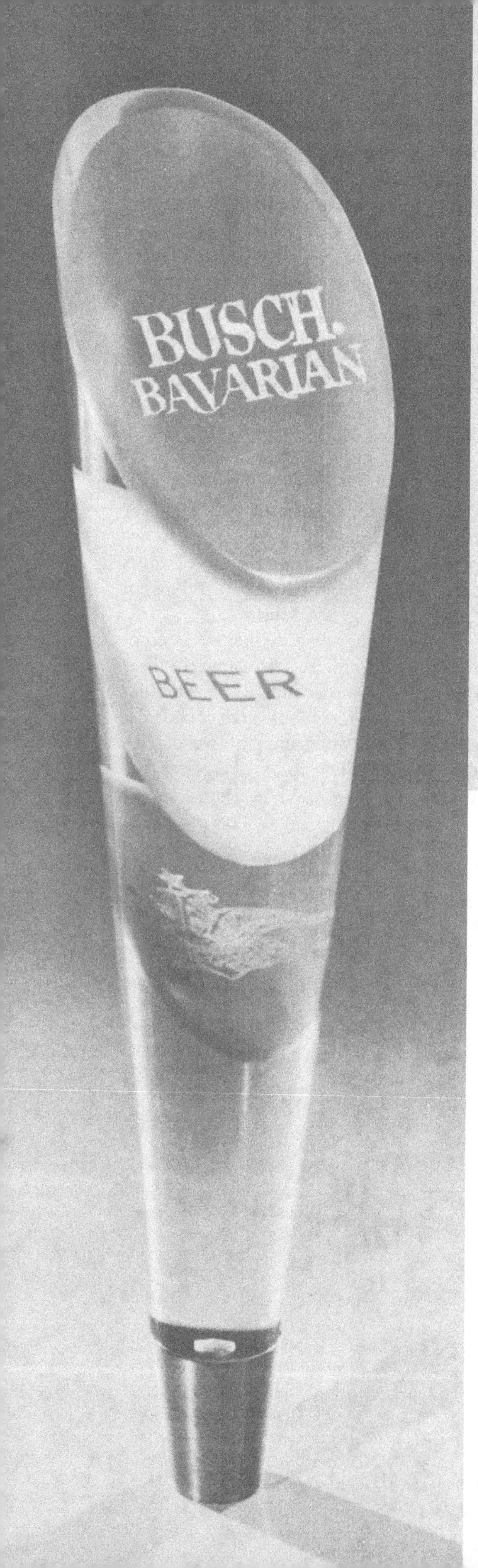

"The Busch Bavarian tap marker is an amusing design to possibly become a point of reference while sitting at a bar. The floating discs are provocative and conducive to discussion. The image, fresh and original, has the advantage of accenting the Busch name over competition. The material is clear plastic, with solid, colored plastic discs imbedded. The typography is gold stamped on the discs."

"For the Alkyd-Cote Paint label, the color swatches were taken out of the swatch-card and placed on the label. Printing cost of the label is slightly higher, but less costly than producing a separate color-swatch booklet.

"Additionally, the new idea lends itself to exciting promotional possibilities—'Pick your color from the swatch on the label'."

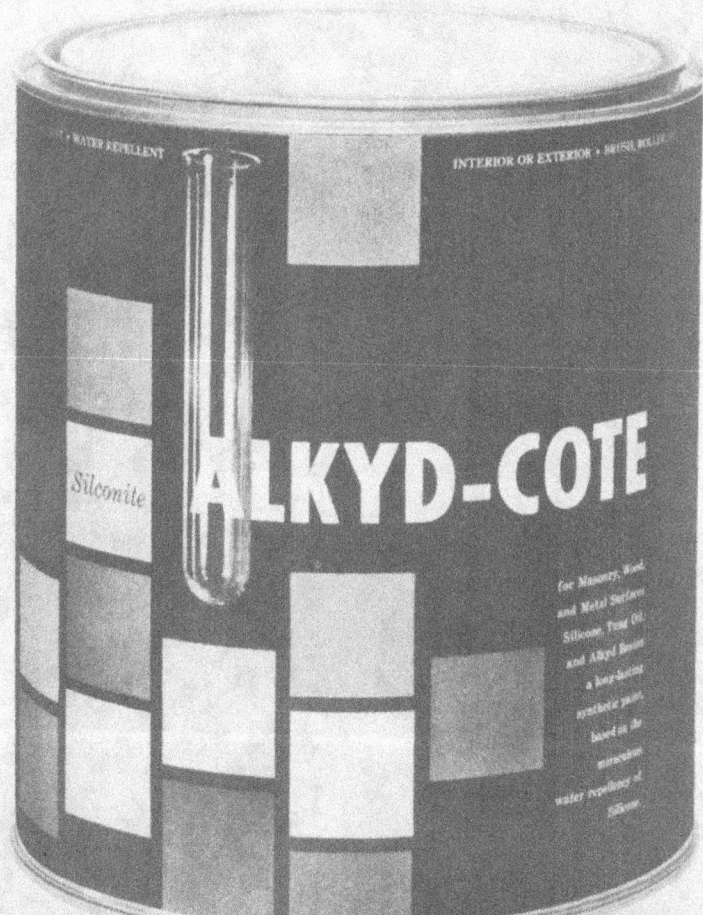

"The new Milani Low Calorie Dressing bottle is restated on the sides of the corrugated box. Whereas the corrugated box is principally used for shipping, the container is now designed to perform a secondary function, that of a display container. In multiples, it is visually demanding.

"The rubber plates used in printing on corrugated restricts one to simple, bold forms. Fine line typography is not possible. The box is red-orange and white."

"The solid appearance of the design for the Masson package was geared to appeal to men. Brandy and the out-of-doors seem synonymous; hence, symbols of sports, hunting, and fishing.

"The design is a deliberate attempt to express Mondrian's principles in three dimensions—a package. The modular possibilities of the box give the dealer an opportunity for imaginative display development. The colors are primary—yellow, red, blue, and black bars."

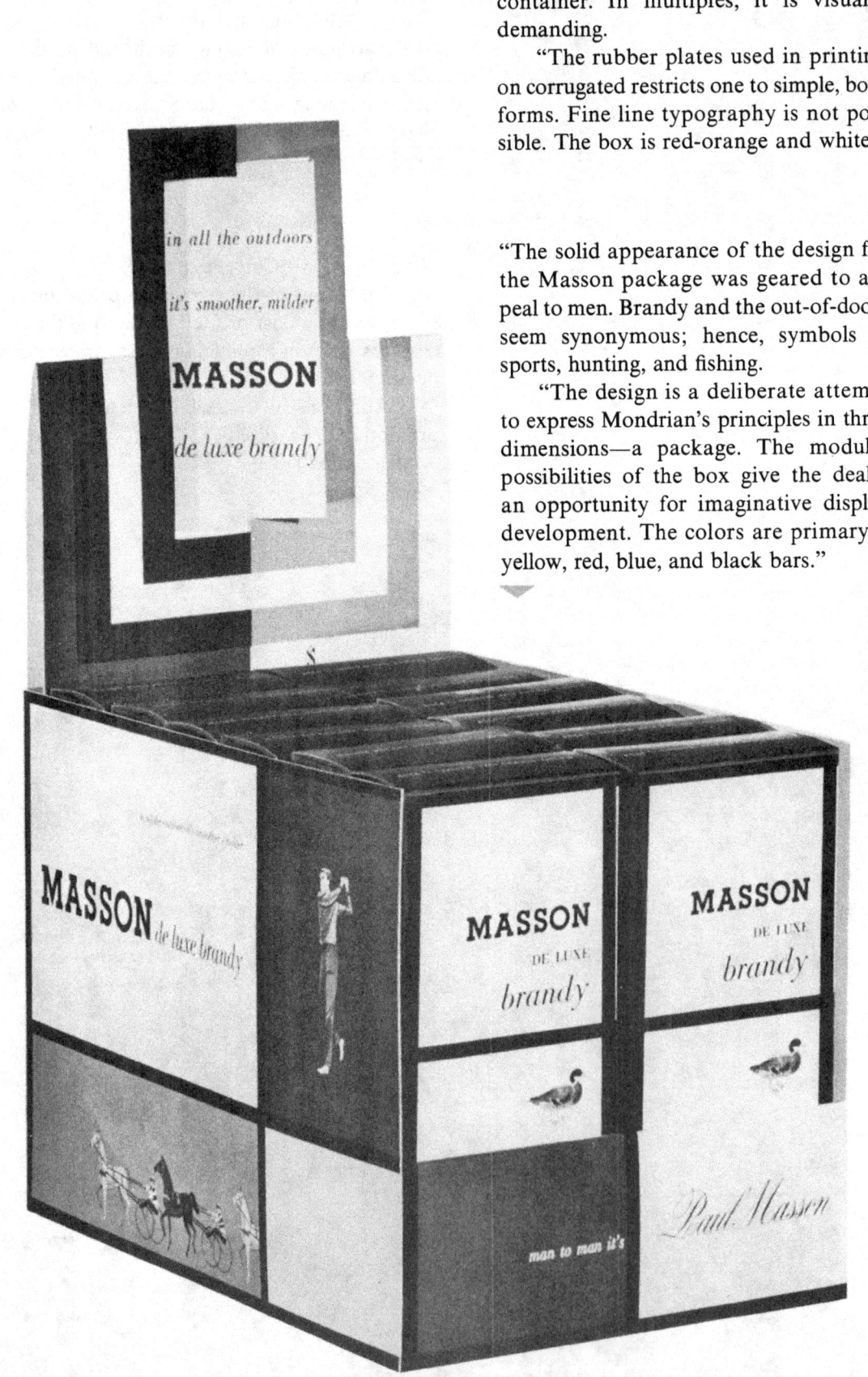

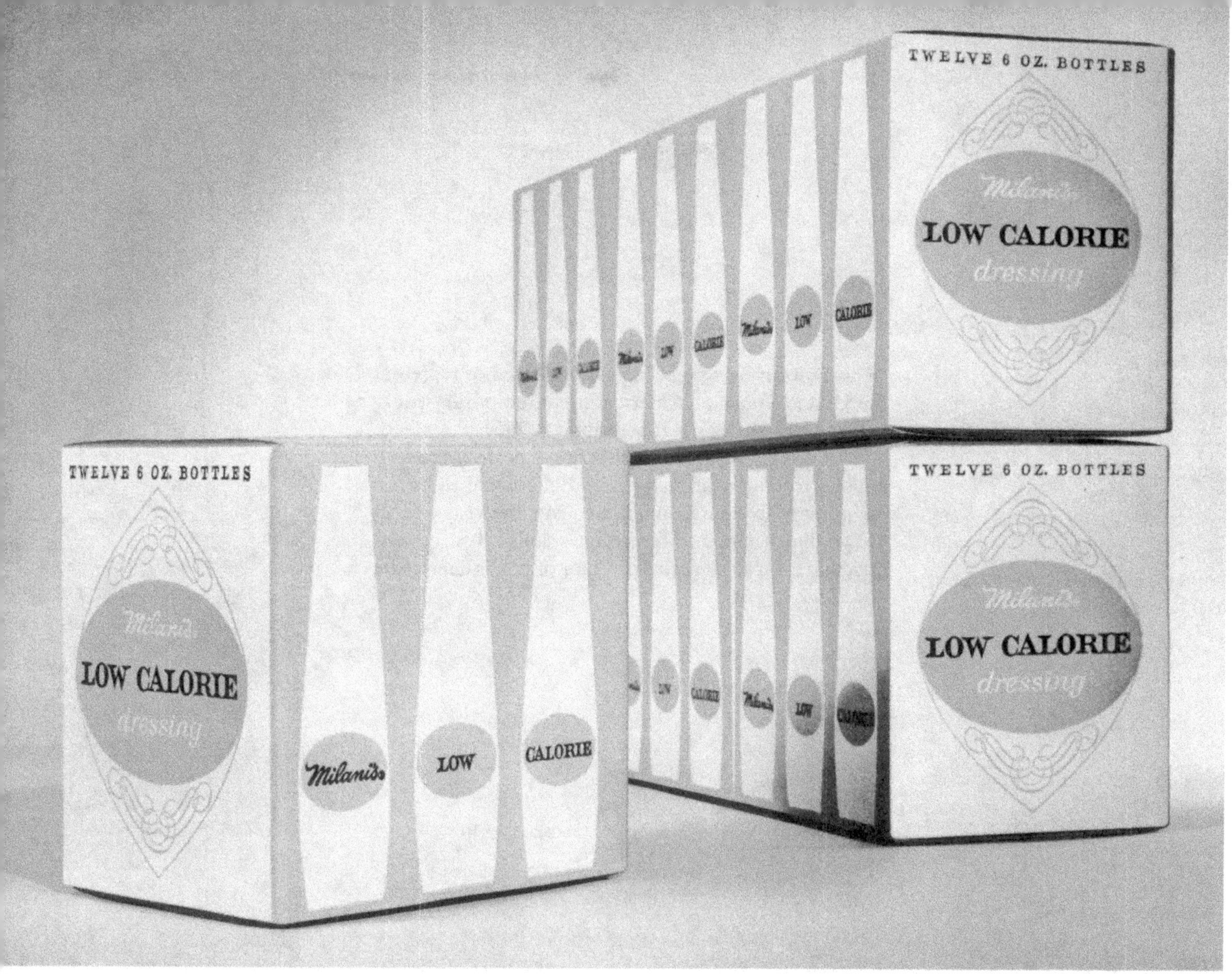

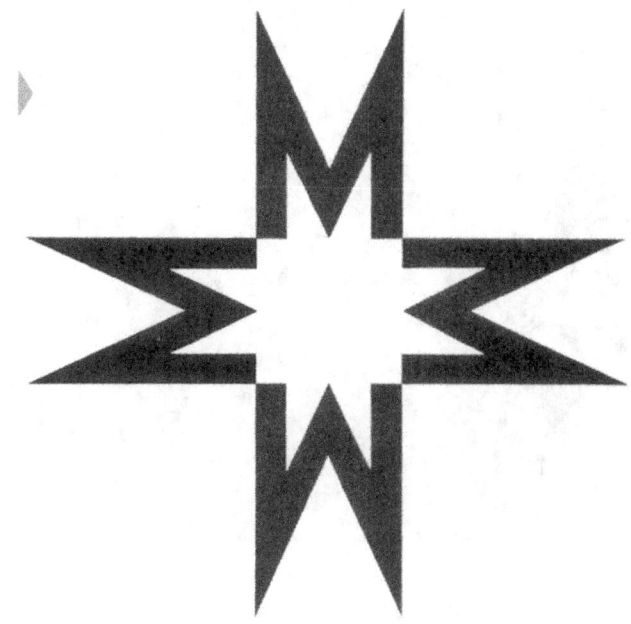

"Problem: To give Manufacturers Trust a strong symbol, with flexibility to reduce or enlarge it to any scale without losing legibility; one that visually imparts excellence, excitement, and authority within the framework of contemporary design. The design is a simple interplay of the firm's initial letter, 'M.' It has found its way onto the cover of the annual report, signs, ads, etc. It has become the basis upon which Manufacturers Trust is developing a new corporate image."

Designs and comments on these pages by GOULD AND ASSOCIATES, INC.

"This Dripcut Savoy package was selected to represent the United States of America in contemporary packaging during the Festival of Britain in 1951.

"A design attempt to deliberately destroy the feeling of a rectangle through linear dimensional elements. An attempt to create, simultaneously, the visual effect of two dimensions and three dimensions. Must be seen in actual form to be realized. Color of box is chartreuse and black."

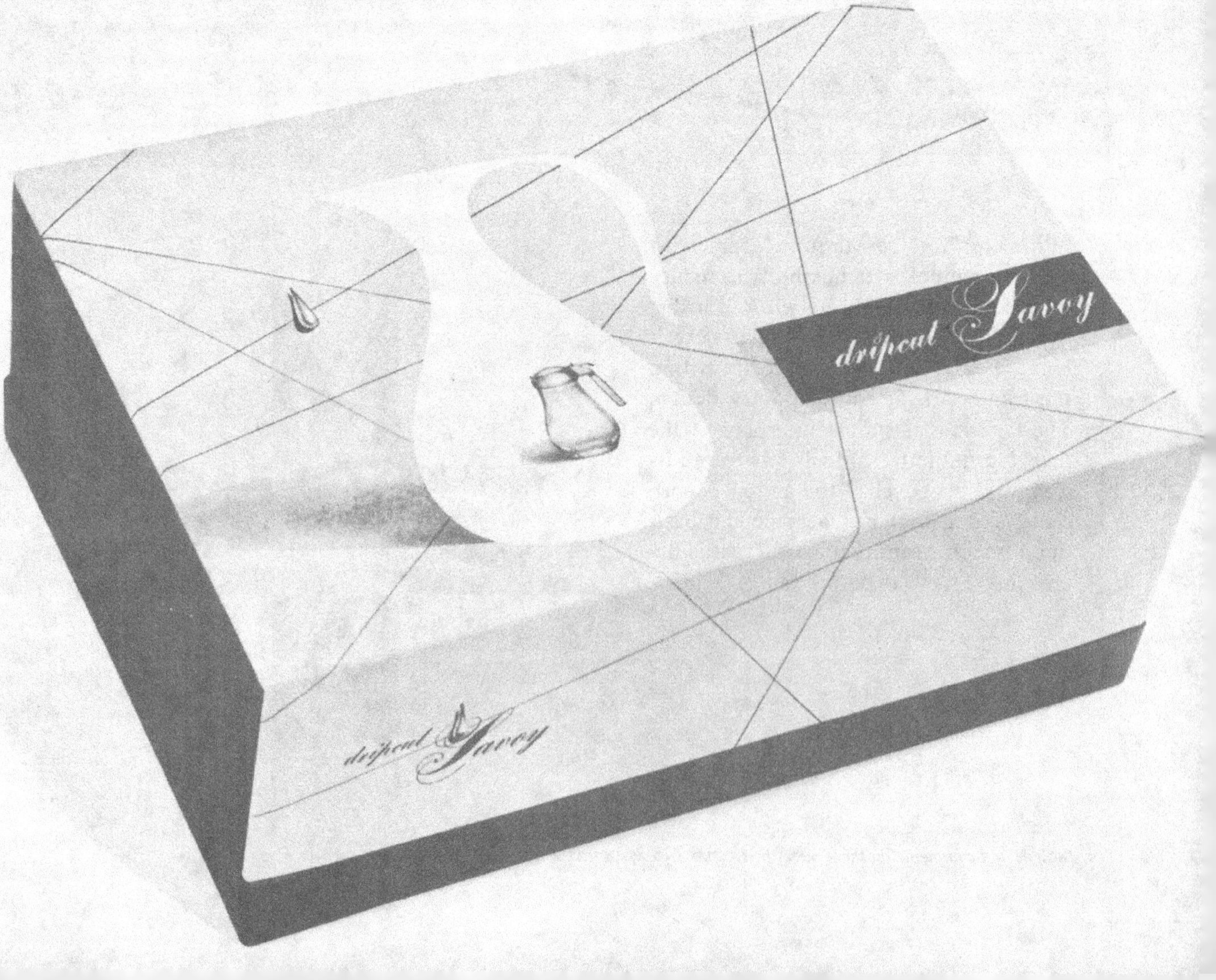

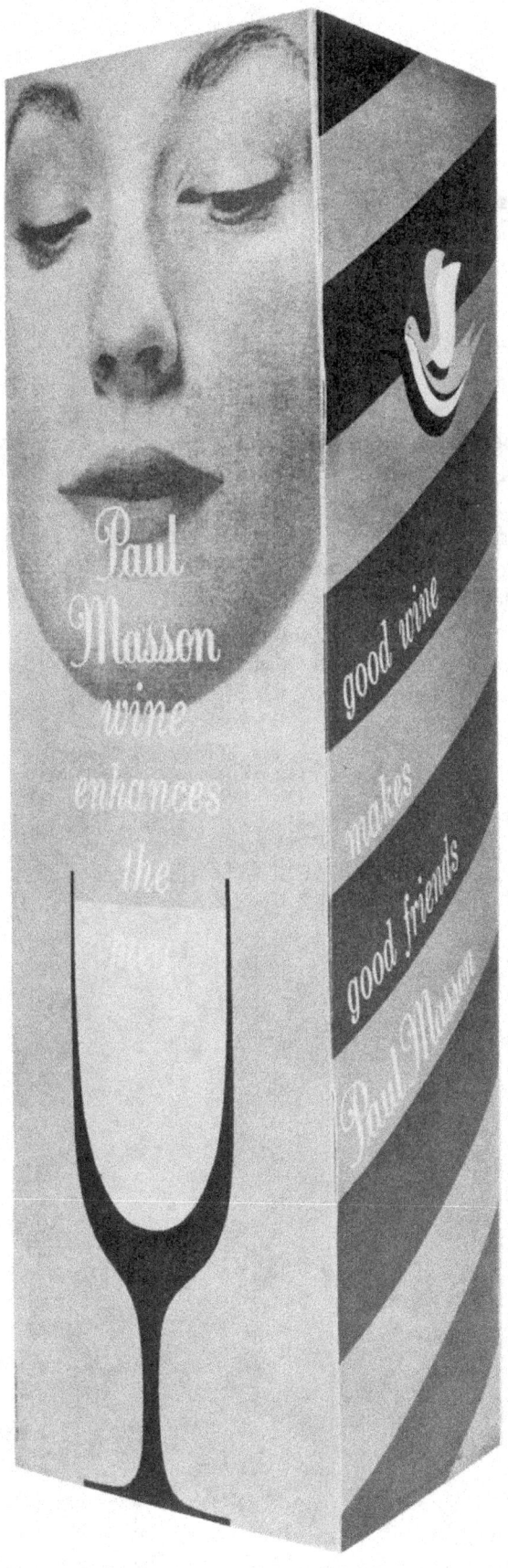

"An attempt at a fresh, new approach to point-of-sale displays. The triangle concept permits the observer a rounded, three-dimensional viewing experience of what is normally a flat, static, two-sided piece. The colors are blue, olive, pink, and black."

"This display consists of a revolving plastic drum lit from within. The heat generated by the lamp inside creates an air turbulence, causing the air to rise. As the air passes through an angled fin, a rotation develops turning the drum. The design 'moves' as the drum spins, and the message on the drum is continuous. The triangles are multicolored."

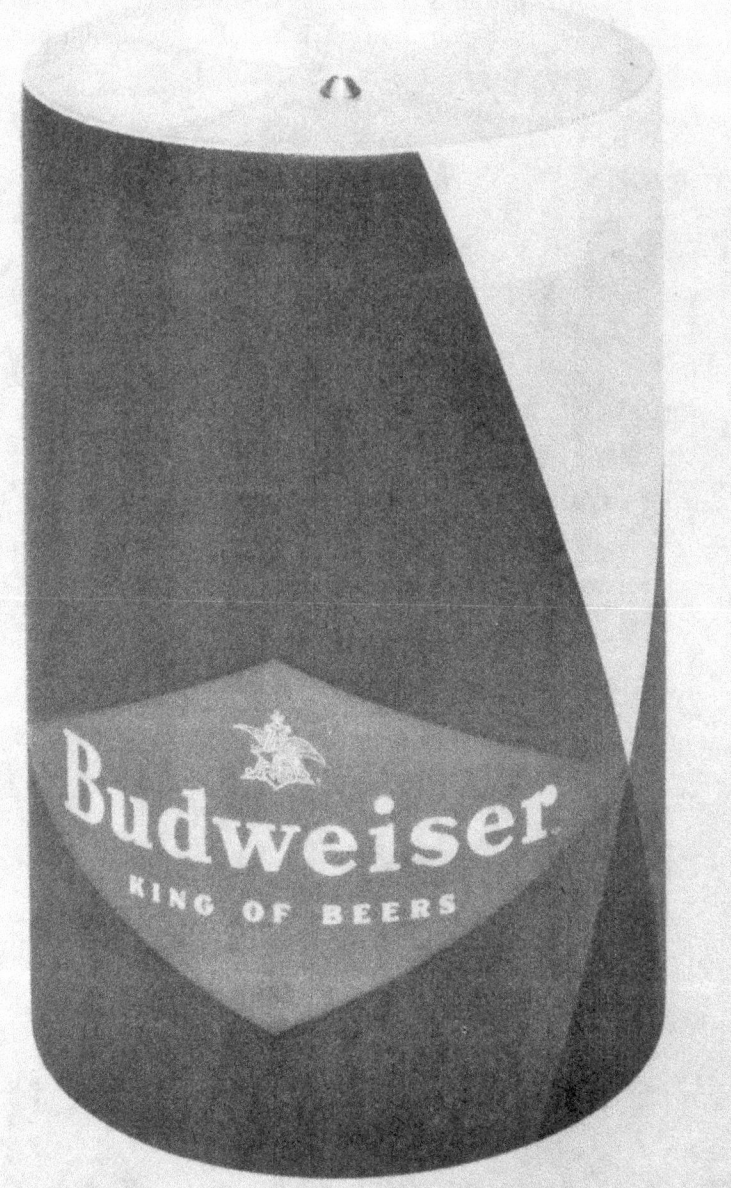

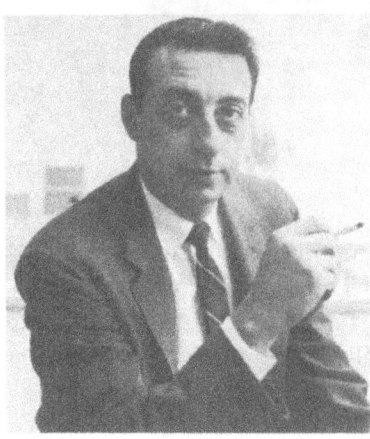

J. CHRIS SMITH
J. Chris Smith Design Associates

J. Chris Smith, head of J. Chris Smith Design Associates, Hollywood, California, is a native of Kansas City, Missouri. Thirty-five-year-old Smith studied art at the Kansas City Art Institute during 1940 and 1941, prior to more than three years of World War II service as a navigator with the Ferrying Division of the Air Transport Command. At the conclusion of hostilities, he took up residence in Southern California and free lanced from 1946 until 1952, at which time he formed a partnership design firm. He founded his present firm in 1956.

Mr. Smith teaches a course in package design at Art Center School in Los Angeles. His firm is active in all phases of advertising and graphic design for industry, with special emphasis placed on packaging and all problems dealing with corporate identity.

His work has been well represented in virtually all national advertising and design competitions, and he has won well over 24 major national awards, in packaging alone, in the past five years. His work has also been published in both national and international publications.

JOB:	B-Z-B Brand Honey Flavor Syrup
CLIENT:	The Honey Company
PROBLEM:	To design a package for a new honey product
SOLUTION:	"Due to the fact that the product was to be marketed along with competing maple syrups, the basic design was developed within the honey-cone design to quickly convey the idea of a honey syrup. Alternate Gothic was chosen as the type for the product name, as the most legible within the close confines of the design."

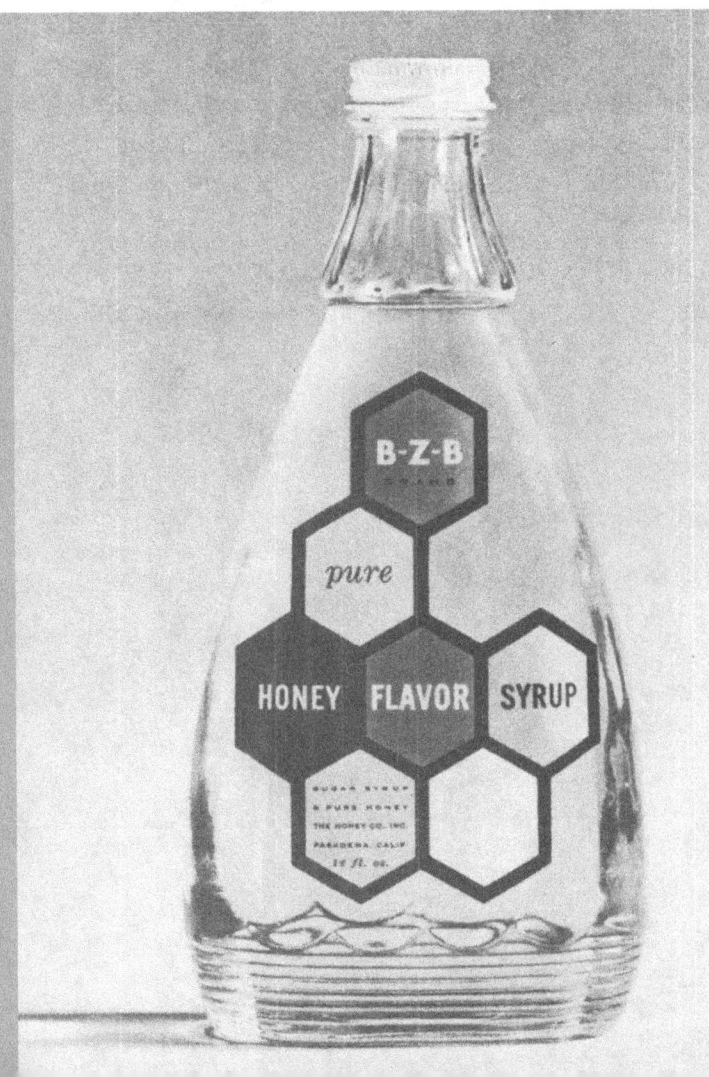

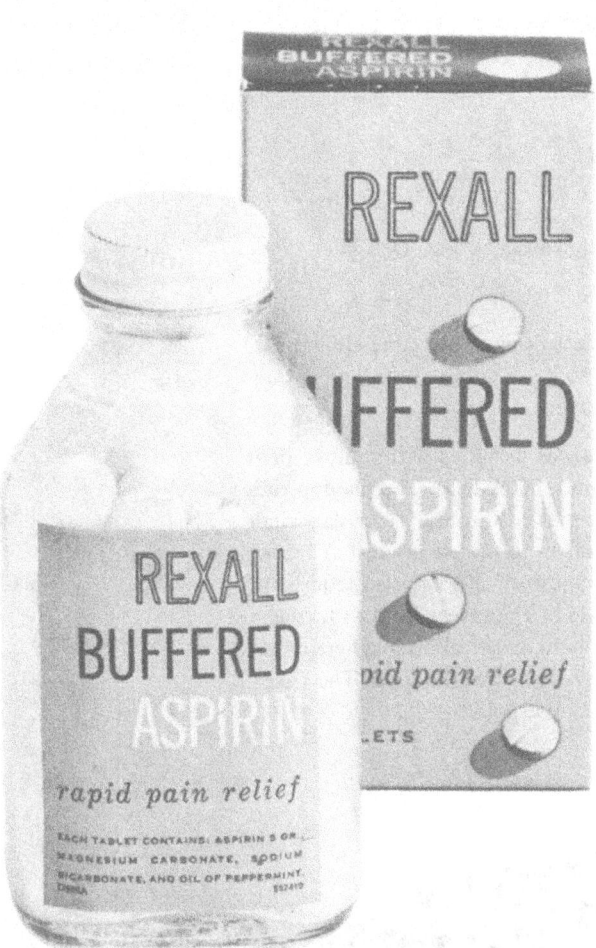

JOB: Rexall Buffered Aspirin

CLIENT: Rexall Drug Company
Larry Goodwin, art director

PROBLEM: Redesign existing aspirin package to increase its effectiveness against competing nationally advertised brands.

SOLUTION: "The design was solved within the framework of an ethical-drug look, as to both color and type selection. The clean, crisp Alternate Gothic for the product name was used effectively in both outline and solid form to accent the key word, 'buffered,' and to set it apart from regular aspirin."

JOB: Dixie Fry

CLIENT: Prepared Products, Inc.

PROBLEM: Redesign of an existing product to enhance shelf appeal.

SOLUTION: "Design was predicated on the unusual use of appetite appeal and the use of off-beat color to set it completely apart from all competition. The hand-lettered style of 'Dixie Fry' was a cleaned-up version from the old package to help retain identity. However, it was closely integrated into the over-all design by alternating the design colors."

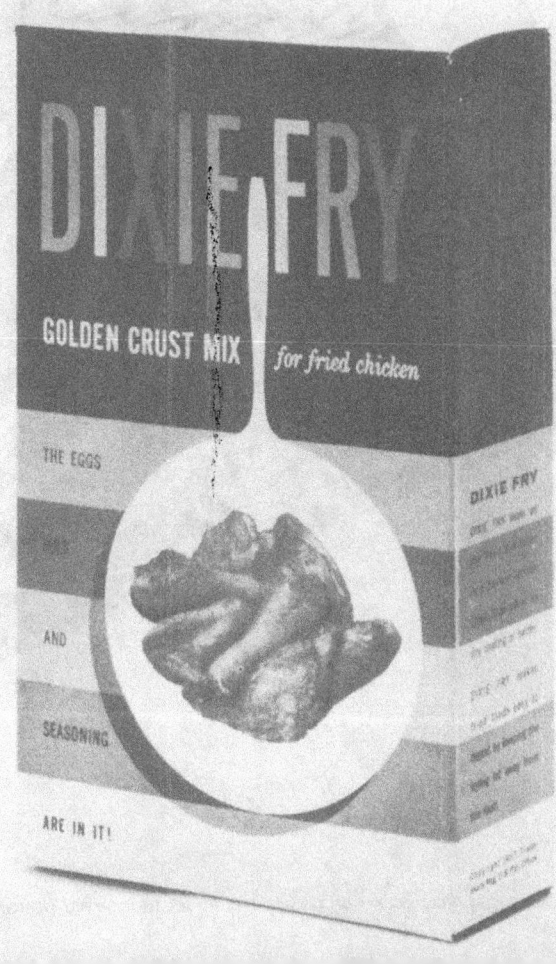

JOB: Showdown Game Box Design

CLIENT: Lord & Freber, Inc.

PROBLEM: Complete design of a game similar to poker to be distributed through toy and department stores.

SOLUTION: "Game was designed with multicolored rings on a black field. The playing cubes can be viewed through a circular window and shaken to arouse interest. The single word 'Showdown' was hand lettered in the style of Engravers Bold to further the rather bold, carnival atmosphere created by the basic over-all design. The base of the box is gold."

Designs and comments on these pages by J. CHRIS SMITH DESIGN ASSOCIATES

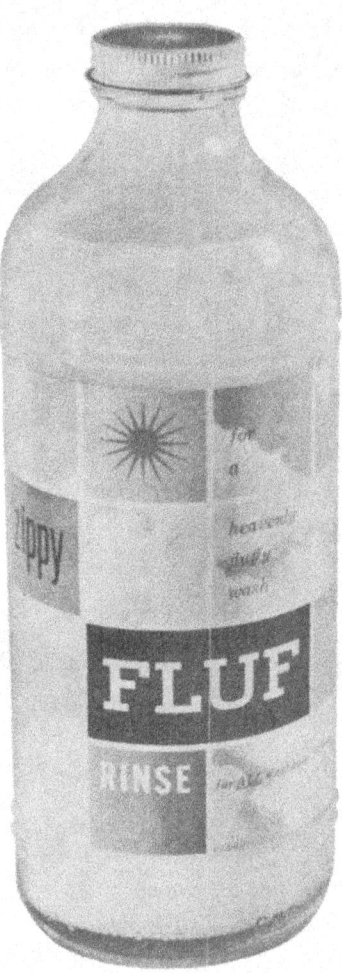

JOB: Fluf Rinse

CLIENT: Zippy, Incorporated

PROBLEM: To produce a package for a new product to be marketed by this company.

SOLUTION: "The design approach was keyed directly to the phrase, 'for a heavenly fluffy wash.' The black panel containing the single word 'Fluf' in a bold Stymie face was in sharp contrast to the billowy clouds and general over-all lightness achieved in the label itself."

JOB: Zippy Starch

CLIENT: Zippy, Incorporated

PROBLEM: Redesign of existing starch package to enhance its appearance at point of sale.

SOLUTION: "The simplicity of the rectangular design. the freshness of the color, and the straightforward approach in the selection of type were all arrived at in an effort to convey the feeling of the ability of this product to produce the desired end result of sun-fresh, starched clothes."

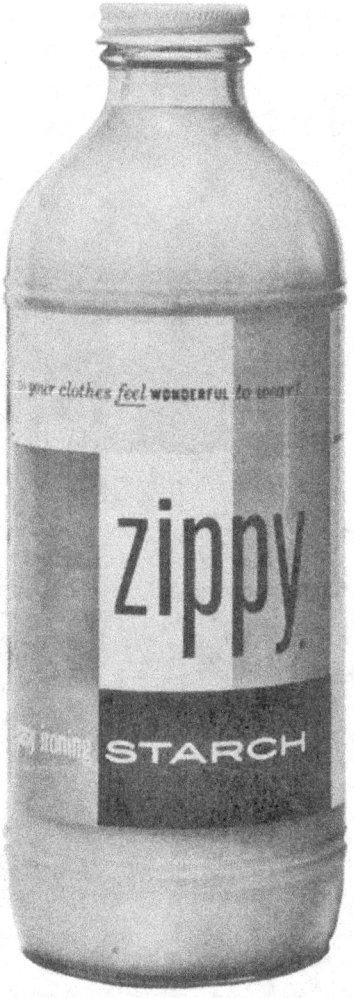

JOB: Crystalite

CLIENT: Mytinger and Casselberry, Inc.

PROBLEM: To design a package for a vitamin product
          to be sold as a companion to a more
          expensive line of vitamins.

SOLUTION: "Since the two vitamin lines are sold
          exclusively by sales representatives on a
          door-to-door basis, shelf strength of the
          design was not a consideration. Rather,
          the solution was to create a package
          whose personality suggested trust and
          reliability, and imparted the feeling of an
          ethical-drug product. The type selections
          were arrived at as a natural means to
          further this impression."

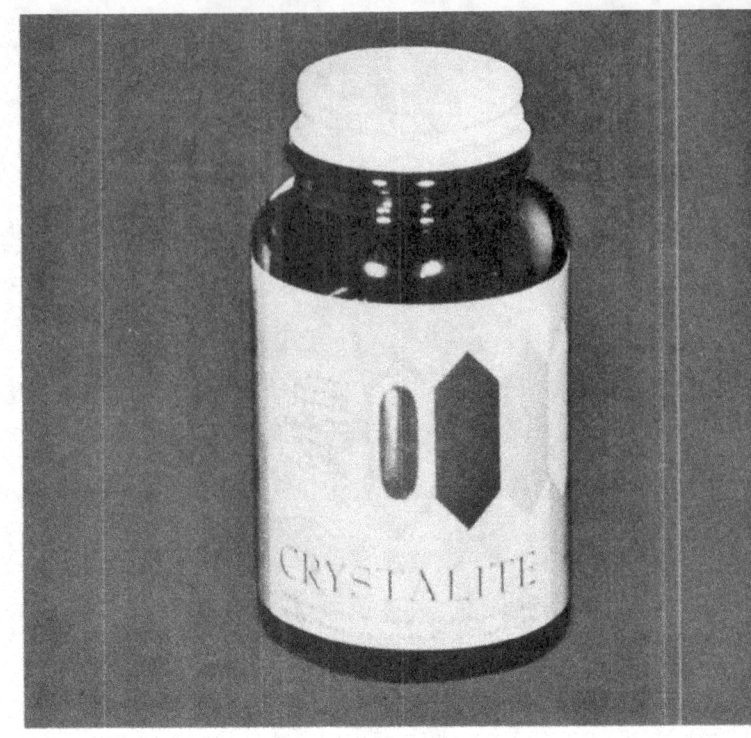

JOB: Golden Dew Cosmetic

CLIENT: Rexall Drug Company
          Larry Goodwin, art director

PROBLEM: To design a specialty line of cosmetics
          for Rexall, marketed under their trade
          name, 'Cara Nome.'

SOLUTION: "Job was executed in one color, with gold
          and embossing. Since the line's function
          was one of cleansing and enriching the
          skin, every effort was made to impart
          a clean yet elegant feeling to the packages.
          Type selections were made to further
          this desired end result. The single, golden
          drop was used not only to reflect the
          name, but to give the prospective buyer
          the feeling of a rare, precious product."

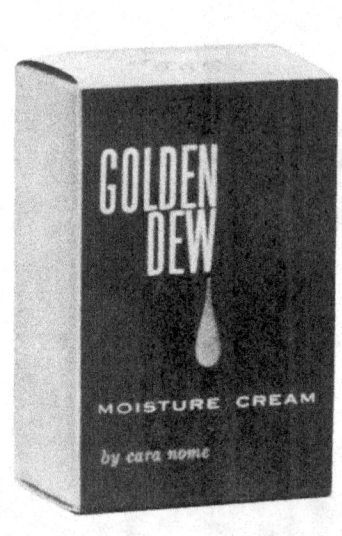
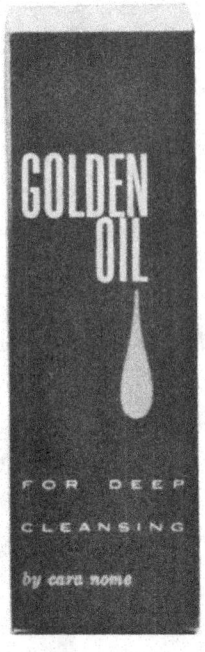
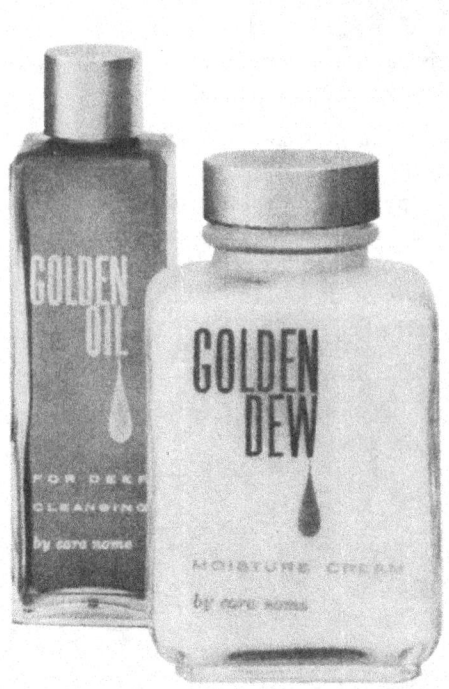
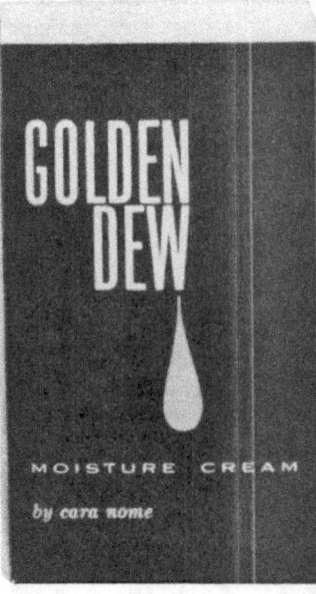

JOB: Betsy Ross Grape Juice

CLIENT: The Real Gold Company

PROBLEM: To redesign their grape juice package in an effort to stimulate sales by giving the product more shelf appeal.

SOLUTION: "The label was keyed, through over-all design and color, to give it a gay, party feeling, which was felt to be all important. However, due to the restricted areas for the name, created by the design, type choices were made which would achieve maximum legibility without the design being made to suffer."

Designs and comments on these pages by
J. CHRIS SMITH DESIGN ASSOCIATES

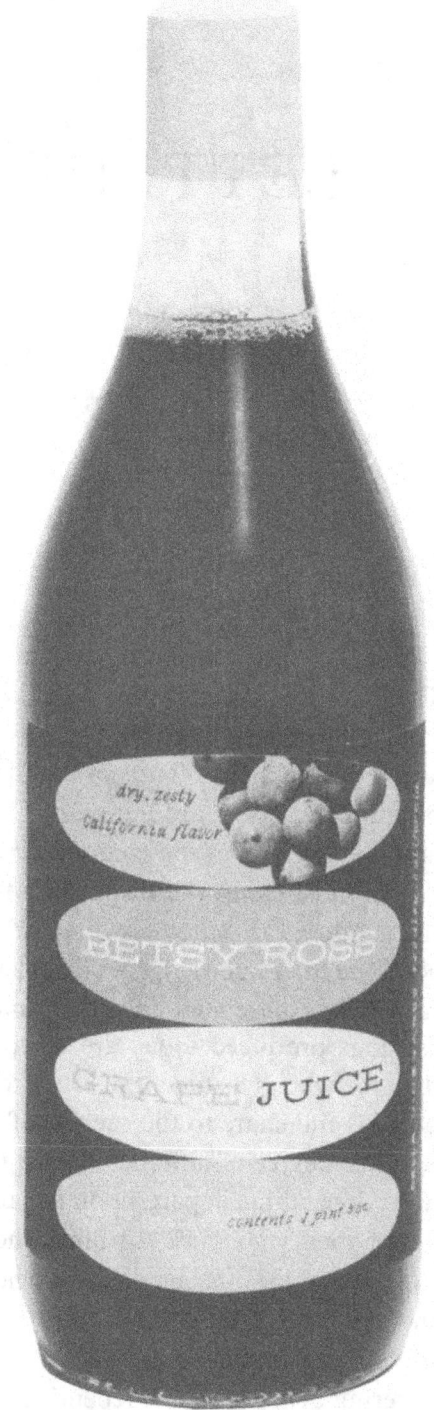

LETTERING

The lettering examples shown on the following pages give a partial indication of the great range of letter styling that can be designed through objective thinking by art directors and lettering artists. The possibilities for creating variations in caption styles and combinations of styles are limitless. Their development depends only upon the knowledge and imagination of the men involved in creative work.

In most cases, the inspiration for an outstanding and effective caption stems from the art director. Many art directors have made a deep study of letter designs, and they combine their knowledge with objective artistry in planning advertising headlines. Almost invariably, these men have the same love of letters as does the lettering artist. The best captions produced today are usually the result of a meeting of minds between an art director who is a student of letter forms and a creative lettering specialist. Each contributes his full share to the success of the job.

The degree of latitude allowed the lettering artist by the art director varies considerably, depending, in part, upon the art director's knowledge of lettering and his confidence in the men who work for him. Though it may be an anomaly, I have found, through experience, that the art director who is well informed about lettering and type designs is the one most likely to give the lettering man the greatest free rein.

Often, time does not allow for a carefully worked out caption indication, and the lettering artist must be depended upon to interpret the feeling and the color indicated on the layout. I believe that the best results are obtained when the art director and lettering artist meet together to discuss the caption before the finished work is begun. Often, during these discussions, new and better ideas evolve. Through personal contact with the art director, the lettering man can also become better informed as to how much latitude he will be allowed in lettering the finished art. Generally speaking, the lettering specialist looks to the art director for the original planning and arrangement of a caption but appreciates the opportunity to add his thinking to the problem.

Once the caption is in the hands of a lettering specialist, its successful completion depends, not only upon his design ability, but upon his knowledge of the effects his instruments can produce. A majority of captions can be done with standard drawing pens and brushes. But when special effects are called for, ingenuity is required in the employment of various instruments, such as personally "barbered" brushes and reshaped pen points. The letterer must also know the effects that can be obtained by working on many different paper surfaces. For the most part, he must acquire this knowledge through his own experiments. The basics of the lettering art can be taught in schools, where information is also provided on the effects produced by various tools, but a good lettering specialist always continues to search for new ways of producing specific effects.

Just as has occurred in the illustration field, where artists, willingly or not, have been classified as specialists in figure drawing (male or female), head drawing, still life, automobile illustration, etc., there are lettering artists who have been placed in the position of specializing within their specialty. In some cases, this has occurred through their own choice. Calligraphers may prefer to draw only letters that can be produced by spontaneous stroking with flat pens; men who handle brushes and speedball pens with facility may prefer to do only the free-style expressions produced with these tools; and others, who favor the pointed pen, may want to concentrate their work on built-up letter forms. However, some lettering artists unwillingly have been placed in a particular category by some art buyers who tend to classify the artists as being proficient only in certain areas of letter styling. Such limited proficiency does exist of course, but, generally, a lettering artist is capable of producing a wide range of lettered expressions and is skilled in the use of many drawing instruments. Lettering specialists who wish to broaden their scope, especially individual free lancers, must prove to art directors that they have greater capabilities by showing examples of their different approaches to letter interpretations.

The comments of the lettering artists (and, in some cases, of the art directors), which accompany many of the lettering examples shown here, should be helpful to art students and beginning lettering specialists. These comments can also serve to make young layout men more aware of the need to establish close rapport with the lettering artists who supply the finished art for captions.

Brushscript lettering, uninhibited by tradition, offers great opportunities for individual expressions and unusual effects. One may speculate whether the scripts should be called "lettering" or be considered a form of controlled writing, but the question is academic since only skilled lettering men can consistently produce competent script captions. While most brushscript captions are done under control, the brush strokes often produce some "happy accidents," which, when judiciously used, can add much to the spontaneous quality of the caption. Nonetheless, lettering artists should be able to produce a specific version of a script, as required by an art director. The desired effects are rarely achieved on the first write-out. As a rule, many write-outs are made. Occasionally, one of the complete lines will work out well enough so that it can be retouched and used in its entirety; but more often, words or segments of words are selected, assembled into a caption, and retouched into reproducible form.

A variety of tools are used in an effort to get specific effects. Variations in paper textures are also taken into consideration. Pointed brushes, chiselled brushes, ruling pens, speedball pens, and flexible pens are used to produce varying results. Many lettering artists "barber" their brushes and reshape speedball pens to their own satisfaction.

Brush and pen scripts serve many purposes. In addition to expressing various moods, they can impart a distinctive quality to captions or logos. They also can combine well with many conventional type forms and lettered forms to produce a pleasant change of pace in an otherwise sedate line.

In the future, we may expect to see many new and attractive versions of the scripts. The only actual requirements, in an otherwise unrestricted expression of lettering, are those of good taste and readability.

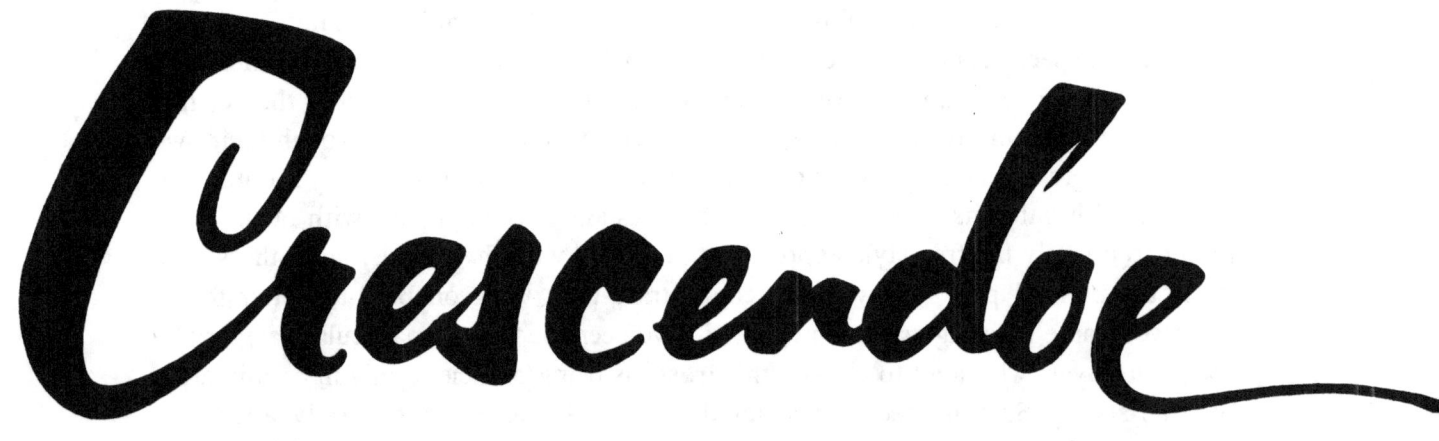

Agency: Leber & Katz, Inc.
Client: Crescendoe Gloves, Inc.
Art Director: Rene Gruau
Lettering Artist: Rene Gruau

Fortisan...a _Celanese_ contemporary fiber

Agency: Ellington & Company, Inc.
Client: Celanese Corporation of America
Art Director: Lynette Logan
Lettering Artist: Lynette Logan

Sleeping Beauty

Client: *The American Weekly* Magazine
Art Director: Abril Lamarque
Lettering Artist: Frank P. Conley

FRANK P. CONLEY: "'Sleeping Beauty' and 'Love in a Bottle' were both done with round speedball pens which I had flattened on the sides to a long, narrow shape. They were written a number of times, and there was some piecing together in the case of 'Love in a Bottle.' Just a little retouching here and there on these. The ink was somewhat thinned in order to get a free flow. These scripts were done on smooth duplicating-machine paper."

Love in a bottle

Agency: Harris & Company Advertising, Inc.
Client: Hotel Nacional de Cuba, an Intercontinental Hotel
Art Director: George R. Buchanan
Lettering Artist: Al Angelo—Schaller-Angelo

World Famous

You're Prettier than you think you are!

...and you can prove it with a Palmolive bar!

Agency: Ted Bates & Company, Inc.
Client: Palmolive Soap
Art Director: William Sheldon
Lettering Artist: Larry Ottino—Fenga & Donderi, Inc.

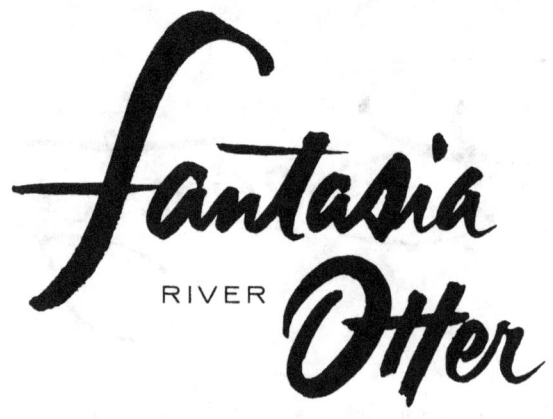

Fantasia RIVER Otter

MORRIS GLICKMAN: *"The 'Fantasia Furs' was one of many I submitted for the design of a logo. This was done in brush. The problem here was to get a fashiony-smart logo, simple and easy to read, and distinctive."*

Agency: Leber & Katz, Inc.
Client: Fantasia Furs
Art Director: Herbert Paulen
Lettering Artist: Morris Glickman

Zest

Agency: Benton & Bowles, Inc.
Client: The Procter & Gamble Company
Art Director: James E. Clark
Lettering Artist: Frank P. Conley

FRANK P. CONLEY: *"Patterned after a suggestion by Art Director Ed Witalis, the 'Zest' logotype was written freely many times with a pointed water-color brush until an acceptable one was achieved. Only a minimum of retouching was needed."*

New Flower Lane

Agency: J. Walter Thompson Company
Client: Heirloom Sterling—Oneida, Ltd.
Art Director: Frank Stephenson
Lettering Artist: Acey Cypress

Agency: N. W. Ayer & Son, Inc.
Client: De Beers Consolidated Mines, Ltd.
Art Director: Paul Darrow
Lettering Artist: Susumu Tanaka

Bright messenger of love

SUSUMU TANAKA: *"For lettering this brushscript line, I used a long, thin Albata brush, altered at the tip in order to produce thick and thin strokes. The caption was done actual size, in red, and retouched with white."*

NEW

Lady Sheaffer

Agency: Batten, Barton, Durstine & Osborn, Inc.
Client: W. A. Sheaffer Pen Company
Art Director: William M. Williams
Lettering Artist: Sam Marsh Studios

Now in 4 new colors

as well as pure white

Agency: J. Walter Thompson Company
Client: Lux—Lever Brothers Company
Art Director: Rudy Dusek
Lettering Artist: Rio Studios

Brush letters, like brushscripts can be helpful in interpreting the mood of a statement and in adding an air of informality to an advertisement. They also combine well with conservative type and lettered forms.

Painting separated letters requires a different brush action than that used for scripts—which are produced by keeping the brush on the paper until a series of connected letters have been stroked in. The brush letters are produced by preplanning the individual strokes. The end of the brush is placed on the paper and held in position before the desired stroke is made. More brush control is needed for these styles than is necessary for script writings. The stroking is usually slower and, in most cases, two or more strokes are made to complete a letter. The cut-and-paste method of assembly is generally used, and the letters, as a rule, need quite a bit of retouching.

Brush-letter styling can range from conservative letters, which give the appearance of loosened Gothics, to highly active forms in which the brush effects are clearly evident.

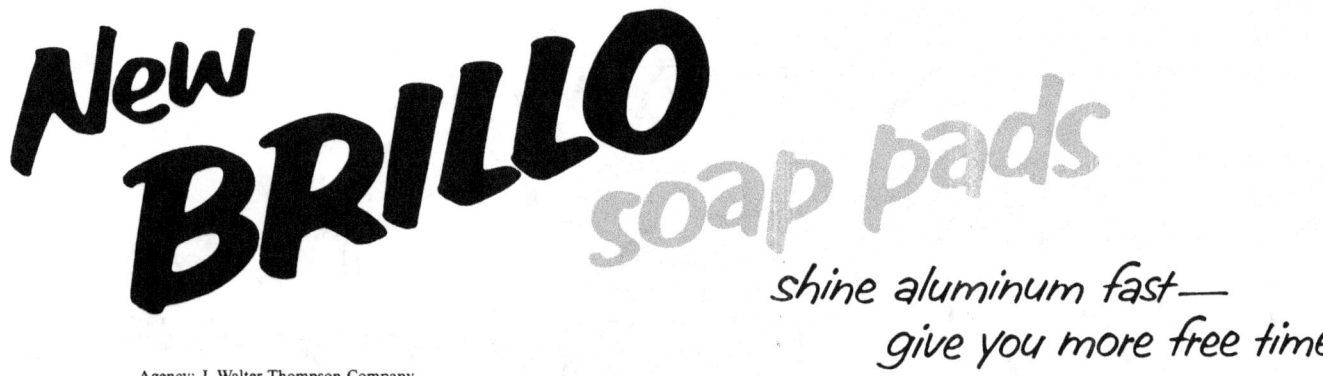

Agency: J. Walter Thompson Company
Client: Brillo Manufacturing Company, Inc.
Art Director: George Booth
Lettering Artist: Harry Watts Studio

Agency: Batten, Barton, Durstine & Osborn, Inc.
Client: Du Pont Cellophane
Art Director: Frank Rupp
Lettering Artist: Tony Violino—KV Studios

TONY VIOLINO: *"I used a chisel-edge HB pencil in laying out the Du Pont Cellophane caption. The lettering was traced down on Strathmore board, outlined with a #290 Gillott pen, and filled in with a brush. Some reshaping of the letters was done with white paint during the final touching up."*

Agency: Lambert & Feasley, Inc.
Client: Listerine Antiseptic—Warner-Lambert Pharmaceutical Co.
Art Director: Walt Peters
Lettering Artist: Bill Reid

"Wow! Our house looks like new!"

Agency: J. Walter Thompson Company
Client: Johns-Manville Corporation
Art Director: Clyde Bartel
Lettering Artist: Frank P. Conley

FRANK P. CONLEY: *"Clyde Bartel's rough indications are always a pleasure to work from as they have a sound lettering knowledge behind them and yet allow the letterer considerable latitude for interpretation.*

"In this case, I used my pet 'mitred' rigger brush (similar effect to sawed-off ruling pen) with India ink. Worked twice size from stat of layout, roughed it out with soft charcoal pencil, placed 1-ply plate over the rough (after fixing, of course), and without penciling, slow-wrote it with the rigger, some heavy weights taking two or three strokes, but mostly using change of pressure for change of weight.

"I placed this under another sheet of 1-ply and redid it. This is my usual method when doing brush letters. Retouched with fine pointed brush and ink and cleaned up with #3 pointed brush for white paint.

"I tried to express the excitement of the words in the lettering—I think I got it."

THE GLAMOUR RIDE TO GLAMOROUS HAWAII

Agency: Foote, Cone & Belding
Client: Lockheed Aircraft Corporation
Art Director: John Groen
Lettering Artist: James L. Wood

JAMES L. WOOD: *"The loose brush lettering for 'Hawaii' was trial-and-error writing, widely used for this style. I just happened to use a brush that I would be helpless without—a Winsor Newton Albata, notched for finger positions like a six-shooter."*

Ivory Liquid DETERGENT

Agency: Compton Advertising, Inc.
Client: The Procter & Gamble Company
Art Director: Robert McDonnell
Lettering Artist: Morris Glickman

Calligraphic letters, stroked out spontaneously with flat pens, were the source material for the earliest type designers and for many who followed. The objective artistry of present-day calligraphy can still exert an influence upon the design of new type expressions. Although modern type alphabets are being widely used, the "old-styles," which stem from calligraphic letters, continue to be of great value in many areas of the graphic design field.

The use of calligraphic lettering in current advertising is limited, but there are times when these personal expressions provide the best solution for a design problem.

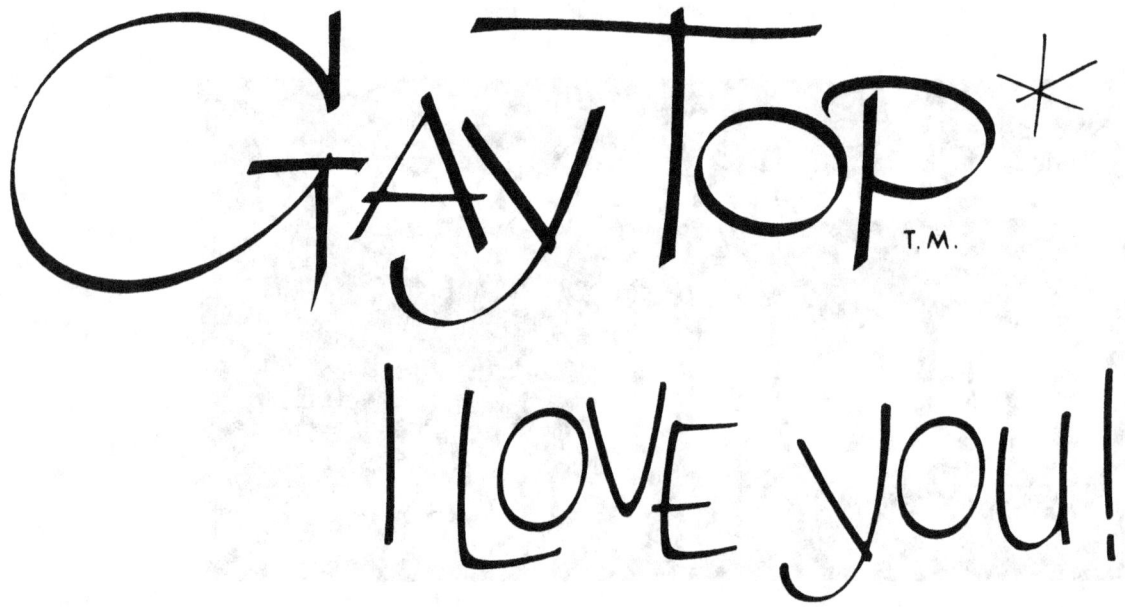

Agency: Edward H. Weiss & Company
Client: Helene Curtis Industries, Inc.
Art Director: Art Meltzer
Lettering Artist: Carl E. Corley—Whitaker Guernsey Studio, Inc.

CARL E. CORLEY: *"The art director was after a rather gay and frivolous kind of lettering descriptive of the name, 'GAY TOP.' I did this lettering several times with a flat pen—picked the one I thought best and touched it up a bit."*

Economy is the big news in the smart set

Agency: J. Walter Thompson Company
Client: Ford Motor Company
Art Director: Richard Hurd
Lettering Artist: Sam Marsh Studios

The Gift of the Magi

Client: Sterling Press
Art Director: Advertising Designers Company
Designer: Lou Frimkess
Lettering Artist: Lou Frimkess

Client: Society of Calligraphers of L. A.
Art Director: Advertising Designers Company
Designer: Lou Frimkess
Lettering Artist: Lou Frimkess

SOCIETY OF Calligraphers LA

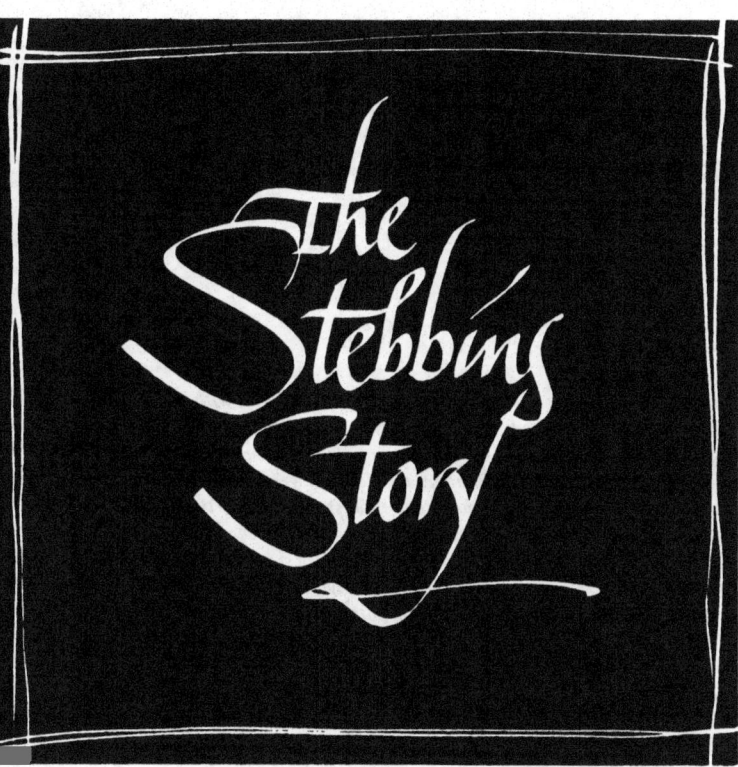

The Stebbins Story

LOU FRIMKESS: *"One might think of the art of calligraphy as being the beginning and the end. Before the invention of metal type forms, all lettering (in the forms that we read today) was done by calligraphers who used flat reeds to stroke out letters. With the development of movable type, the letter styles produced in metal were based on these calligraphic strokes. A great number of type styles, which have evolved through the past centuries, are calligraphic expressions 'frozen' into metal.*

"The design of good type styles today is still dependent upon men who have a thorough knowledge of basic letter forms and who are essentially good lettering artists."

Client: Hal Stebbins, Inc.
Art Director: Advertising Designers Company
Designer: Lou Frimkess
Lettering Artist: Lou Frimkess

Client: Hollywood-Los Feliz Jewish Community Center
Art Director: Advertising Designers Company
Designer: Lou Frimkess
Lettering Artist: Lou Frimkess

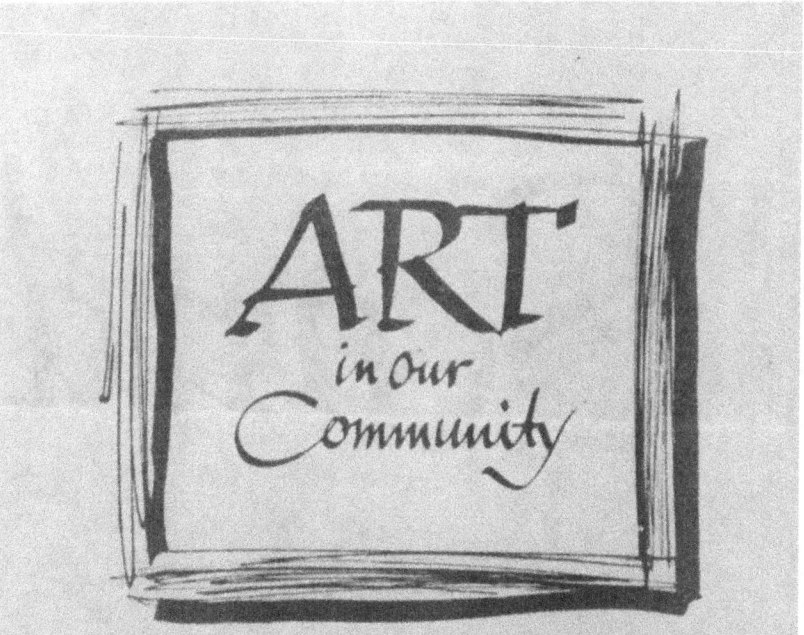

ART in our Community

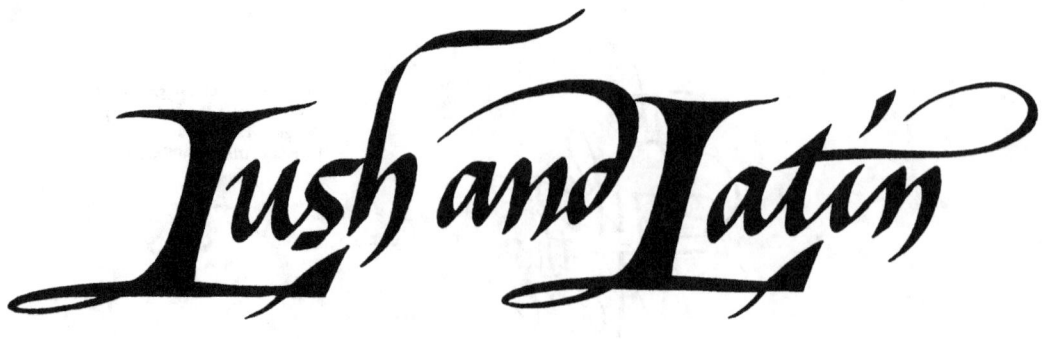

Lush and Latin

DEAN MARTIN

The Lovers of Rome

MAURY NEMOY: "These are examples of my calligraphy, drawn with the broad-edged pen, done for Capitol Records.

"As to my feelings about them and calligraphy in general, I would say that calligraphy, in its freedom, offers the designer great opportunity for creative letter forms. This very personal expression of the artist, can, in many ways, create a mood and visual image, and, because of the fallibility of the human hand, endow the work with a more sensitive interpretation. The personality of the doer will show, and, with an informed mind, he can create letters that are both pleasing and readable.

"I particularly have enjoyed working on album covers, as the subject matter is varied and music in itself is interpreted in many ways. These new challenges will invariably create new visual ways to solve the problem.

"Calligraphy is not confined to the pen, and the work of the Orientals in their brushwork strives to be not only formally perfect but organically vital."

Scandinavia!

Client: Capitol Records, Inc.
Art Director: Marvin Schwartz
Lettering Artist: Maury Nemoy

Agency: McCann-Erickson, Inc.
Client: Chrysler Division, Chrysler Corporation
Art Director: Jeane Bice
Lettering Artist: Richard Isbell—Art Group, Inc.

Enjoy Chrysler's bold new look of success !

RICHARD ISBELL: *"The caption was designed and rendered primarily with a #3 chisel speedball pen, with additional hand drawing with a #4 brush."*

JAMES L. WOOD: *"The calligraphy for this announcement was written with a Rex broad-nib pen; a casual italic hand, loosely done to logically associate itself with water colors."*

Client: Jake Lee
Art Director: James L. Wood
Lettering Artist: James L. Wood

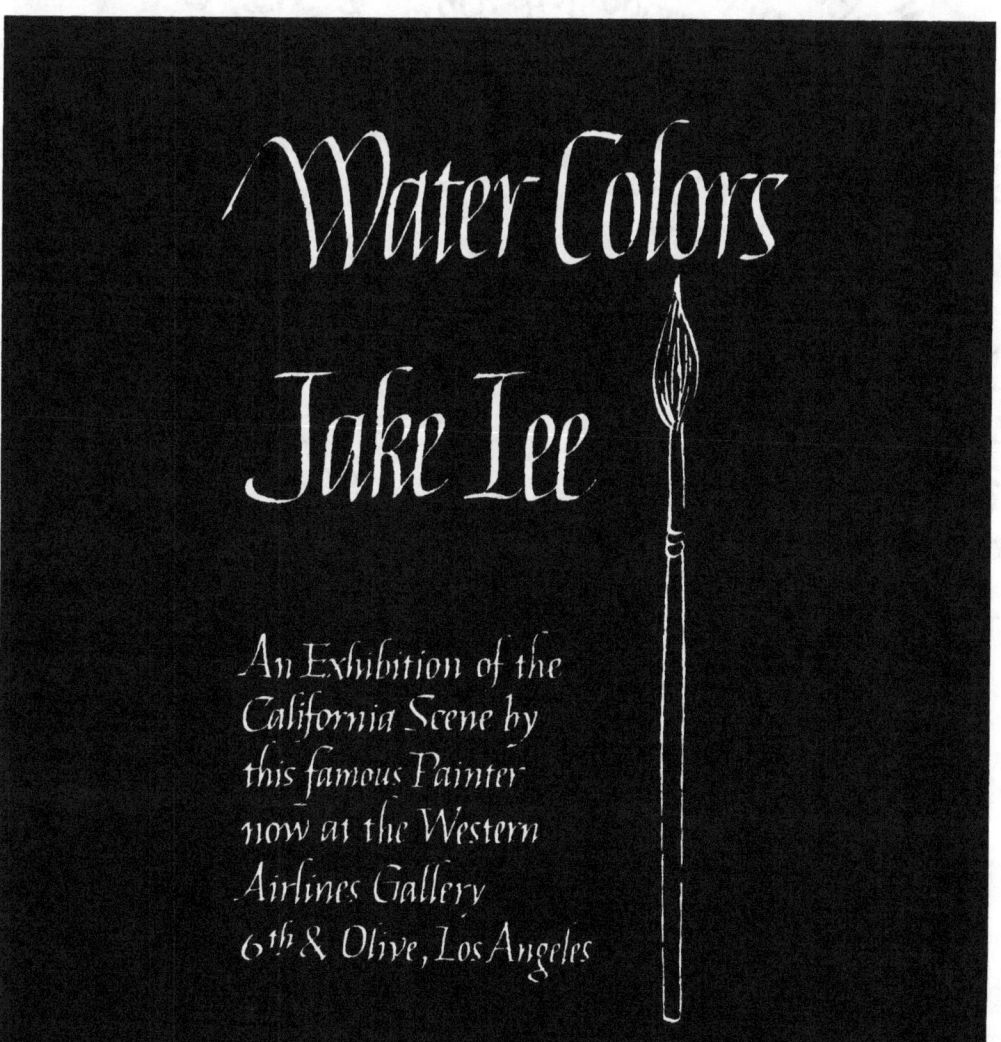

182

BYRON J. MACDONALD: "With the revival of calligraphy in Europe and the fast-growing interest in the art here in this country, we, as a resourceful and imaginative people, should take calligraphy out of its ivory tower and 'put it to work' for all to see—not just for the relatively few who are intrigued by beautiful penmanship.

"There is great opportunity for calligraphy in advertising and in the field of package and label design. The use of type on labels is not, in most cases, a happy solution. The better American label designs are hand lettered, tailored for a particular use.

"I feel that the twentieth century penman should apply his skill to new surfaces, and experiment with new techniques—making calligraphy work in modern business."

"One of a set of six learning cards for children. The cards were mounted on a bottom card with a grommet and turned by the child while reading. This is two-thirds the size of the original and was lettered with a ground-down stub fountain pen."

Art Director: Byron J. MacDonald
Lettering Artist: Byron J. MacDonald
Client: Byron West MacDonald

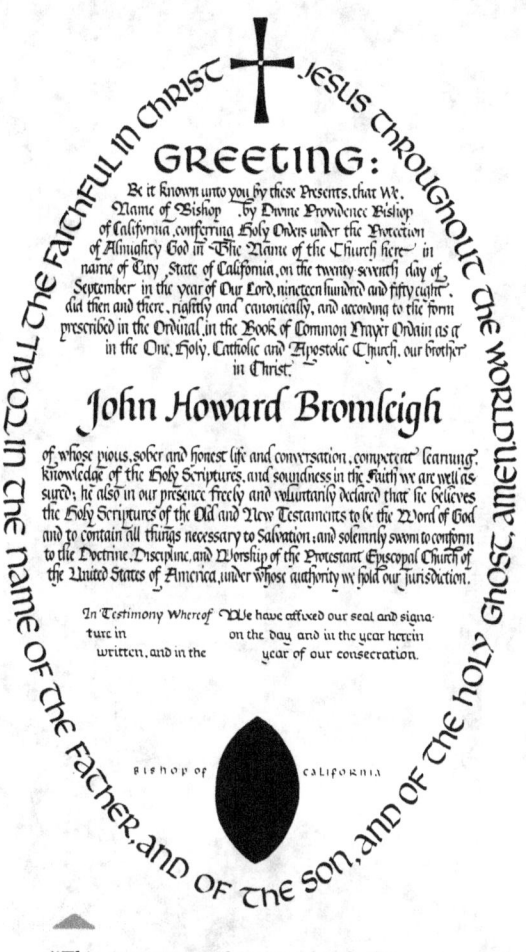

"This is a comprehensive sketch for a proposed ordination certificate, reproduced approximately one-quarter of the original size. The sketch was lettered with a turkey quill."

"Reproduced one-half original size, this was lettered with a bamboo-reed pen."

Art Director: Byron J. MacDonald
Lettering Artist: Byron J. MacDonald

O GOD, who hast prepared for those who love thee such good things as pass man's understanding; Pour into our hearts such love toward thee, that we, loving thee above all things, may obtain thy promises which exceed all that we may desire; through Jesus Christ † our Lord. Amen.

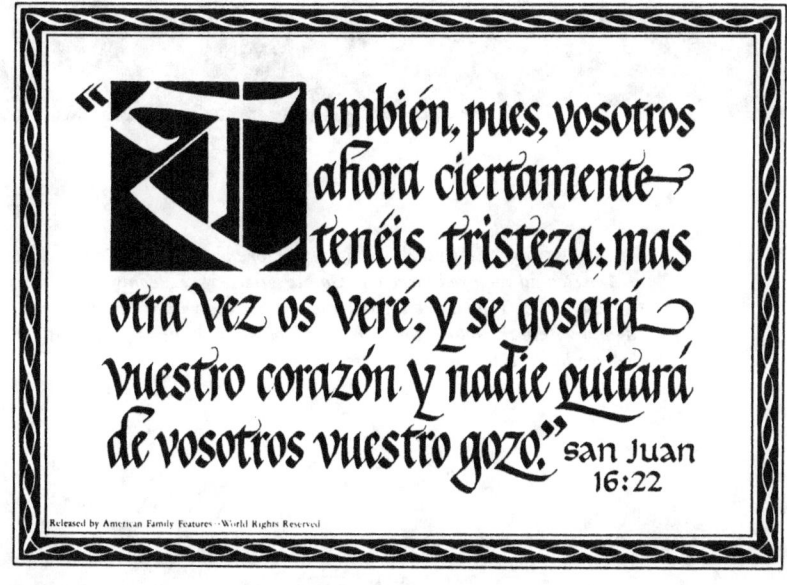

"También, pues, vosotros ahora ciertamente tenéis tristeza; mas otra vez os veré, y se gosará vuestro corazón y nadie quitará de vosotros vuestro gozo." san Juan 16:22

WILLIAM GODWIN ON THE CHOICE OF GOVERNMENT

Agency: N. W. Ayer & Son, Inc.
Client: Container Corporation of America
(This display is part of the Great Ideas Series)
Art Directors: Ed Kysar, Walter Reinsel
Lettering Artist: James L. Wood

JAMES L. WOOD: *"Ed Kysar's strong design for the Container Corporation of America ad required large cap Gothic letters, very cleanly and formally done. Type is the logical answer, but the widths had to vary slightly within the letters on each line to make them line up. Because of this, we lettered it, rather than flex type."*

Cuffs à-la-mode!

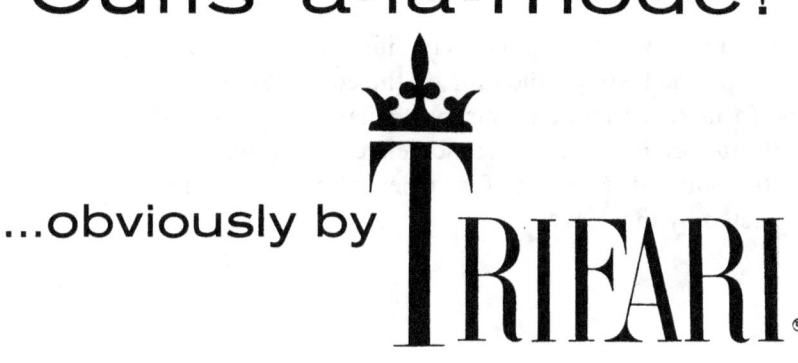

...obviously by TRIFARI.

Agency: Grant Advertising, Inc.
Client: Trifari®—Trifari, Krussman & Fishel, Inc.
Art Director: Mrs. Helen Bertull

RITA MC NAMARA, *Account Executive:* "*Unfortunately, we are unable to give you the name of the designer of the Trifari trademark. It was lettered almost a quarter of a century ago, and records are no longer available. However, the designer is worthy of a great deal of praise for creating a logotype that has retained its freshness, its suitability, and character all this time.*

"*The type used in the remaining areas of the headline is 24 point Standard Extended (large).*

"*The type was specified by Mrs. Helen Bertull who is our art director on the account. The particular selection was made because we wished to keep the layout modern and crisp in effect. The nature of the lettering of the trademark name limits the art director to the kinds of faces that can be used effectively with it. She thought this was a good choice as it did not interfere with the character of the trademark, and actually complements it by its simplicity. She has found this an effective type face for achieving a clean, modern effect with great legibility.*"

apple on a stick

Agency: McCann-Erickson, Inc.
Client: Dorothy Gray, Ltd.
Art Director: Don Shure
Lettering Artist: Irving Bogen

IRVING BOGEN: "*Because the type to be used in all the Dorothy Gray ads was hard and rigid, the art director and I felt that the lettered captions, though in Gothic, could take some softness. The letters were all drawn 'freehand' with a slight curve for all normally straight strokes, and the 'i' form heaviest at the top and bottom and thinnest in the center. Other refinements were added with a view towards 'loosening' the forms to get away from the hardness of the Venus character.*

"*In all, the question I asked myself was, 'Given a job to do that emulates type, how far can I get away from it?' I'd like to see a little less fear of illegibility and a return to greater freedom in lettering.*

"*This job was done on 2-ply, kid-finished bristol, with a Gillott #170 pen, then 'cleaned up' with Permo White and a #2 sable-haired, pointed brush.*"

The lettering examples shown on these facing pages, though entirely different in conception and design, are all efforts to portray the specific feeling called for by the copy. While many other expressions of lettering also perform this function, this particular group presents evidence that many dissimilar styles of interpretive lettering can be effective. Although no particular style need be considered as the only "sure" choice for achieving a desired effect, some styles are often automatically suggested by the copy.

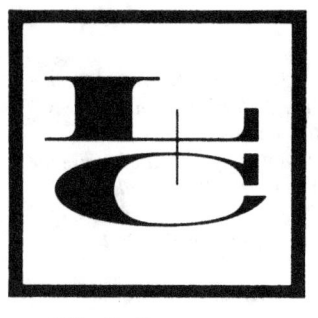

Ron Cleveland **ARCHITECT**

DOYALD YOUNG: *"The vertical line drawn through the initials was employed to signify partnership. A strong weight was needed for display, but thin hairlines were held to suggest the precision of an architectural organization."*

Client: Leach, Cleveland, & Associates
Art Director: Sterling Leach
Lettering Artist: Doyald Young

Captain Tom's Fish Bake

Agency: Young & Rubicam, Inc.
Client: Hunt Foods & Industries, Inc.
Art Director: Robert Wheeler
Lettering Artist: Mortimer Leach

MORTIMER LEACH: *"The art director felt that the headline copy for the Hunt's Tomato Sauce advertisement was reminiscent of early New England days and called for the use of Caslon, which was widely used in that era. It was decided that Antique Caslon be used to simulate the crude, hand-press printing done in those days.*

"I inked in the letters roughly with a Gillott #170 pen, trying to maintain a ragged texture. The caption was completed by making additional indents into the letters with white paint, using a #2 pointed brush."

MORTIMER LEACH: *"The copy suggested the use of a lilting and yet smooth-flowing line of lettering. Contained within a two-column magazine ad, the letters had to be somewhat condensed, but this was relieved by swinging some of the curving hairlines through the following letters. The line was inked in with an Esterbrook #356 pen and retouched with white."*

ENGLAND'S MOST HAUNTED HOUSE

Client: *The American Weekly* Magazine
Art Director: Ralph Finch
Lettering Artist: Frank P. Conley

FRANK P. CONLEY: "*The inspirational feeling for this caption was supplied by Ralph Finch, the art director. Lettering on blotting paper seemed the logical way to capture this feeling and further express it. I lettered this twice on ordinary blotters, 4 inches by 9½ inches, using a somewhat worn #3 pointed brush and India ink, without preliminary sketches, and the caption shown here was selected.*

"*The method of execution was to maintain simultaneous control of speed and pressure of the brush. A slight additional pressure, and a pause, produced the blobby ends. It takes a good deal of concentration to produce letters this crazy and still retain a good readable pattern.*"

HERITAGE
DESIGN ✳ CRAFTSMANSHIP

Agency: Ellington & Company, Inc.
Client: Heritage Furniture, Inc.
Art Director: Charles Shelander
Lettering Artist: Frank P. Conley

FRANK P. CONLEY: "*This is a logo for a manufacturer of fine furniture, used not only in the ads but on furniture, etc.*

"*The original conception was by Charles Shelander, a man with exquisite taste. It was done in two weights to cover various uses, in pure Roman.*

"*I referred to an alphabet done by Cresci of Rome in 1560 for inspiration but had to take it from there for unity and interest of the design. The contrast between the tall letters of 'Heritage' and the small, wider letters of 'design* craftsmanship' with their letter spacing, does a lot for this from a design standpoint. Things like the sweep of inner serif of the 'G,' and the dynamic drawing of the symbolic substitute for an ampersand help to give the whole thing a distinctive flavor.*

"*The execution was on 3-ply, kid Strathmore with #303 and #290 Gillott pen points, plus a bit of white.*

"*I laid it out in ink for preciseness and traced it on a light table.*"

Coty FRENCH SPICE

MORRIS GLICKMAN: "*French Spice was rendered in brush, an experiment in cutting a #5 brush to give the informal effect. The feeling I wanted was a 'Frenchy' poster-style form with a little fashion flair.*"

Agency: Batten, Barton, Durstine & Osborn, Inc.
Client: Coty, Inc.
Art Director: Martin Stevens
Lettering Artist: Morris Glickman

'The Orchestra Sings'

Agency: Young & Rubicam, Inc.
Client: Capitol Records, Inc.
Art Director: James Stitt
Lettering Artist: Mortimer Leach

These examples of cut-out letters were done by William A. Coppock of San Francisco. Well known in the lettering field, he has thorough and broad experience. Constantly striving for new effects, his work shows the results of thoughtful study. Mr. Coppock's description of an approach to cut-out forms is presented here.

WILLIAM A. COPPOCK: "Genuinely creative lettering artists are usually experimenting with new methods and approaches to lettering problems in order to come up with something different, something unique. Lettering should reflect the special qualities of the tools used. For example, script takes on the special character of the brush or pen. Many of the twists and accents of script are controlled accidents and are not contrived.

"Recently, increased use has been made of the razor blade and thin, solid-red zipatone paper, in the designing of headings. When used with imagination and skill, a fresh charm results, which would be quite impossible to attain in the conventional way.

"Here are some examples of silhouette lettering and a description of the method:

"1. Lay out the heading on tissue and carefully trace down on white board with blue chalk.

"2. Press down solid-vermillion, matte-finish zipatone over traced-down lettering, but do not burnish.

"3. Using sharp razor blade, carefully cut the lettering along the blue lines (which appear black when covered over with the red paper), and remove background as you cut. Burnish *now*.

"4. Clean off any chalk remaining on the white paper with a draftsman's dry cleaning pad, get negative photostat, touch up where needed, and get positive stat, to size.

"It is important to use vermillion zipatone because it photographs black, yet is transparent enough to see the blue tracing beneath."

STORY OF WALNUTS

Agency: McCann-Erickson, Inc.
Client: Diamond Walnut Growers, Inc.
Art Director: Dean Smith
Lettering Artist: William A. Coppock

Agency: McCann-Erickson, Inc.
Client: Coca Cola Bottling Co. of Sacramento
Art Director: John Feeley
Lettering Artist: William A. Coppock

WIN A $278 EVINRUDE

This lettered text, done for a Foremost advertisement, was drawn approximately one-half size larger than reproduction size, as shown on a segment photostated from the original art.

As an experiment, Mr. Coppock photostated some of the letters to four times the size of the original lettering and assembled them into the words "hand lettering." This blowup shows the phenomenon that occurs when letters are greatly enlarged from their original size. The textures which result from extreme enlargements are almost impossible to duplicate in any other way.

Reproduction size

It's not sherbet! It's not ice cream! It's <u>strawberries</u>- and nothing but strawberries! The big, bright, blushing kind... gently crushed, sweetened and frozen into something new and very special. We call it Strawberry Crush. And some hot day soon - like today, maybe - you're going to call it <u>wonderful</u>!

Size of original lettering

into something n

Crush. And some

g to call it <u>wonder</u>

Agency: Batten, Barton, Durstine & Osborn, Inc.
Client: Foremost Dairies
Art Director: Robert Biancalana
Lettering Artist: William A. Coppock

hand
lettering

Formal and semi-Formal scripts continue to be of value in present-day advertising. The air of grace and dignity expressed by these forms limits their use to advertisements and designs which logically call for this effect, but these opportunities are not rare. Free-style variations of the Formal scripts offer possibilities for personal interpretations in which the words give the impression of an elegant form of feminine handwriting. Currently, many slim and refined brushscript captions, which retain much of the formal beauty of the pen scripts, are appearing in magazine ads.

The Penn Mutual "Million Club"...

MICHAEL R. LOMBARDO: *"The Formal script lettering shown here was reproduced from the comprehensive layout, made by the Martino Studios. The reason for using the comprehensive lettering was to retain the freshness and freedom that might be lost in finished lettering."*

Agency: The Aitkin-Kynett Company, Inc.
Client: The Penn Mutual Life Insurance Company
Art Director: Michael R. Lombardo
Lettering Artist: Willie Martino—Martino Studios

The fabulous **PHILCO**
Slender Seventeener

JOSEPH OBRANT: *"The combination of letter styles shown here began with setting the logotype in Futura Medium and creating another logotype for 'Slender Seventeener.' Since this TV set is very slim, I wanted a condensed, easy-flowing script. 'The fabulous' was set in Bodoni Italics as a balance for the two logos."*

Agency: Batten, Barton, Durstine & Osborn, Inc.
Client: Philco Corporation
Art Director: Joseph Obrant
Lettering Artist: Willie Martino—Martino Studios

DOYALD YOUNG: *"The problem here was to design words which would fit pleasingly in a 13-by-24-inch vertical page. The obvious solution for filling the area was to draw the capitals with wide-swinging hairlines. A #170 Gillott pen was used for these words, which were drawn in large size."*

Client: Albert Van Luit & Co.
Art Director: Theodore Ramsay
Lettering Artist: Doyald Young

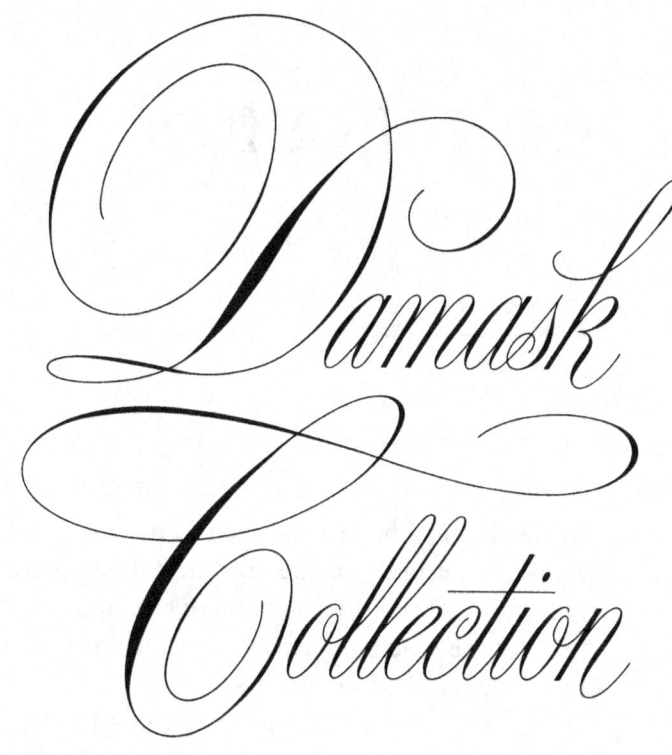

Client: William Craig Smith
Lettering Artist: Doyald Young

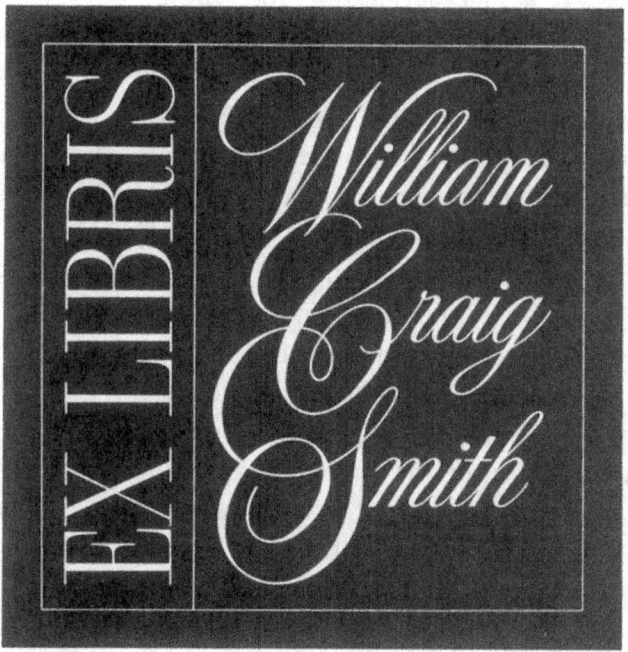

DOYALD YOUNG: *"The letters were drawn with a #170 Gillott (which seems to be a very versatile point). Formal script and Bodoni were chosen for their compatibility. The script capitals were designed to form an interesting pattern within the rectangular shape of the background. I wanted to draw them in one continuous line (for no particular reason), but try as I might, the 'W' simply would not join!"*

Agency: Young & Rubicam, Inc.
Client: Serena by Modess
Art Director: Raymond Todd
Lettering Artist: Sam Marsh Studios

CONCLUSION

In this book, I have attempted to present a representative picture of the current uses of type and lettering in the graphic arts field. And I have also attempted to describe the thinking that precedes the design and applications of letter forms. My objective has been to offer the reader sufficient data and examples to allow for a comprehensive evaluation of this facet of commercial art.

During the past few decades, there has been a slow but steady change in advertising and sales-promotional designs. The degree of change has accelerated considerably within recent years. Many advertisements, packages and displays appearing today show a tendency toward more objective and less inhibited approaches to the problem of selling a product. While a completely radical change in design thinking within the advertising business and its related fields is unlikely in the immediate future, there are definite indications that the physical appearance of sales-promotional designs produced in this country will change much more rapidly within the coming generation than in the past.

At the present time, type designs appearing on the market are still largely based on the "best of the nineteenth century." Lettering artists and photo-lettering organizations are producing variations of these redesigned forms for display captions. This pattern probably will not change for some time. However, the competition among producers of letter forms may quite possibly result in the eventual development of letter styles that depart from traditional forms. Acceptance of these styles of the future by graphic designers, typographers and the public will depend, of course, upon the soundness of such designs and their potentials for general use. It is not likely that these as yet unthought of styles will replace the best of the traditional forms, but they will instead open a wider range of choice for advertising designers.

It is logical to expect that the transition to new letter expressions will be spearheaded by men with sound, practical experience as lettering artists. Practicality as well as artistry is the key to the development of successful new letter stylings. In recent years, type designs that have attempted to break with tradition have not offered a potential for general use, but, inevitably, skilled men who deal with the development of letters will eventually succeed in producing objective letter styles that will take their place beside the best of our present-day forms.

In my opinion, the increasing competition among the related fields of letter designing will continue to stimulate efforts toward improvement of letter designs, but the competition will not seriously affect the status of any of these fields in the foreseeable future.

www.ingramcontent.com/pod-product-compliance
Lightning Source LLC
Chambersburg PA
CBHW081119170526
45165CB00008B/2492